RICH KIDS

Also by Paul Barry

The Rise and Fall of Alan Bond
The Rise and Rise of Kerry Packer
Going for Broke

RICH KIDS

PAUL BARRY

BANTAM BOOKS
SYDNEY • AUCKLAND • TORONTO • NEW YORK • LONDON

RICH KIDS
A BANTAM BOOK

First published in Australia and New Zealand in 2002
by Bantam

Copyright © Paul Barry, 2002

National Library of Australia
Cataloguing-in-Publication Entry

Barry, Paul, 1952- .
Rich kids: how the Murdochs and Packers lost $950 million in One.Tel.

Includes index.
ISBN 1 86325 338 6.

1. Packer, Kerry. 2. Murdoch, Rupert, 1931- .
3. One.Tel (Firm). 4. Business failures—Australia.
5. Telecommunication—Australia. I. Title.
II. Title: How the Murdochs and Packers lost $950 million in One.Tel.

384.0994

Transworld Publishers,
a division of Random House Australia Pty Ltd
20 Alfred Street, Milsons Point NSW 2061
http://www.randomhouse.com.au

Random House New Zealand Limited
18 Poland Road, Glenfield, Auckland

Transworld Publishers,
a division of The Random House Group Ltd
61–63 Uxbridge Road, London W5 5SA

Random House Inc
1540 Broadway, New York, New York 10036

Typeset by Bookhouse, Sydney
Printed and bound by Griffin Press, Netley, South Australia

10 9 8 7 6 5 4 3 2 1

To Lisa

Contents

Acknowledgments

I could not have written this book without the help of Jodee Rich, who spent many hours talking to me, answering questions and telling me his version of the One.Tel Story. He also gave me invaluable help in persuading key people to talk, such as Mark Silbermann, Kevin Beck, George Savva, and many others.

This book also could not have been written without the help of the people who worked at One.Tel. Many were willing to tell me their story, and some were prepared to meet me several times to ensure I got things straight. I want to thank them all for their courage and frankness, even if I can't name them individually. They know who they are.

There are many others who have helped make this book what it is. Most important is my wonderful researcher, Lisa McGregor, who found some of the best people and stories, and looked after our gorgeous young twins while she did it. I couldn't have chosen a better partner in either venture. Thank you.

Among the others I want to thank are the staff at the Fairfax Library, who tracked down people, companies, articles, addresses and information that I would never have found myself. Several journalistic colleagues also helped me unselfishly. Sandy Plunkett, formerly of *Business Review Weekly*, covered the Imagineering story extremely well in the late 1980s. More recently, Neil Chenoweth, Aaron Patrick and Trevor Sykes at the *Australian Financial Review* have helped me on One.Tel, as have Kate Askew, Anne Davies, Elizabeth Knight and Jeni Porter at the *Sydney Morning Herald* and Natalie Apostolou at *Communications Day*, and last but not least, Geoff Elliott and Mark Westfield at *The Australian*. Thanks also to Grant Butler of Editor.com, author of *Where's the loot?*. I hope I can return all these favours one day. It is fashionable to snipe at journalists in Australia, but I believe they did their job on One.Tel extremely well.

Gervase Green and Pam Spies from the Australian Stock Exchange dug around for documents for me and unearthed some extremely valuable records for Imagineering. Finally, I want to thank Richard Potter of Phillips Fox for his advice, and everyone at Random House. My special thanks to Fiona Henderson, whose regular food parcels kept me going, and to my very talented editor Vanessa Mickan. As always, it has been great fun.

Prologue

One.Man

If Jodee made a mistake, it was that
he didn't fight to the end.

Jodee Rich, 2001

I first meet Jodee Rich two months after the collapse
of One.Tel. We are alone in his lawyers' office on the
23rd floor of Sydney's Glasshouse, and he wants to talk.
He's dressed casually in cream pleated slacks, boat shoes,
and a blue moleskin shirt, and he's smaller than expected.
He has thin grey hair and pale, almost papery, skin,
which make him look older than his 41 years.

It's no surprise that he looks a bit rough—he's been
through a lot in the previous few weeks. The company
he founded has been snatched from him and shut down.
He's been branded a liar and a criminal by the press,
and attacked by politicians from both major parties. He
has incurred the wrath of the most frightening man in
Australia, Kerry Packer, who has threatened to remove

'his right testicle'. And he has offended the nation's most powerful media baron, Rupert Murdoch, who owns two-thirds of Australia's newspapers. He is also being investigated by a large contingent of Australia's corporate cops.

Worst of all, his dream is in ruins and people are saying he's failed again. Eighteen months ago the media were calling him a genius. He was hip, cool, clever, and a billionaire to boot. Now there's an almost $2 billion black hole. For the second time in a decade, his shooting star has come crashing down to earth.

Despite all this, he is bright, charming and relaxed. He doesn't seem angry or bitter. He's not even self-obsessed, or not obviously. He exudes an air of calm righteousness, like a Christian who's about to be thrown to the lions. But rather than God, perhaps his faith is in Jodee. His detractors say that he thinks he *is* God and that's his problem.

In the months to come I will ask him what mistakes he made and whether he would do things differently next time round, but the best he will offer is that he grieves for a wonderful company, which should never have been allowed to fail. If Jodee made a mistake, he says—lapsing suddenly into the third person—it was that he didn't fight to the end. It was that he left One.Tel when the Packers and Murdochs insisted he go. It was their refusal to put in another $132 million at the end of May 2001 that killed the company.

Across Australia, when this minor *mea culpa* is aired on the TV news, you can almost hear the guffaws. Many who worked for One.Tel can't believe he's saying this, and certainly don't think it's true. They know the state the company was in.

But self belief is the key to being an entrepreneur, and Jodee Rich has it in spades. It was what persuaded the Packers and Murdochs to put almost $1 billion into One.Tel and stay around till they lost it. It was what drove the company to acquire 2 million customers and made it a household name in Europe. It was what propelled the company on its meteoric rise.

On this, my first of many meetings with Jodee, he looks me in the eye, grins a Cheshire cat grin, and reaches out to touch my wrist. It is as if he assumes we are already firm friends, that I am already on his side. It is not how journalists or authors are usually treated, but Rich is an unusual man. He has that capacity to focus on the person he is with, to make them feel special, to cast a spell. He is clearly used to getting his way.

There is no doubt that he used this power to seduce James Packer. Those who watched them say they were like brothers or best friends. They talked of life and love and powerful fathers. They went on trips together. They were forever on the phone. They shared the dream. Their intimacy and trust was vital to the rise of One.Tel. And now they no longer speak.

Jodee Rich also seduced a willing public. Here was a

company that ate cash from the day it was floated on the Australian Stock Exchange, and gobbled up almost $2 billion of other people's money in its short life. Yet the markets valued it at more than $5 billion—almost as much as the entire Packer empire—only 18 months before the crash.

Rich Kids is the story of an era when huge fortunes were made and lost in the mad dot-com and telco boom. It is also a story of James Packer's and Lachlan Murdoch's business brilliance, or lack of it. But above all, it's the story of One.Tel and One.Man, Jodee Rich, without whom none of this could ever have happened.

1

Rich Kids

*Your first choice of business as
an occupation is realistic.*

Vocational guidance to Jodee Rich, aged 16

Jodee Rich is not your average guy and the Riches are not your average family. They're rich, eccentric, and decidedly different.

Back in the 1980s for example, at the wedding of his younger sister Nici, the bride, groom and guests all danced in the nude. It was held in the garden of the Riches' home in Sydney's Eastern Suburbs, with the well-known comedian Vince Sorrenti acting as marriage celebrant and taking charge of the ceremony. The guests gathered around as Sorrenti, in the guise of the Reverend Doctor Love, with a red ribbon around his penis, stood at one end of the swimming pool while the pregnant bride and her attendants swam under a wooden bridge towards him, roses clenched between their teeth. There was much laughter, fun and cheering, the formalities were completed, and the marriage was made.

Then the music started, and everyone began to conga naked round the garden. Jodee's mother led the procession, like a big bare-breasted fairy, wearing nothing more than a happy smile and a white see-through skirt. The bridesmaids were similarly attired, with flowers in their hair, like sprites from *A Midsummer Night's Dream*. The other guests wore nothing at all.

The conga complete, they all jumped into the pool and drank champagne. In the wedding pictures some 20 men and women, including Jodee and his wife Maxine, jostle for space in the Jacuzzi, like an aquatic version of that famous cover for Jimi Hendrix's *Electric Ladyland* album. Later, they all put their clothes back on and ate pork spareribs in the garden. The Riches are Jewish, but clearly not orthodox in any sense of the word.

By all accounts it was a lovely ceremony, but it was not something you would expect to see down the road at the Packer compound. Nor is it the sort of atmosphere in which the typical entrepreneur is raised. But Jodee Rich and his family are hardly typical. His mother Gayl is a warm, vibrant, red-haired woman with boundless energy and enthusiasm, who has spent much of her life pursuing Eastern philosophies and searching for a spiritual alternative. The Riches' current family home in Bellevue Hill has a sandstone pyramid in the garden, in which Gayl sits to meditate. There is also a tower on the corner of the terrace, Moorish in style, which serves the same purpose.

In the 1970s, Gayl was something of a hippie, flirting with the teachings of the Sunyassins, or orange people. In the 1980s, she opened a shop in Paddington called the Crystal Seven Life Changing Centre. 'Seven is the most sacred number which has been a mystical figure since the beginning of time', Gayl told one journalist. 'I do everything in sevens, my whole life is in sevens', she explained to another.

At Crystal Seven, Gayl sold precious rocks and crystals, gathered on her travels around the world. She also did colour therapy, read people's auras and conducted laughter workshops, because it doubled as a healing centre and salon. There were always people passing through—artists, film-makers, sculptors and others she'd befriended around the place.

In many ways, Jodee is more like his father, Steven. A book called *Stump Jumpers*, which profiles several successful immigrants to Australia and includes a chapter on the elder Rich, makes these similarities very clear. Both Steven and Jodee have millions of dollars but claim not to be interested in money, except as a measure of success. Both name happiness as their goal in life, and believe you achieve it by pursuing your own goals and by leading not following. Both also believe that their contribution to society and the world is important.

Steven was born in 1926 in Frankfurt, the son of Hugo Richheimer, a rich cigar manufacturer who fled to London with his family when Hitler came to power. In 1941, they moved to America because the British were threatening to intern all Germans, even if they were Jews, and changed the family name to Rich.

Steven went to school and university in New York, joined the company Hunter Douglas, which had been started by his family, then moved to Australia in 1953 to set up its operation here. Ultimately he ran all its international activities. In the late 1960s he started Traveland, with David Jones and John Fairfax, and built it into an extremely successful travel business. He also acquired coffee plantations in New Guinea and property investments on Australia's east coast.

One friend who has known him many years says Steven Rich is much liked and respected in the business community. But he's no soft touch. His old friend Sir Peter Abeles, another refugee from the Holocaust, who was head of Ansett Airlines when it bought Rich out of Traveland in 1986, described him as 'an extremely shrewd businessman and a tough competitor'. He added that he drove a hard bargain. Another who knows him well says that he is 'authoritarian' and believes that 'more people fear him in business than like him'.

One businessman who does like him says he is 'warm, charismatic and a lot more interesting than his son.' Unlike Jodee, he also has an active social conscience.

He has been the deputy chairman of the Salvation Army's Red Shield appeal since 1971 and has long held one of the movement's highest honours. In addition, he appears to have few of the fears that rich men have. If you look in the Sydney White Pages you will see his home address and telephone number prominently displayed.

By several accounts Jodee's father is flamboyant and fond of tricks. One man recalls sitting in his office discussing a deal. Halfway through the conversation, Steven reached under his desk to press a button, whereupon his secretary announced: 'There's a call for you from the United States'. Rich apparently laughed and said, 'Oh shit, I've pressed the wrong button—I meant to call for coffee'.

Steven and Gayl first met at the Queen's Ball in Adelaide in 1954, which suggests they were both well connected socially. They met again on a plane soon afterwards: Gayl was a hostess for TAA, and Steven was on one of his many business trips. They married in 1956 in New York—because Steven had been recalled to the USA—and it was there four years later that John David Rich was born. By 1963, they were all back in Australia for good, but Steven still flew all over the region for work and often took the family along too. The Riches did not believe in nannies, which was another thing that set them apart from most millionaires.

'Jodee' as he soon came to be known, was Steven and Gayl's first child, their only son, and by all accounts, the apple of their eye. This, says a friend, 'is one of the problems'. Gayl never tired of telling people how clever he was and how well he was doing at school. She was convinced he was a genius, and told him there were no limits to what he should strive for and achieve. She told Jane Cadzow of *Good Weekend* in 2001 that she had never once had to reprimand him, and only worried that he was too good.

By the time Jodee went to school at Cranbrook, in Sydney's ritzy Eastern Suburbs, the Riches had settled into a five-storey mansion complete with elevator in one of the city's most expensive harbourside neighbourhoods, Darling Point. There, Jodee had plenty of space to get away from the crowds of people with which Gayl filled the house. Unlike his mother, he rarely brought friends home and seemed to cut a lonely figure, occupying a floor almost entirely to himself.

At Cranbrook he is remembered as a shy, serious boy, a model student who never made trouble. He would sit at the front of the class, putting his hand up eagerly every time the teacher asked a question, always getting the answer right. He was extremely small, very bright, and bad at sport. Not surprisingly, he was sometimes bullied.

In one respect, however, he was a typical Cranbrook boy, because the school was full of rich kids like him. Some years later, James Packer went there, as did Warwick Fairfax and a hundred other sons of Sydney's money-making elite. One of Jodee's contemporaries was

Rodney Adler, who became a key backer of One.Tel and whose millionaire father was notorious for his deals with Alan Bond.

Rodney and Jodee first met in an economics class, a suitable place to begin in view of the business they would do together down the years. But things did not get off to a great start. Jodee, as always, sat right at the front, poised to provide an answer if one was required. Rodney and his mates sat down the back, fooling around and making trouble. The precocious Rich was an obvious target. 'When we walked past his desk we'd push his books over or clip him round the ear', says Adler. Famous stories are also told about Rodney throwing Jodee's pencil case out the window, and Adler confirms them proudly. 'We threw a lot more than that, I can tell you', he says today.

Despite the teasing, it wasn't long before the two teamed up. 'After a time', Adler explains, hinting at wide experience in these matters, 'you hate the person, you pity them, or you like them. Jodee I liked'. Despite their obvious differences, the two had plenty in common. Both were rich, both were smart, both stood out, both were champions in their respective class—Rodney the king of the bad boys, Jodee the king of the swots.

While Adler was branded by some as 'uncooperative, lazy and always talking', Jodee was a teacher's dream. According to Rob King, his economics master, 'He was extremely focused and driven to get good marks. He knew where he was going. He wanted to be the best'.

It says much about the clientele at Cranbrook that discussions in economics were often sidetracked into talk of tax-avoidance schemes and parking assets in one's wife's name. At the tender age of 16, several of Jodee's classmates were already directors of thriving family companies that would guarantee them a comfortable adult life.

Jodee was already keen to get ahead on this score, too. By the age of nine he was investing in the stock market using money his mother had given him. By the age of ten, he was lunching with his father and David Rockefeller in the New York boardroom of Chase Manhattan Bank. By the age of 12 he was breeding tropical fish and selling them at school. 'It was obvious that he was going to make a lot money', says King.

Jodee tells the story of how, still aged 12, he marched into the Edgecliff branch of the Bank of New South Wales, where he could hardly see over the counter, to ask for an overdraft. He had decided to lease aquariums to Sydney businesses, but needed finance to expand. Annoyed, but undaunted, by the manager's refusal to lend to one so young, he wrote a letter to the managing director to complain. According to Jodee, a reply to the local manager, authorising a $500 overdraft limit for the pre-pubescent entrepreneur, is still sitting in his file at what is now a branch of Westpac.

Jodee's first corporate customer was one of his father's companies. Family connections soon led to more business and before long he was going round the city after school every Friday with a bucket and brush to clean out the tanks. He was buying the tanks wholesale, breeding the fish himself, which was no mean feat, and getting his mother Gayl to create the aquascapes. His favourite fish was the *Cribensis*, an endearing little brightly coloured specimen no bigger than your thumb, and one of the few fish that makes a nest for its eggs and doesn't eat its young.

Three decades later, Rich can still produce a price list from 1972 with 'J.D.R. Fisheries—Proprietor J.D. Rich' on the cover, along with his own pen-and-ink drawing of exotic sea creatures. It says something about the man that he can still lay his hands on this—perhaps he's been keeping it for his biographer—but the brochure itself tells even more about him. There are 15 pages of extraordinarily precise specifications, which the 12-year-old entrepreneur has meticulously typed, or had typed for him, into a list.

You want elbow junctions? J.D.R. Fisheries has a bewildering choice, from the '356 for 394 tubing (388.0602)', all the way up to the '756 for 794 tubing (587.0506)'. You want diaphragm stem-springs or rubber feet? Proprietor J.D. Rich has them too. He also has plenty of *Anacharis egeria densa*, *Ottelia alismoides* and other marine plants to provide a suitable habitat.

Best of all, young J.D.R. promises cheap prices and a unique product—just like at One.Tel. There's ten per cent off all orders over $20 and 'weekly specials' on four varieties of fish, including Exotic Swordtails, which are imported from Singapore and are 'possibly the only ones obtainable in Australia'.

By the age of 16, Jodee's fish were so popular that he was employing his friends to clean the tanks. He was charging businesses $1,000 a year for the full fish service, and stashing money in the bank. Little wonder that when he went for vocational guidance to a psychologist hired by Cranbrook he was told: 'Your first choice of business as an occupation is realistic . . . you would find routine work intolerable. You need an occupation which offers variety, challenge, and the chance to do your own thing'. The psychologist had nothing but praise for the teenage tycoon. The personality test showed him to be 'warm, sociable, bright, intelligent, experimenting, critical, resourceful, stable and highly creative'. His performance with numbers, reasoning and accuracy put him almost off the top of the scale.

But the teenage Jodee was still not liked by many of his classmates. 'The boarders and footballers thought I was very odd', he says. 'I was selling fish tanks, trading shares, doing well in science and maths, and I didn't like football.'

He was also 'arrogant . . . intimidating . . . not a natural sort of friend', according to one boy in his year.

'And he wasn't a mainstream person. He was far more centred on himself.' He seemed to enjoy putting people down, which was another thing he had a gift for.

Even his friends wondered what to make of him: 'When he greeted you he always had a big gleeful smile and acted almost too friendly', says one. 'It somehow never appeared genuine. He was very hard to read.' Apart from girls, he did not pursue the things that boys of his age normally regard as important. He was not remotely interested in sport and had no desire to be a prefect.

He was too busy doing other things. By 1976, when Jodee was in Year 11, Cranbrook had acquired a primitive computer—a huge, programmable calculator the size of a PC—that ran on punch cards. Jodee and a couple of others took to staying after school to teach it noughts and crosses. Some of the footballers thought it fun to reach through the window and turn off the power to wipe out the program. But Jodee never got angry. He would look at them witheringly and say, 'You don't realise how important this is', then reload the punch cards and start all over again.

Even then, according to Rob King, Jodee 'was always thinking about making money, and he already saw computers as a way to do that'. He certainly had most of the necessary skills to turn a profit. On a school skiing trip, King taught him to play poker and explained about bluffing: that to make a lot of money you had to stake a lot of money. Jodee grasped the concept enthusiastically. He did not need to hear it twice.

Despite all his extra-curricular activities, Jodee still had time to act in plays, write poetry and contribute to Cranbrook's school magazine. He also won academic prizes, narrowly missed becoming dux and scored in the top one per cent of the state in the HSC. He excelled at almost everything.

In 1978, at the age of 18, he left school and went to Sydney University to study medicine, as his father had done many years before. After only a year he decided he wasn't altruistic enough to become a doctor, and switched to economics and law, as his father had also done. In the tussle between his spiritual side, inherited from his mother, and his father's capitalist genes, the capitalist came out on top.

Even in a group of 450 university students Jodee's cleverness still stood out. But his style was even more striking. While others cycled or caught buses to uni, Jodee would rock up in his Porsche and park it in the staff car park—if he bothered to come at all. Instead of going to lectures, he commissioned an old friend from Cranbrook to take notes for him so he could devote his energies to trading gold with Rodney Adler. In Australia the bullion price was going through the roof, and the two young tycoons had worked out they could buy cheaply on the Hong Kong or London market and sell to Australians at a premium.

Before long, he was thinking about other ways of cashing in. By 1979 he had discovered that he could get access to a big American database called The Source, using a phone line, an ancient acoustic coupler and one of the first Apple Macs. Armed with this information, which was extremely valuable to anyone operating in the bullion markets, he and Adler set up a company called Sourcenet, to write trading software for the Australian branch of a UK investment bank, Hill Samuel.

The two men were not yet in their 20s, but they were soon doing the same for other banks and brokers, and supplying the Apple Macs as well. Jodee was working flat out from home, while Rodney was doing a bit in the evenings. According to Adler, it was not long before Rich decided he wanted to get serious about the business: 'He said to me, "Either you're with me 100 per cent or you're not"'.

'Even then Jodee wanted to do things in a big way', Adler explained to *BRW* in 1991, 'but he needed big amounts of capital behind him and I was perceived as a bit of a handbrake'.

Rodney was being groomed to take over the family business, FAI, and already had his future mapped out, so he sold his half of the business to Jodee for $10,000 and they parted company.

Young Jodee had not yet finished his degree, but the personal computer market was about to explode into activity and he was desperate to get his new venture going. He would finish his economics course at the same time as building the business. Launched in March 1981, it had a clever, catchy name that fitted well with the times: 'Imagineering'.

2

Jodee's Rocket

I did it all off my own bat. I went to a private
school, my parents are wealthy, but I borrowed
money from the bank, not my father.

Jodee Rich on Imagineering, Daily Telegraph, *1987*

In 1986, shortly after Imagineering went public, Jodee
Rich found himself on the *BRW* Rich List. At the
tender age of 26, he was judged to be worth $23 million,
prompting one breathless scribe to claim that he was
'the youngest and richest self-made millionaire this side
of the Indian Ocean'.

In interviews with journalists, he was eager to point
out that he had done it all himself. He boasted that he
had started the company with $20,000 from his fish
tank earnings and a $30,000 bank loan. 'I did it all off
my own bat', he told the *Daily Telegraph* in early 1987.
'I went to a private school, my parents are wealthy, but
I borrowed money from the bank, not my father.'

In fact, this was not strictly true, because young Jodee's rocket had been helped into orbit by Rich family companies, which had lent him money and guaranteed repayment of Imagineering's enormous overdraft. The first two years had seen the company lose $130,000 and come close to failure, and Steven's help had almost certainly been critical to its survival.

That is not to say that Jodee didn't deserve most of the credit for Imagineering's meteoric rise. It was his idea, his energy that got it moving, and his talent and nerve that made it such a success. But *most* of the credit was clearly not enough for Jodee. As to why he needed to claim he had done it without help, Rodney Adler believes that all boys with powerful fathers want to show they can do it on their own. 'We all feel a special pressure to prove ourselves', he says, 'and Jodee is no exception'. For the record, Jodee says Adler's explanation is 'absolutely wrong'.

Twenty years on, it is hard to remember what the world looked like when Imagineering set up shop in 1981, but it was certainly very different from today. The Apple Mac had only just been invented, the IBM PC was still two years away from being launched in Australia, and most computers were huge machines that filled a room. At this stage, Microsoft was only a minnow, and Lotus, the software giant which developed 1-2-3, did not even exist. The revolution was waiting to happen.

Despite the opportunities to build an empire and make a fortune, as many computer entrepreneurs did, Imagineering was never going to be a Microsoft, nor Jodee a Bill Gates. For all its success and acclaim, Imagineering would always be more of a Harvey Norman: a distributor of other people's products—and a good one—rather than a high-tech creator of its own.

In the first 18 months, the new business had a pretty rough ride. It lost a pile of money and looked like it might go bust. But when the micro-computer boom arrived in 1983, the Australian market began to grow at 40 to 50 per cent a year, and it was impossible to go wrong. According to Dan Keller, who joined Imagineering as a salesman a few months after IBM launched its PC, 'Things were really hectic. You would have five or six calls banked up at a time, and you could make as many sales as you could take phone calls. Every month it was doubling'. Keller's record was 230 calls in one day. 'It was extremely intense', he says, 'but there was a great vibe, a great buzz, and Jodee was like the Messiah. He had the vision, and we believed in him'.

Many still talk about their days at Imagineering as the most exciting time of their life, and Keller was certainly not alone in finding Jodee an inspiration. But many also had mixed feelings. One woman who joined the company in the mid-1980s regards him as the most challenging person she ever worked for, but also remembers the downside: 'He was a very difficult person to stand up to, he had a short wick, and he didn't entertain fools at all. He was a deeply flawed individual, a misfit'. According to Keller, 'He liked to make an example of people from time to time. You were either in the in-crowd or you weren't, and he always let you know'.

But Jodee's style inspired commitment, either through fear or loyalty, and most were happy to put in long hours and work at weekends. Jodee did so too. He would often be seen in the office at seven or eight o'clock at night dressed in shorts and a T-shirt, after a spell at the gym.

When the boom arrived, Imagineering quickly stole a march on its rivals by securing exclusive rights to the top-selling American software products. The first of these was a spreadsheet program called VisiCalc, which had been developed by students at Harvard and was then the only product of its kind on the market. VisiCalc already had an Australian distributor, but this did not stop Jodee jumping on a plane to San Francisco and marching in to see its manufacturer. For the next six months, he told Visi Corp's boss, Gerry Diamond, that Imagineering would do a far better job than his existing Australian agent. Finally the man gave in. Jodee was given sole rights to sell VisiCalc in Australia, which meant that every retailer in the country would now have to buy it from him.

It helped that Jodee's father owned a travel business, which meant he got free flights, but it was far more important that he had the nerve to do such a thing. As one of his friends at the time observed, 'Jodee played it cutthroat. He did everything in a big way and he spoke the US suppliers' language. They lapped it up'.

Those who came knocking on Imagineering's door— for VisiCalc or anything else—found a different Jodee, who was warm, welcoming and eager to help. 'He had that hustler style, but I liked him', says Joe De Simone, who ran an up-and-coming Melbourne computer dealership and flew up to Sydney to talk to the company after it had been going for about 18 months. 'You walked in the door and immediately knew they wanted your business. They made you feel special.'

The team at Imagineering not only tried harder than their rivals, they were also prepared to take risks. When De Simone asked for some software on trial, to see how good it was, they packed him off with $30,000 worth and wished him luck. Soon he was putting orders their way, along with everyone else, and the company was growing like mad.

Having notched up sales of $1.6 million in its first year, Imagineering topped $5 million the next. By mid-1984, sales had again doubled, to $10 million, and it was making a profit—a healthy $500,000 after tax.

By this time Imagineering had opened an office in New Zealand, was employing 45 people, and was on the way to having 1,500 dealers in Australia. It also had a computerised sales and ordering system, which allowed it to promise customers who placed orders by 3.00pm, that they would have their goods by 10.00am the next day.

When business threatened to flag, Jodee's quick thinking kept Imagineering ahead of the pack. In 1984, with sales of VisiCalc tailing off, he set about snaffling the new top seller, Lotus 1-2-3, which was being handled in Australia by a rival company, Sourceware. Hoping to win their business with a direct approach, he caught a flight to Boston and presented himself at Lotus HQ, where he sat around for six hours waiting to see the chief. His mission ended in failure because no one was prepared to see him, but he was told that two executives would be in Australia in six weeks time and he could raise the matter with them.

He discovered that one of the executives was an Italian from Chicago called Chuck Digate. Over the next few weeks he phoned Digate's secretary constantly, eventually to be told that the executive was on his way to Australia and would be stopping in New Zealand on the way.

Once again, Jodee didn't lose any time. He found out that Digate was staying at the Sheraton Hotel in Auckland, pitched up in the lobby and took him out to dinner, where he waxed lyrical about Imagineering and what a great company it was. By the time Digate and his sidekick landed in Sydney they were ready to sign up. And any doubts they may have harboured were soon dispelled. They were met at the airport by a BMW bearing the number plate 123, which Jodee had bought for the occasion, and whisked to Imagineering's offices in Ultimo where they were greeted by the entire team, waving Lotus banners. 'We got the deal', says Jodee, 'because we were committed and we pitched hard'.

There was just one small problem. The Lotus executives wanted Jodee to share the business with Sourceware because they reckoned the company and its gentle American managing director, Doug Ruttan, had done a decent job. Jodee told them this really wasn't an option.

Poor Sourceware, with its modest office suite in Chatswood, had no answer to the sort of campaign Jodee was waging. 'We were a small outfit and there was no way we could compete with that sort of financial backing and tactical sophistication', Ruttan told *BRW*. 'We were gazumped well and truly.'

The Lotus coup was followed soon afterwards by a similar capture of Ashton Tate, which manufactured a hugely popular database program called dBase III. When Ashton Tate came to Sydney to appoint an exclusive distributor, they made it clear that the highest bid would win. Jodee promised to outgun and outspend the existing agent, Arcom Pacific, who went into receivership six months later.

By the end of 1985, Imagineering was so far ahead of its competitors that it had staked out half the Australian market. Sales had doubled in a year—yet again—and profits had done even better. The company had outlets in Hong Kong and Singapore, plus an office in Los Angeles keeping an eye on new products and trends in the market.

After four years, Jodee now had a business that could be sold to others, and an opportunity to make some money. In December 1985 Imagineering was floated on the Australian Stock Exchange in a deal valuing the company at $12 million. The Rich Family Trust pocketed $4.8 million after selling 40 per cent of the shares, while another family company, Beaulieu Holdings, retained the other 60 per cent. Soon afterwards, Jodee made his debut on the *BRW* Rich List as its youngest member, aged 26.

Imagineering itself got no cash from the deal, but its stock exchange listing would allow Jodee and Steven to ask their new shareholders for money in the future. And a look at the balance sheet suggested it would have to do this, if it wanted to keep on growing. Despite its sales and profit growth there was remarkably little in the bank, and virtually nothing in the way of assets, except 'goodwill'. The punters buying the stock for 50 cents a share were getting net tangible assets of just 3 cents, and lots of promise.

There had been a bit of bother in setting the sale price. The brokers Ord Minett, who underwrote the issue by promising to buy the shares if no one else wanted to, had agreed to value the company at 12 times its 1985 earnings. But when the 1985 figures came in, the profit fell well short of the magic $1 million that Jodee had set his heart on.

Jodee suggested a simple solution to the problem: if they changed the company's year end from June to

August, they could lose two months from 1984 and gain two better ones in 1985. This would take the company's after-tax profit over the million mark, so they could stick a price tag of $12 million on the company.

Shenanigans or not, the buyers had nothing to complain about, because the shares soon took off like shooting stars, doubling within a year of the float and doubling again within the following four months. The company was topping every sales target that Rich set for it. He was talking big, and delivering even more.

The press had decided, with that easy way of theirs, that the boy must be a genius, just as his mother had always said. And Jodee was happy to agree. In interviews, he was bold, brash and supremely confident. 'I've always felt good about myself', he told one journalist. 'I guess that's helped me through the bad times.' Whatever they were.

However, some noticed he was a little bit odd, and felt he didn't quite ring true. Even the *Daily Telegraph*, which rarely goes beyond the golly-gosh approach to Great Aussie Success Stories, noted in 1987:

Although he is a very personable young man, there's something slightly stilted about him. He sits very still. His voice is very quiet. Before he answers any question he gives a wide engaging smile. Apart

from that smile, his face remains almost expres-
sionless.

It was a reaction that people would have time and again
over the next 15 years.

The *Telegraph*'s profiler, Fran Hernon, recounted a
story from a young woman who had sat next to him at
a society ball and also found him strange. 'He talked a
lot about cars and he made it really obvious that he had
a lot of money', the woman reported, 'not in an arrogant way, but as if that made him a better person'.
Hernon clearly didn't like him much, but tried to give
him the benefit of the doubt, concluding: 'Maybe Rich
is young enough not to have learned how to be humble.
Maybe he is simply shy'.

Channel 9's Helen Dalley, who was then writing for
Australian Business, didn't appear to warm to him either.
In one of the earliest profiles, written in 1984, she
observed:

> Nothing breeds ego and pride like success. Of his
> riches he says: 'I've probably made my first
> million—maybe I have, maybe I haven't—but it's
> not the money that turns me on'. What does turn
> him on, he says, is the parry and thrust, the
> negotiating, making software a household word—
> and women. 'I love getting a good sale and enjoying
> a lovely lady', he says. Flamboyant in life as in
> business, Rich drives to the Thredbo ski fields

throughout winter in his silver BMW with the computerised radar detector under the bonnet. 'This car is an ego trip, but I feel I've earned it.'

Two years later Jodee's ego trip had obviously become even more powerful, because he had traded up to a Porsche 944 Turbo. His executives also had boys' toys. The car park at Imagineering was full of BMWs, Porsches and Mercedes, with number plates like APPLE and IMAGIN. One day a red Ferrari made an appearance—which was not seen as a clever move. It didn't do to out-horse the boss.

Jodee was keen to claim he didn't care about such stuff. 'People think that all you do is drive fast cars and eat out a lot', he told the *Telegraph*, 'but it's not that way at all. The things I most enjoy are the simple things in life'.

He had confided to Helen Dalley that he was still a boy at heart. 'I'm like an average 14-year-old. I love dancing at Rogues. I love eating out and the movies.'

But 14 and average were two things he was not. Nor was Imagineering an ordinary company. Jodee was a fan of Californian philosophies like est and Insight, which laud the power of positive thinking, so the company had teams and champions, and brass gongs that were rung when a sale was made. In theory there were no hierarchies, and limitless possibilities for the 'Imagineers' who worked there. Jodee delighted in telling the story of a 16-year-old employee who shook his hand and told him he wanted his job one day—a homily he would still be repeating 15 years later.

Jodee's democratic zeal even extended to refusing to be branded a whiz kid. 'That implies that other people can't do what I have done', he told one journalist in 1988. 'But they can.' It was as if 28-year-old multimillionaires were just two a penny.

Jodee was also responsible for motivational weekends, where everyone could get to know each other, and themselves. On one occasion in the Blue Mountains, all the managers were made to abseil off the top of a cliff, with Jodee egging them on by saying: 'A company that jumps together stays together'. On another, they sat round a room and had to say something about themselves—then had to listen while the group leader tore each person apart on the basis of what they had said.

Dan Keller recalls one speaker at a management love-in talking about the importance of not wasting other people's time, after which Jodee introduced a rule that the last person to turn up to a management meeting—late—would have to shine everybody else's shoes. He included himself in the deal, and it worked wonders.

Till then, Jodee had been notorious for not arriving on time. Rob Stirling, who ran a company called Datascape that distributed computer printers, tells how Jodee would be running late for talks on a business deal and ring up to ask: 'What sort of paddle pops do you want?'. When he arrived, he wouldn't apologise, just hand paddle pops around to everyone, and they would all sit around sucking them in negotiations. 'It was a trick, a magician's trick', says Stirling, who witnessed it on several occasions. 'He had lots of these tricks. They were designed to take the upper hand.'

At one such meeting, Jodee made Stirling a generous offer. Just before the deal was to be signed, he rang up to say that he needed to come in and see him again to talk it over. He arrived, gave Rob a paddle pop and said, 'The deal's off'.

'I was really angry', says Stirling. 'All I wanted to do was shove the paddle pop up his arse, but you know, I had this wet thing in my mouth. It's hard to feel powerful when you're sucking on a paddle pop.'

The tricks didn't stop Stirling from joining Imagineering soon afterwards, and their magic obviously worked. By August 1986 the company's sales had doubled again, beating all forecasts, and the future seemed limitless. They had opened new offices in Wellington, Brisbane and Taipei, and they had moved to bigger and better ones in Sydney, Melbourne, Hong Kong and Los Angeles. The company was selling software to Grace Bros, Myer, K-Mart and Dick Smith, and had been named International Dealer of the Year by 3Com, the American company that now makes the Palm Pilot.

They were also getting even further ahead of their rivals by winning yet more contracts with top US suppliers. As usual, they pitched for new business with flair and extravagance, as one of Jodee's competitors inadvertently discovered at a trade show. As the rival stood there, looking a little lost, a young man came up to him to say, 'We'll pick you up and take you to the airport, and there'll be a private jet to take you down to the snow'. Sadly, the promise was never followed through. An Imagineering rep had mistaken him for a visiting executive from a big US software developer.

Jodee also knew how to play tough when it was needed. For several months Rob Stirling talked to the Japanese printer company Fujitsu in the hope of selling their products. After doing things gently and politely, he had still not managed to make them decide. Jodee resolved to have them in for a meeting, at which he would try to get them over the line. According to Stirling, two Japanese gentlemen duly came to the new HQ at Rosebery, in the old industrial heart of Sydney, to be asked whether they were ready to sign. 'They said, "Well, there are a couple of things we'd just like to clear up". And Jodee said, "Well, I think you've fucked with us long enough. If you're not going to sign, then fuck off", or words to that effect. There was a stunned silence, and then they apologised and signed up.'

Another version of this story has a different punch line. According to one of Imagineering's managers, 'Jodee was his usual self. He had his hands in his pockets, was playing with his pen, looking at the ceiling, while these guys were dressed in suits, sitting upright, very formal. Suddenly out of the blue he says, "In order to know what diseases I've got, I need to know who's fucking me". There was commotion. The interpreter suddenly started interpreting madly, everyone looked embarrassed, and the meeting came to an abrupt end'. But once again, Jodee got the business. Later he would retell the story and fall about laughing.

There was a constant stream of visiting suppliers from the USA and Japan who needed to be entertained. One of Jodee's competitors was impressed to see him out on the town with Bill Gates, who was a guru in the industry even then. Jodee now admits he was trying to grab Microsoft's business from its local distributor.

But often Rich left the carousing to others. When the vice president of sales and marketing from one of the industry's big names came out, threatening to terminate his company's deal, Jodee called a young Imagineer into his office to brief him on the visit. He expected to hear about their commercial relationship, but instead, he says today: 'Jodee closed his office door and started talking about this guy, saying, "He's a bit of a party boy, he's quite a nocturnal person, and he enjoys going out hard. And you need to know something else, he likes cock". I nearly fell off my chair, I was completely shocked. Jodee tried to calm me down. He said, "I'm not suggesting you do anything about it but I'm sure he'd enjoy the company of a good-looking young guy like you". I said to him, "Before I explode, are you saying you want me to distract this guy by introducing him to fags?". He smiled at me and said, "You got it"'.

The 1980s, of course, is still famous as the decade of excess, and in this regard Imagineering could compete with the best. Its Sydney parties at the Regent Hotel and Rogues nightclub were always more lavish than anyone else's, and the company's extravaganzas at Jupiter's Casino on the Gold Coast were the stuff of legend. Known as High Rollers, because they rewarded dealers who had made large amounts of money for Imagineering, these events were famous throughout the industry. If there was one invitation you wanted to get, it was this one, and since it could only be earned by hitting sales targets, it was a great way to get products moving. The formula was simple: charter a couple of jumbos and fly 500 or 600 people from Sydney and Melbourne up to the Gold Coast for a weekend of free accommodation, free food, free booze and free fun.

At the time the computer industry was notorious for its testosterone-charged young men, so there were always plenty of attractive young women on show. There were soapie stars and models to present the sales awards— which is what the party was about—and, for those who went parasailing, there were bikini-clad blondes (complete with 'Safety Instructor' sashes) to strap people in for their flights. Most who earned the right to go were young, single and out for a good time. When sun, surf and stimulants were added to that cocktail, it was no surprise that the parties were wild.

'It was biblical, Cecil B de Mille, a weekend of debauchery', says one man who still marvels at the memory. 'An obscene amount of money was spent on it. You would spend the day at the beach, then there would be a formal dinner in the evening. And afterwards you would get down and have fun. All the big software manufacturers would leave plastic bags in your room, called "care packages". Inside were combs, toothbrushes, trinkets, playing cards and the companies' badges, and then there were condoms and lubricants. There were also little hazelnuts that looked whole, but when you cracked them open, there were condoms inside.'

The beauty of the High Rollers concept was that Imagineering's suppliers could be persuaded to pay for almost everything. You would go to the Ashton Tate pool party for cocktails, then to the Persist Memory Boards dinner, and at bedtime there would be an IBM mint on your pillow. In the morning, you'd go down to breakfast and be greeted by a vendor's tablecloth. On the boat trips, the name of the sponsor would be all over the side. It was two or three days of advertising nirvana. 'It made the sponsorship at the Atlanta Olympics look like child's play', says Joe De Simone.

The last High Rollers happened in 1988. It was the end of an era. According to its organiser, Stefan Wasinski, it was then the biggest party in Australian history.

Imagineering chartered five jets to fly people up to Queensland and had marching bands on the tarmac to greet them. Wasinski is convinced it was worth it, and is adamant that it boosted sales by millions.

And without it, of course, we would not have that famous picture, taken at Jupiter's, of Jodee and Maxine Rich in their shiny red devil suits.

3

Crash and Burn

Jodee had this fundamental belief that he could
do no wrong . . . he just wasn't prepared for
things not going well.

Dan Keller, Imagineering manager

By the middle of 1988, Jodee's rocket was heading off into the stratosphere. Sales for the six months to February had doubled from the previous year, forecasts were being revised upwards again, and everyone had their eyes firmly on the heavens.

The latest great success was hardware, which now made up more than two-thirds of the company's sales. Having introduced its own IBM clone, the Ultra PC, in 1987, and opened a new factory in Taiwan, Imagineering was selling the machines as fast as it could put them together, and still had a huge backlog of orders.

The share price was also climbing, so Jodee and his father took the opportunity to reward themselves by granting the Rich Family Trust a couple of million share options which would be triggered if the share price hit $2.00. They also took advantage of the sunny outlook to raise $17 million from the company's shareholders and place $7.2 million worth of new shares with Australian institutions, almost all of which were snapped up by Bankers Trust at $1.50 apiece.

According to the company's broker, the shares were still an outstanding buy: Imagineering was predicting another record year, had extended its exclusive agreement with Lotus till 1990, and was embarking on yet another program of expansion. It was opening new offices in Bangkok, Manila, Seoul, Jakarta, Adelaide, Canberra and Perth, and had just tripled warehouse space in Sydney to cope with the huge demand for its PCs.

But even as 1989 began, interest rates and inflation were shooting skywards, the boom was going bust and business was getting tougher by the day. By May, Imagineering shares were falling fast, but Jodee was still relentlessly upbeat, boasting in the half-year results that the company was still growing rapidly and that profits had risen by 46 per cent. Even more growth was on the way, he promised, and there wasn't a cloud on the horizon.

The truth was otherwise, as Jodee should have known. A closer reading of the accounts showed Imagineering had actually made a loss for the six months to February. And inside the company, all systems were stretched to the limit. According to one of the senior finance people, 'it had grown so fast there were no structures in place. You just couldn't keep up. The structures just couldn't handle the size of the business'.

It was not only in the finance area that Imagineering had problems. One of its promises to dealers in 1985 had been to get goods on their doorsteps in under 24 hours, but this was now a distant memory. The huge demand for the Ultra PC meant it was taking a week to fill orders. And when the computers arrived, they often didn't work.

Joe De Simone, who by now was one of the company's biggest dealers, had begun to experience difficulties in early 1988. He was selling batches of 50 computers to TAFE and other colleges and getting seven or eight of them back. Then he was finding it impossible to get the machines fixed, because Imagineering had no spare parts. 'It created a huge amount of work for us and caused us a lot of anguish', he says.

The root of the problem was in Sydney, where Imagineering was supposed to test the Ultras after bringing them in from Taipei. Instead of running the machines for 24 to 48 hours to ensure that the components were compatible and everything was working, the company was rushing them out to customers. De Simone reckons they were being tested for only two hours, resulting in a shocking failure rate.

In September 1988, dealers had begun complaining to journalists that it was taking a week to get a new PC delivered, and three weeks to get it put right. One reported that Imagineering was so overloaded he could not get any sense out of them. 'The lines of communication seem filled to capacity. We had to continually reintroduce ourselves. It seemed at times the left hand didn't know what the right hand was doing.'

Rich had responded publicly that everything was under control. They were fixing the problems—by taking on staff and boosting production—and the critics were just being negative. 'There's an attitude out there that implies a company can't keep up with explosive sales growth without getting to the point where it can't cope internally any more. That's nonsense.'

It wasn't only Imagineering's customers who were telling Jodee to slow down. At board meetings, his fellow directors had been begging him to do the same. As one of his most senior managers, Graham Pickles, told *BRW* after the crash, 'Jodee has an extremely strong personality and enormous energy. He worked around the clock and pushed very hard for the company. It was like he wouldn't take his foot off the accelerator. Others in the company weren't so comfortable with that pace. There were some extremely heated boardroom debates'.

Back in December 1985, at the time of the public float, Jodee's father had recruited three of Australia's best businessmen to keep an eye on the company and provide a steadying hand. Their presence as non-executive directors was supposed to reassure investors that the business would be run in a disciplined fashion, but by 1988 these grey-haired captains of industry were shouting from the back seat of Jodee's rocket and not being heard. The young space cadet was at the controls, and he wasn't stopping for anyone.

One of the old hands trying to get Jodee to ease back the throttle was the then boss of McDonald's Australia, Peter Ritchie, who was widely regarded as one of Australia's top managers. 'The company was growing far too fast', he says today. 'It couldn't service the dealers, it couldn't get the product out, it didn't have the people or the finance. There were creaks and groans all over the organisation. We all told Jodee that it couldn't go on the way it was going. We told him for two years. But we weren't able to get through to him. The outside directors were just talking among themselves.'

Another of the hugely experienced minders was Brian Scott, whose career spanned Harvard, Stanford, a family business and a host of government inquiries. But he, too, was ignored. 'The business was travelling too fast. It didn't have the controls we would have liked. We told Jodee he had to consolidate, slow down. He didn't listen.'

Scott and Ritchie had two detailed sessions with Jodee on top of the regular board meetings, but it was to no avail. 'He wasn't exactly rude', says Scott, 'but he made it clear that he was only there because he had to be. He thought anyone over 35 who didn't understand computers had no role to play'.

If Scott or Ritchie had been chairman of the board, they might have been able to enforce their views, but this position was held by Jodee's father. As the arguments raged about the company's course, Steven Rich consistently took his son's side, making it easier for Jodee to keep gunning the engines. 'It was a mistake for Steven to be chairman', says Brian Scott today. 'It should have been someone who was completely independent.'

It was not just his fellow directors that Jodee ignored. According to Dan Keller, 'At the end of the day, Jodee would do what Jodee wanted to do'. Or, in the words of Imagineering's general manager, Chris Spring, 'He wouldn't listen to suggestions of slowing down, even from the executives he respected a great deal. He would say that we were defeatist'.

Arguing with visionaries is never easy, and taking on the Messiah is several degrees harder, so many did not bother to speak up. According to Peter Ritchie—and many others since—this is why Jodee will always get his way. 'Nobody's ever strong enough to stand up to him. He doesn't want to hear the truth and no one wants to tell him, because he's so dominant.'

I tell this to Jodee in 2001 and he looks genuinely surprised, as if no one has ever mentioned it before. Yet it's certainly not the first time it's been said, and he could have read it many times in countless articles. In a way it illustrates the point—that listening is not his forte.

At our next two meetings he brings it up again. It has really hurt him, he says, to think that people might say this about him. He has canvassed several friends and they have all told him he's an excellent listener. He can't understand how others don't agree. I suggest that maybe it's because it's almost impossible to get him to change his mind about anything—as I myself am discovering. He doesn't accept that either: 'That is absolutely wrong'.

In mid-1989 the storm arrived. With a sudden slump in demand came price-cutting and savage competition. Everywhere you looked there was pain. Dealers were going bust, and the Ultra's name was mud in the market-place. As rates soared and stocks of the PC piled up in the warehouse, Imagineering's interest bill took off. From $300,000 a month it was soon pushing $1 million. Yet still Rich appeared unconcerned. Instead of battening down the hatches, cutting staff and getting costs down, he continued to forge ahead.

Inside the company the problems were obvious. According to a couple of senior Imagineers, cash was incredibly tight, bills weren't being paid on time, and the pile-up of old stock was 'horrific'. Much of it was six months old, which made it unsaleable or very hard to shift. The new telecommunications division, which had only just been opened, had a warehouse full of brick-sized mobiles that were twice the size and twice the price of rival brands—Jodee and his Imagineers had not realised how fast technology was moving.

The company's exclusive contracts with US software suppliers had also become a handicap. To win and keep their business Jodee had committed to buying huge quantities, which now could not be shifted. When confronted with the problem, Jodee didn't want to know about the details. 'Just get rid of it', he told his managers. Positive as ever, he commissioned a Ghostbusters-style poster with a Jodee caricature bursting forth from a red-crossed circle, proclaiming 'I ain't afraid of no slow stocks'.

He had once told Dan Keller that he wasn't interested in Imagineering unless it was growing at 100 per cent a year, and he still seemed to think that was possible. 'Jodee had this fundamental belief that he could do no wrong', says Keller, who had been a real disciple in the early days. 'He just wasn't prepared for things not going well.'

To add to the company's difficulties, the sins of the past were coming back to haunt them. In previous years Jodee had given instructions to hide old stock by parking it with dealers like Joe De Simone on a sale-or-return basis, then counting it as sold. This had only postponed the crunch, and was now making it worse.

'That was Jodee's management style', says one senior Imagineer. 'Everything we did was like a stay of execution. Everything was a day-to-day proposition. And towards the end it got harder and harder.'

With the dealers also swamped with stock, there was no way they could be persuaded to take more. In fact, several of the biggest ones were going bust, so bad debts were also a worry. Much of the money owed to Imagineering had been outstanding for 90, 120 or even 150 days and was clearly not recoverable—a problem that would also plague One.Tel a decade later.

As the company's shares dived still further, Imagineering announced at the end of July that it would put its year-end back four months. This meant that Jodee and his team could put off telling the world how bad things were until December.

Then, suddenly, salvation was at hand. For months, Jodee had been looking for a rich investor, or 'Big Brother', to ride to the company's rescue. He had targeted ten companies in the USA and Asia, and eventually persuaded one to buy into the business. In September, Imagineering informed the Stock Exchange that it was negotiating for 'a significant investment' in the company. Four weeks later it announced that a Hong-Kong-based multinational, First Pacific, had agreed to pump in $18 million. Without this money, as soon became clear, Imagineering would have been unable to survive.

Typically, Jodee had struck a remarkable deal with his saviour. In addition to injecting $18 million (in exchange for around a quarter of the company) First Pacific had agreed to buy one-fifth of everyone's shares at double the market price, which would allow the Rich family to take out $3 million in cash. It was also granting Jodee three million options and signing him up for a new two-year service agreement.

The documents filed with the Australian Stock Exchange (ASX) revealed that Jodee had promised the purchaser a small profit for the year—somewhere between breakeven and $4 million. He had also given a raft of guarantees that nothing had been covered up—specifically, that Imagineering's finances were accurately portrayed in the audited accounts to August 1988 and the unaudited accounts to June 1989.

There was nothing unusual in these guarantees but First Pacific was wise to have demanded them because the due diligence process, in which any purchaser is allowed to examine the books, had been most unsatisfactory. Jodee had told the investigating accountants, Price Waterhouse, that they had only 14 days to look at the company—a ridiculously short time—and had instructed them that they could only talk to him or one of his executives, whom we shall call Ken White, although that is not his real name.

These were extraordinary conditions to work under and had caused the accountants great grief. They had been denied access to board minutes, which are normally considered vital because they give clues to the real issues in the company, and had not been allowed to set eyes on many of the documents they wanted. As a consequence, they had been unable to throw much light on the true state of the business. The accountants recorded that questions had been asked about various matters, and answers received from management. But they could not say whether the answers should be trusted. In the absence of supporting documents or discussions with line managers, it was simply not possible for them to verify what they were being told.

On the occasions that they did talk to people below Rich and White's level, they received the impression that the Imagineers had been told what to say, and in at least one case this was true. One senior manager told me in 2001 that he was briefed on the story to tell, and provided with false documents to back it up. He told me: 'I used to get a computer-generated report every month that told me what stock I had. One day, in late 1989, Ken White came to me quietly, he was looking very sheepish, and he said to me, "Look, we're selling the company, the auditors are here to review a few things. Do you have a current report?". I said, "yeah". "Well, when you sit down and talk about it, don't use yours, use this one"'.

The manager acted out the process for me, including an awkward-looking White surreptitiously slipping him a document.

'He called it a revised report. He didn't say "This is a forgery" or anything like that, but the way he looked at me I knew there was something amiss. He said, "Have a read through it, and then come and see me if you've got any questions". I read it, and the report said that the total value of the unsold stock was something like $10 million less than it really was. The difference between the two was enormous. I'm not the fastest guy but I thought "My God, that's an eye-opener". I was gobsmacked. I thought, "What am I going to do now?". I went and saw Ken White and pointed out the differences, and he said, "Just go with what it says, forget the differences".

'I made notes in my diary at the time, to cover my arse: that White met me and that I questioned the discrepancy. I wrote that White explained to me, "Disregard the original report and work off this one". I also remember really clearly writing, "Basically, I'm fucked"'.

The manager says he never discussed his concerns with anyone else, least of all Jodee, because he 'knew it was pointless'. He was also sure that Jodee knew already: 'You can't be the managing director and claim ignorance'. This was especially true of Jodee, who had always run the company from top to bottom. He was still the largest shareholder, still the managing director, and still at the controls. In the words of another top-level manager: 'It was still Jodee, Jodee, Jodee'.

If First Pacific *had* been lied to about the company's finances, it was inevitable they would soon discover it. Two weeks after getting its $18 million, Imagineering confirmed its profit for the year to 31 August 1998 had come in bang on target, at $1 million. Three weeks later, Jodee was forced to make a special announcement that this had become a $4 million loss, because $5 million of expenditure had been improperly 'deferred', or left out of the calculations for the year. It was also announced that Imagineering would fork out $3 million to First Pacific in compensation.

Behind the scenes, a second firm of investigating accountants, Arthur Andersen, now went through the business for First Pacific, looked at the books, and found that the finances were drastically worse than Jodee had indicated. Or as one of them put it, 'Imagineering was in deep shit'. The $18 million had just disappeared into a black hole.

A big debate now followed about whether the business could be salvaged at all, or whether First Pacific should just treat it as a bad dream and walk away. Not surprisingly, the purchasers were extremely angry about what they were uncovering in the company and felt that they had been, to coin a phrase, 'profoundly misled'. There was much talk of suing the Riches, and of suing Price Waterhouse for negligence, but in the end the talk did not lead to action. It was all uncannily similar to what would happen with One.Tel a decade later.

After three months of detailed work, and several discussions between Andersens and the board in Hong Kong, First Pacific decided it was worth throwing more money at the problem, because there might yet be some value in the business. In the meantime, they started to clean up the mess.

At the end of March 1990, Imagineering shocked the market by confessing it had crashed to a $52 million loss in the 16 months to December, or roughly three times what the company had made since going public four years earlier. Undoubtedly, the business had deteriorated since August, when Jodee had claimed a $1 million profit for the year. Four extra months of losses explained some of the reversal, but the main reasons for the appalling result lay elsewhere.

The accounts showed that Jodee and his team—who were now taking orders from an angry Big Brother—had been forced to write off $14 million in goodwill and a further $17 million in bad debts and obsolete stock, which had been festering in the warehouses and rotting in the dealerships. It was hard to believe that Jodee had been unaware of this problem when he made his promises to First Pacific.

Jodee's annual statement to the shareholders shed no light on what Imagineering's new benefactor felt about all this bad news. Implausibly, it suggested that he and First Pacific were getting on famously. In fact, his days were already numbered.

Some journalists obviously hadn't noticed the debacle. Or perhaps the offer of exclusive access to the talented Mr Rich was still impossible to resist. A few days after the huge loss was announced, the *Daily Mirror* told its awe-struck readers:

> Australia's youngest multimillionaire rides a bicycle to work ... Sydney's Jodee Rich [who] is worth about $30 million ... [and] employs 600 people in a commercial empire which includes Taiwan, New Zealand and the US ... said there was no better way to start the day. 'I get to the office refreshed and relaxed', he said. 'But I hate it when it's pouring with rain, which seems to be quite often lately, because I can't ride my bike.' Mr Rich, who works 12 hours a day, attributed his financial success to doing what he loves best—bike riding, windsurfing and sailing. 'I never planned to be wealthy', he said. 'It's just a by-product of doing what I enjoy.'

Ten out of ten for timing. It really deserved a prize. Remarkably, the *Daily Telegraph* would run almost exactly the same story 11 years later, after One.Tel collapsed.

Imagineering was now in severe danger of going under. According to one manager, 'It was becoming an ugly place to be. We had been hugely successful and now we weren't, and it was like Jodee couldn't care less any more'.

By April 1990 only 160 employees were left in the company's Australian computer division, compared to the 390 who had been there at the start of 1989. Worse still, the accounts had been given a 'going concern' qualification by the auditors, which meant that Imagineering was surviving only with the grace of its bankers and First Pacific. Its biggest creditor, the ANZ Bank, had made it quite clear it wanted its $38 million out.

In May the company's shareholders received an expert report from Arthur Andersen telling them that their company needed lots of money and needed it quick. Imagineering's two other banks, Westpac and the Commonwealth, were also threatening to quit. They were only prepared to throw more money at the company if First Pacific pumped in another $20 million—and First Pacific had decreed that it would only do this if it were given Imagineering on a plate.

This was bad news for the shareholders, including Jodee, who would effectively lose two-thirds of their investment. But the alternative was far worse. Without the re-financing, there would be a fire sale of assets, which would bring shareholders virtually nothing if they were lucky, and nothing at all if they weren't. The company was hopelessly insolvent. Nor was there any hope of a miracle. Imagineering had lost $6 million in the first four months of 1990 and was forecast to lose more in the future.

Jodee and the other shareholders therefore had no choice but to agree, and in July 1990, First Pacific took full charge. Two months later, Jodee was removed as managing director and disappeared 'on sabbatical'. At the same time, his father Steven agreed to quit the board of directors.

The endgame was now in play. In February 1991 a thumping $41 million loss was revealed. Then, in May, the company failed to lodge an annual report and its shares were suspended. By this time the Taiwan computer plant had been shut down, warehouses and offices had been closed all over the place and another huge batch of obsolete stock had been written off. A further 70 staff had been sacked.

The only way for First Pacific to save face was to privatise the company, which it did for $1 million, or just 10 cents a share. This was one-80th of what people had paid at the top of the market, one-60th of what Bankers Trust had paid in October 1988, and one-20th of what Imagineering's shares had been floated for in 1985. But the mandatory experts' report judged it good value nevertheless. On their calculations, the shares were worth minus 80 or 90 cents apiece, and the company faced continuing losses, which could only be met by First Pacific, who had already sunk some $70 million into the company.

Under the offer, the Riches would be paid around $350,000 in cash, or given an IOU for $417,000 that could not be redeemed until April 2001. They agreed to accept the latter, either through altruism or under duress, and pocketed an extra $10 for agreeing to cancel 750,000 stock options.

Inevitably, the post mortems now began. The whiz kid had failed in the eyes of the market; his promises had been broken; he had been proved to be fallible or worse. Rodney Adler told *BRW* that his old friend had wanted too much too soon. 'Jodee's vision built Imagineering, and he deserves credit for that. But when the economy went bad, perhaps his experience didn't balance his gall and vision.' Not everyone was so kind. The headline on *BRW*'s cover read 'Saga of a son who failed'.

According to Adler today, the loss of Imagineering was, 'An incredible blow to his reputation and it really, really, upset him. He didn't become a hermit, but he withdrew into his shell. You didn't see him, he wouldn't return calls, he just disappeared'.

Of course Imagineering was not the only fatality in the industry because computer sales had grown at top speed for seven years and then hit the wall. But few who worked in Jodee's team had kind words for their captain after the crash, and few remember him fondly today, even if they still find him fascinating. One told me he would do anything 'for fame and fortune. I used to have a healthy respect for him, but I think his business skills leave a lot to be desired'.

Many criticise his lack of attention to detail. Others observe that he is pathologically incapable of caution.

'He is an adventurer, always looking for the next peak to conquer', says one former director. 'He is always in danger of going too far.'

'He's a thrill seeker and an adrenaline junky', says an ex-senior manager. 'Skiing fast is one way to get it. Putting your company at risk is another.'

Jodee himself claims to have learnt lessons from the disaster, like not using debt to build a business and not tolerating managers who can't do the job. But humility is clearly not one of them. When I ask him what went wrong, and why so many people accuse him of not listening, he assures me that he did listen, but his hands were tied: Imagineering would have lost its exclusive software contracts if he had slowed down, and none of the directors wanted that.

We move on to the company's financial health. I suggest that First Pacific put around $70 million into the business. He says this is 'absolutely wrong' and he will bring the papers to prove it. I tell him that $33 million was put into the business in two rights issues in 1986 and a placement in 1988. He informs me this, too, is 'absolutely wrong' and he will prove it. I tell him that I believe the business was insolvent by December 1989, because it had a going concern qualification from its auditors, was haemorrhaging cash, and only surviving on First Pacific's money. His reply is, as ever, 'That is absolutely wrong', and goes on to add, 'The business was never insolvent'.

'At no stage?' I ask him.

'Correct.'

The next day I produce the figures confirming what I have said, but he doesn't want to look at them or discuss the details. So how does he explain all the criticisms? Well, to coin a phrase, they are 'absolutely wrong'. He suspects that his former fellow directors and executives just want to blame it all on him. 'I cannot accept for one second that all these intelligent people', he says, pointing to a picture of his management team, 'can maintain that they were not involved in what went on. Your accusation is that Jodee [he has slipped into third person again] was running as fast as he could and everyone else was telling him to slow down, and that's just not true'.

Jodee may be right, of course. It seems in his eyes, he always is. He reminds me that Imagineering, now renamed Tech Pacific, is once again a successful business, worth several hundred million dollars. So it's absolutely wrong to say that his company collapsed.

But Jodee Rich took Imagineering to the very brink of bankruptcy. The people who backed him lost millions of dollars. And *he* no longer owns it.

4

Welcome to One.Tel

Optus was young and naïve,
and Jodee took us to the cleaners.

Optus executive

After his ignominious exit from Imagineering, Jodee Rich went on holiday for nine months with his wife Maxine, a successful corporate lawyer whom he had married in a glamorous ceremony at the New South Wales Art Gallery in December 1987. Together, they went helicopter skiing in the Rockies, skiing in the Alps, and to cooking school in France. In the hope of picking up some tips, perhaps, Jodee also spent six weeks at the Wharton Business School in Pennsylvania, doing the advanced management program for mid-life executives.

Maxine Rich is tall, dark, pretty, rich, thin and smart—and almost universally liked—which has made some people ask uncharitably how Jodee managed to catch her. As it happened, they had known each other since their teens, and been childhood sweethearts. They were introduced by Maxine's elder brother, Phillip Brenner, who was Jodee's best friend at Cranbrook, but their relationship hadn't started well. In August 2001, after his second spectacular corporate crash, Jodee told *Good Weekend* that Maxine disliked him so much on first meeting him that she told her brother, 'I never want to see that boy in the house again'. Presumably, Jodee told this story to demonstrate that he was much nicer than he seemed, or that, however long the odds, he could be guaranteed to overcome them.

Certainly, his determination to become a pilot suggested he did not give up easily. He had taken flying lessons in the late 1970s, while still a student, and been so frightened the first few times that he threw up. Despite that, he took to the air again in the last days of Imagineering and still found it torture: often he would wake sweating in the middle of the night, convinced he was going to crash and die. Yet he persevered, and now put in the hours needed to win his commercial licence, flying bigger and faster planes, all the way up to Lear jets. His mother told friends proudly that no one in history had learnt to fly so many planes so quickly.

By the early 1990s he had become passionate about it: he loved flying planes and clearly got huge satisfaction from teaching others. And, unlike most people, he was rich enough to have it as his hobby. Despite all the disasters at Imagineering, in which shareholders had lost almost all their investment, Jodee had salvaged some $8 million from the company, which was more than enough to pay for his own private plane.

In 1992, to the great joy of his flying instructor at Bankstown Airport, he bought himself a Cessna Citation jet from the Commonwealth Bank. According to Jodee, the bank was selling it cheap after repossessing it from another casualty of the late 1980s boom and bust.

He used it briefly to work as a charter pilot, ferrying all sorts of people up and down the east coast, including the New South Wales Premier, Nick Greiner. In 1993, he flew down to Canberra late one night to pick up Kerry Packer and his son James, whose private DC-8 had developed engine trouble. With a strong southerly tailwind they were back in Sydney in 25 minutes, which was much faster than Kerry normally managed. To Jodee's great surprise, Australia's richest man failed to recognise him. He rationalised that Kerry hadn't expected to see the famous former whiz kid in the uniform of an airborne taxi driver.

When he wasn't flying, skiing or supervising the building of a splendid new house in Vaucluse for him and Maxine—they had lived in the garden flat of the Riches' family home in Bellevue Hill since their marriage—Jodee was back at Sydney University, studying for a second degree, in biochemistry. He had always been interested in the ageing process, and wanted to find a scientific way to reverse it. He took vitamins, dietary supplements and all manner of tonics to keep himself young. Friends said he was paranoid about growing old.

By August 1994, after four years out of the rat race, he was itching to get back into the fray, make more money and create another empire. And so, as Jodee tells the story, the idea of One.Tel was born. Sitting in a ski lodge at Thredbo one night, after a hard day on the slopes, he and a skiing buddy got talking telephones . . . as you do. Jodee said to his mate: 'Why don't we start a telephone company for normal people?'.

It wasn't quite as bizarre as that, of course, because his buddy was Brad Keeling, the marketing whiz at Imagineering, who had left to become managing director of Australia's biggest and fastest-growing mobile phone dealer, Strathfield Car Radio.

As both men knew well, the mobile phone promised to be the computer of the 1990s. The market was growing at 100 per cent a year, and there was money to be made. Over in the UK, independent phone companies were already making a mint by buying network access from the big carriers and reselling it to the public with a different brand name, and several in Australia, such as Digicall and First Direct, were trying it too. With the market newly deregulated, and with Brad and Jodee's talent for pulling in customers, there seemed to be no reason why they couldn't make a success of it.

The difficulty would be to persuade Telstra, Optus or Vodafone to let them into the game. Telstra had already decided not to use resellers because it did not want upstart rivals pinching its customers, but Optus was known to be keener. And Jodee knew Bob Mansfield, the company's boss, who was a close friend and colleague of the former Imagineering director, Peter Ritchie. It took just one meeting, a couple of weeks later, to sell him the concept. 'Bob thought it was a great idea', says Rich.

Unlike Telstra, Optus was desperate for customers. It had spent billions of dollars laying out a network and sorely needed to get some calls. To use an airline analogy, its planes were flying empty, and it had to get bums on seats. It could sell spare capacity to Rich at almost any price and still do better than before. But Jodee's pitch offered Optus more than that. Through direct marketing to young people, tradesmen, companies and sports clubs, he and Keeling would be able to attract a whole range of customers that Optus might otherwise miss.

Mansfield and his marketing people were impressed and sent Jodee off to write a business plan, with the help of three number crunchers from Optus's finance department. He was supposed to be finishing his degree and preparing for exams—as he had been when he was starting Imagineering—but once again he would have to find the time to do both successfully.

Within three months, his team had written a 16-page draft, codenamed Project E, which was an absolute masterpiece of business prose, the snappiest bit describing the key objectives thus:

> Use a highly integrated voice and data processing system to customise the end user interface, maximise internal efficiency, and leverage the customer base. Use internal systems to provide the support for unique partnership.

It was a miracle that it didn't go straight in the bin. But the idea was better than the language, and Optus was keen to proceed. The big carrier set only one condition for getting involved, which was that Jodee should find a corporate backer to put in some money. He already had just the man in mind: his old schoolmate, Rodney Adler. He was always keen to back new ideas, on the basis that only one in ten needed to work for him to make a profit, and he still had faith in Jodee, despite Imagineering. Adler had just one problem: 'Jodee said "I want to be a mobile telephone reseller". And I listened for a bit and didn't understand a word of it. So I said, "Fantastic, fantastic. Please explain"'.

Adler sent him to see a variety of people who did know what a reseller was. And despite his odd appearance, Jodee managed to sell them the idea. One recalls that the 34-year-old Rich looked pretty weird after four years in the corporate wilderness. 'He had long hair that grew out of the top of his ears, which he had waxed into points.' Yes, really. 'He looked just like an elf', this witness swears today, 'and he had these strange manner-isms, like stroking you'. Once again, one can only marvel that One.Tel got off the ground.

Adler's next step was to give Jodee office space at FAI and introduce him to his business analyst, Diane Nolder, whose job it was to sort the wheat from the chaff among the projects that came Adler's way. Smart, straight-talking and honest, Nolder did not think much of Project E at first. The business plan was so scanty and lacking in detail that she could see no obvious reason to recom-mend it. When she told Adler this, he was so clearly unhappy that she went back to have another look.

Within a matter of days, Jodee had persuaded Nolder to change her mind. He was so enthusiastic, so confi-dent, so sure he had a winner, that she couldn't help but be swayed. The more she asked for details, the more he convinced her he was right. She had seen hundreds of projects cross her desk and scores of budding tycoons walk through her door, but Jodee stood out as the best entrepreneur she had ever seen.

There were other things that made his idea look good. The mobile phone market was growing twice as fast as the PC market in the early 1980s and the two big carriers couldn't cope with the rush. It would obviously suit Optus to have an outfit like One.Tel help sign up customers, connect them and deal with their bills.

But the core of its appeal to FAI, or any other backer, lay in the extraordinary deal that Rich had negotiated with Optus. Not only had the carrier agreed to pay big subsidies to One.Tel so it could pump out cheap handsets to customers, it had guaranteed to sell calls at a rate that would give One.Tel a fat margin, and had promised to give the company $170 for every new connection.

Better still, Optus was committing itself to paying an extra 'loyalty' bonus of $120 in cash for every customer that One.Tel signed up—which was $120 more than anyone else in the industry was getting. This not only ensured that the company could survive without financial support from FAI, it almost guaranteed One.Tel's success. In the words of one of the Optus analysts working on the project, 'It was a gift, the like of which you've never seen'. This man was so impressed that he joined One.Tel soon after, became a director, and ended up making a killing on the shares.

It is hard now to understand why Optus offered such a generous deal, but James Packer had already been lined up by Jodee as a potential One.Tel shareholder, and it was likely that it made sense to keep the Packers sweet. Not only was Kerry a major player in Optus Vision at the time, and a shareholder in the parent company, but young James was leading the fight against Super League on the Packers' and Optus Vision's behalf.

A simpler explanation from a former Optus executive is that Jodee's negotiating team, led by the current second in command at Telstra, Ted Pretty, was just too good: 'Optus was young and naïve, and Jodee took us to the cleaners'. An experienced telecommunications lawyer who observed the process agrees: 'The Optus team just wasn't good enough. They didn't understand what they were giving away'.

Some of FAI's directors also had trouble appreciating how good the deal was. Having worked through the night to get the board papers ready, Diane Nolder was called in by FAI's chairman, John Landerer, to explain why FAI should risk its money. Even though the company was being asked to invest only $950,000, he was openly sceptical, and said it would be on her head if One.Tel was a dog. Luckily, she was tough enough to stick to her guns.

In Nolder's view, the risks were extremely low because Optus was so keen on the project that it would be eager to make it work. And if the worst came to the worst, it would probably rescue the company to stop One.Tel's customers being snapped up by Telstra. On the other hand, success could bring a bonanza, because Optus might buy the company for a great deal more, to prevent it becoming a threat.

After some discussion, the board of FAI voted to give Jodee the thumbs up, which left One.Tel needing only final approval from the Optus directors to get going. Jodee had assured them he had no desire to build a network or go head-to-head with the carrier. He would just bring in customers, so that Optus could focus on Pay TV, cabling Australia and other big ticket items. This was what everyone wanted to hear, and the board duly agreed to put in $1.5 million. It was a remarkably small amount of money given where One.Tel would end up.

With Optus and FAI on the bandwagon, others now rushed to jump on too. Back in August, Rich had asked James Packer to invest in the company after running into him at the airport (as Jodee tells the tale), or after Bob Mansfield had suggested they talk (if you accept a different version of the story). They already knew each other slightly, according to Jodee, because his brother-in-law, Phillip Brenner, had dated James's sister Gretel.

At that stage, the 27-year-old heir to the Packer fortune was lukewarm about the idea. He had run it past Brian Powers, head of the family's investment company Consolidated Press Holdings, and been told it was too small and too much of a distraction from the Packers' core businesses in TV and magazines. But with the proposal looking a certain winner, James was now hot to trot and prepared to risk some of his own money, which he had made on a couple of recent property developments. Meanwhile, Jodee had become far cooler about sharing the spoils with anyone else, and had decided he had all the capital he needed.

Letters and phone calls went back and forth, and it looked as though Packer would have to miss out because Jodee was not prepared to budge. Then Rodney Adler intervened. He and James had known each other for many years and had both been at Cranbrook, though several years apart. They lived in the same part of town, moved in the same social circles, tapped into the same networks and had already made money together in property. Rodney told Jodee it would be good for One.Tel to have the Packers on board. It would doubtless also do wonders for the share price if the company ever went public.

Jodee was still concerned: 'I wanted to know who we were going to be partners with', he says. 'I wanted to know if it was James or Kerry, and I made James promise it would be his investment.'

To squeeze this important passenger onto the bus before it left, another 500 shares had to be issued. James was given five per cent of the new company for $250,000, a proportion of which he had to hold through Jodee's unit trust, Kalara Investments. This allowed Ted Pretty, who had led negotiations with Optus, to be fitted in too.

Kalara would control One.Tel, with just over 50 per cent of the shares, most of which belonged to Jodee. Keeling would have five per cent, although this was not made public. Optus would have 28 per cent and Rodney Adler around 17 per cent. All up, the company would have around $4 million to play with.

In early March 1995 the shareholders of the new company gathered in Adler's boardroom at FAI to sign all the documents. As Jodee stood silhouetted against the window, one of those present noticed his long ear hairs, lit up by the rays of the bright autumn sun.

Two months later, on Monday, 1 May 1995, One.Tel officially opened for business in brand new offices at the top of the Castlereagh Centre, a shiny steel tower in Sydney's CBD, 100 metres from Martin Place. The launch was a strange, low-key affair, with a handful of the company's new staff hitting the phones while an electronic scoreboard counted calls (to God-knows-who). There were streamers, half a dozen journalists, and a large rent-a-crowd of friends and hangers-on from the Eastern Suburbs. As one woman tartly observed, she appeared to be the only poor person who had been invited.

It was garish and corny, but it also had flair. The red telephone box, which would become a One.Tel trademark, held centre stage. Tim Shaw, the man from Demtel, acted as master of ceremonies, and Rodney Adler cut the ribbon. His wife, Lindy, quipped that she had expected Superman to leap out of the phone box, but there was nothing so exciting. As Maxine Rich, heavily pregnant with their second child, looked on, Jodee made a speech about the sort of outfit that One.Tel would be. There would be a flat management structure, no hierarchies, and everyone would be encouraged to lie on the grass.

There was already a hint that these freedoms would be rigidly enforced. Everyone had been made to wear a One.Badge, so that even Bob Mansfield had One.Bob pinned to his lapel. Of One.James Packer there was no sign. He was said to be off in Europe.

Jodee's pitch outlined what the new company would offer. It would be a re-packaged, re-branded Optus service at lower cost (although that certainly wasn't how he put it), with a single phone bill, One.Bill, for local, long-distance and mobile phone services. It would offer simplicity and convenience. There would be no more absurdly complicated tariff plans. Nor would there be any question of taking on Optus or Telstra. One.Tel would not be tempted to set up its own telephone network or become a rival carrier, he promised. 'One.Tel will not be competing with its most valued customers.'

For a company that would soon be worth billions, the birth had a pretty quiet reception. There were no great fanfares in the press. An industry newsletter, *Communications Day*, scooped its rivals by getting wind of the occasion three days before, but no one followed it up. The only people who seemed to be interested were the boys from Telstra. Grahame Lynch, then editor of *Communications Day*, remembers Telstra's corporate affairs department was very keen to give him the spin: 'The line they were spreading was basically that the mobile phone industry was dodgy, that there were lots of dodgy dealers out there . . . and that One.Tel was in that mould. Telstra basically raised question marks over the credibility of Brad and Jodee, saying, "Look how desperate Optus are. They're turning to these guys to run their company". They were keen to point up Jodee's failure with Imagineering, and keen to cast doubt about Brad's character'.

In fact, Telstra was doing a lot more than that to cause trouble for its new rival. Just two weeks before the launch, it had set the New South Wales Fraud Squad onto Brad Keeling over a crime it alleged he had committed in his last days at Strathfield Car Radio.

It was no secret that Keeling and Strathfield, which just happened to be Telstra's biggest mobile phone dealer, had parted on bad terms. According to the company's owner and founder, Andrew Kelly, who was asked about Keeling on ABC Radio the day after One.Tel collapsed, 'He failed to come back from holidays in January [1995], so we basically fired him, the board fired him, or we got him to resign'.

The full story was far juicier. Three weeks before the One.Tel launch, Keeling sued Strathfield for damages in the Federal Court. Three weeks after the launch, his ex-employer filed a cross claim and promised to raise 'serious allegations of misappropriation of moneys and fraud'. In the interim, the New South Wales Police were told that Brad had pocketed around $200,000 in unauthorised bonuses.

Seven months later, with One.Tel already hauling in thousands of customers, Keeling was summoned to Surry Hills police station and charged with three counts of 'cheating or defrauding' Strathfield 'by obtaining bank cheques totalling $150,000'. Six months after that, the mud began to fly. When the case came to Sydney's local court for committal in May 1996, Keeling's lawyers accused Strathfield of conspiring with Telstra to invent the charges against him so as to 'bring about irreparable damage to the company, One.Tel'.

It was soon revealed that it was Telstra, not Strathfield, which had made the original complaint. Somewhat bizarrely, the head of Telstra's Investigations Unit had phoned the commander of the armed hold-up unit of Sydney's Major Crime Squad to set the police on Keeling's tail. Shortly afterwards, Detective Senior Sergeant Helen Gilbert was sent to a meeting with Telstra, Strathfield and a bevy of lawyers, to be briefed on charges that might be brought. According to DS Gilbert, Telstra offered to help the police in any way possible and was 'very keen to assist'.

And assist they certainly did. Not only did Telstra provide an Avis hire car to the fraud squad for the entire investigation into Keeling—which lasted seven months— but the court was told that the national carrier had quite possibly bankrolled the whole enquiry. Naturally, they showed an extremely close interest in how the case was going, and made regular calls to the officer in charge.

Before the case was tossed out of court in September 1996, with all charges dismissed, Telstra's lawyers tried to explain why Keeling's dealings with Strathfield were any of their business, but they failed miserably. The most plausible explanation was that they wanted to damage

One.Tel and Optus. They may have also had personal reasons to get back at Keeling, who had made himself spectacularly unpopular in his last months at Strathfield.

Keeling and Telstra had argued constantly about Strathfield becoming a reseller like One.Tel, which had clearly caused friction. They had fought even harder over Strathfield's plans to float, which was all ready to go in October 1994 when Telstra suddenly vetoed it to prevent details of its confidential contracts with Strathfield being made public. Keeling was furious, because he had wasted months and would now lose millions of dollars worth of shares. He confessed in court that he had let fly:

> I was very forceful with Telstra about their disallowing disclosure of the contract . . . and therefore preventing us from floating . . . I had very heated arguments . . . very heated arguments, yeah, pretty much blew the relationship apart.

Those who have been on the wrong end of a blast from Brad Keeling say that he can be seriously offensive when he wants to be. Many still blanch at the memory of tirades they have witnessed. One ex-Telstra executive who dealt with him throughout this difficult period says: 'In my whole life I've never witnessed anything as bad as I have when I was dealing with that guy . . . I remember being in a meeting once when he ordered a Telstra guy off the premises, someone who worked on the Strathfield account, and for absolutely no reason.

He yelled at him: "Before we start anything, you get the hell out of my building now"'. Years later, the man still loathes Keeling with a passion: 'He is all about money and ego. The ego is so big you can't jump over it. You've never met anything like it. To feed it was almost impossible. And it just got bigger and bigger. After he won the court case, you didn't want to be anywhere near him. He thought he was indestructible'.

There is virtually nothing in the public domain about Brad Keeling's background, apart from some scant details of his business career. He has managed to keep himself out of *Who's Who in Australia* and other such reference works and refused several invitations to be interviewed for this book, but friends say he was brought up in the Northern Suburbs and went to Shore, the Sydney Church of England Grammar School, in North Sydney. Keeling is four years older than Jodee Rich, which means he was born in the mid-1950s, and several centimetres shorter, which makes him around 170 cm. Grey-haired, clean cut, always casually dressed, he certainly does not stand out in a crowd, and was able to walk past photographers unrecognised when the press was staking out One.Tel's offices after the collapse in 2001. Even at the height of One.Tel's success, he preferred to keep a low profile: he was rarely seen at big parties or glitzy social events, continued to live quietly on the North Shore, rather than in the flashier Eastern Suburbs, and seemed to devote most of his spare time to skiing.

Many people were puzzled that Jodee chose him as his partner in 1995. The two men were not close personal friends and had barely seen each other in the four years since Imagineering's implosion. As one of his fellow Imagineers puts it: 'It was a constant source of amazement to lots of people when Jodee set up business with him. They seemed like such an odd couple. Jodee was so smart and Brad wasn't'.

Despite his admitted talent for marketing, Keeling seemed to many people to be precisely the wrong sort of person for Rich to team up with if he wanted to avoid repeating his mistakes. In the words of one former senior executive who had watched young Rich's rocket crash and burn: 'Jodee desperately needed a strong financial manager. But none of the people he brought in from Imagineering fitted the bill, least of all, Brad Keeling'.

At Imagineering, Brad had always been Jodee's golden-haired boy, though few could understand why. He was notorious with the finance team for his habit of blowing budgets and building everything up to be bigger than Ben Hur. As one accountant recalls, 'He spent money with a vengeance. He spent millions on sponsorship, advertising and promotion', and continued to do so even as the company careered towards disaster.

Joe De Simone, one of Imagineeering's biggest dealers, was also amazed. 'Having those two guys in charge of One.Tel was just unbelievable. There was no doubt in my mind One.Tel would explode. I thought they would put some smart people in to control Jodee, but Brad just pumped him up even further. He didn't learn anything when he set up One.Tel. The same exuberance was there, the same high-risk strategy. The business was built on hype and promise. You might as well have put your money on a horse. At least you knew the odds.'

One accountant who had worked closely with Jodee and Brad at Imagineering reckoned it *was* worth a wager—but not that it would succeed. He bet his friend $100 that the new venture would go broke, then sat back to wait for his payout.

5

One.Happy Family

A happy team means happy players.

One.Tel's Beliefs and Values

One of One.Tel's first employees was a big bluff yachtie from Auckland named Paul Fleetwood, who, at 40-something, was twice the age of most of the other new recruits. Two days before the launch he had been running an Optus dealership in Double Bay, but he had been told to link up with a bigger dealer or close down, so he had come along to Brad and Jodee, who hired him on the spot.

There were 19 of them on that first day, huddled at one end of a huge L-shaped office occupying the entire 28th floor. Jodee had managed to rent the space at fire-sale rates and picked up some old Oregon bench tops for everyone to sit at. Stocks of mobile phones and accessories were piled up in boxes, and throughout the day a queue of dealers would form waiting to collect them.

Fleetwood had been warned by some of his friends and Optus contacts that it would all end in tears. 'Just look at what Jodee's done before', they told him. But One.Tel went gangbusters almost from the start, and after the first few weeks the new team could barely keep pace with sales. Paul would come in at 5.30am to connect customers signed the previous day, and find Brad Keeling had beaten him to it. He rarely got home before 8.00pm and once came back to the office in the middle of the night because he had so much left to do. Jodee was also working these crazy hours.

When one or two of the new recruits complained about the pressure, Jodee called them all into the meeting room for a pep talk. At Imagineering, he told them, people had mortgaged their houses to buy the company's shares, the price was falling through the floor, the warehouse was full of stock, and the phones weren't ringing. 'That's pressure', he said. 'Here the phones are ringing, we've got customers. This is fun.'

One.Tel's business plan had promised 16,000 customers by the end of the first year, but after only five months they had already hit their target, and the team had grown to 50 people. Five months later, they had passed 50,000 customers and their ranks had doubled again. 'I would go there one day and there would be another five desks', says a former Optus marketing man.

'I'd go there again and there would be another five rows; I'd go a few months later and they would have expanded to another floor.'

Visitors were struck by the atmosphere that Jodee had created. 'There was fantastic camaraderie', says an Optus executive, who had never seen a telephone company remotely like it. 'It was full of young kids. Everyone thought they could do no wrong.'

Their aim was to be 'fun and friendly', which Brad and Jodee believed to be the essence of Australian service. And they certainly succeeded. To the people at Optus, a company still dominated by engineers in grey cardigans, One.Tel's style and success were both a revelation and a warning. According to the management consultants whom Optus had hired to find 'best practice', their infant rival was as good as anyone else in the world. It was giving customers what they wanted, and doing it fast. It was miles ahead of any other reseller and even further in front of Optus and Telstra. Where the two telephone giants would take 90 to 120 days to get new products or promotions onto the market—because they had to be designed, discussed and run through committees—One.Tel could get them onto the street in 48 hours.

The company's information and billing system, which formed the backbone of the business, was also a marvel. One.Sys could tell salespeople how many customers they had connected, and show call centre staff how many people they had spoken to, or missed. If a customer wanted to know who the babysitter had phoned on a Saturday night, One.Tel could tell them in a flash. There was even a frowning face to warn team members to be especially nice to any customer who had been unhappy with One.Tel in the past. Jodee had decreed that the software developers should sit with the people who used this system so they could see any problems first-hand. And this made it more user-friendly, more readily improved and more easily fixed.

In fact, in those early days everyone sat together. They were all on one floor with no partitions, offices or corridors, and everyone mucked in. They also took turns to wear a yellow fireman's hat for a day. It was the fireman's job to run around for everyone else, loading paper into the photocopier, getting the stationery, running errands, fixing problems and fighting fires. It was one big happy family.

Just like at Imagineering, there were teams and champions, but One.Tel's brand of corporate culture was far more pervasive. They were called One.Team and One.Champ, and the champions had their pictures painted onto the wall. There was also the One.Tel Story, which everybody had to know in case Jodee made them recite it. New recruits were asked to define a team player, to which the correct answer was someone who enjoyed others' success and *shared*. A cartoon on the wall labelled 'Vitamin C' encouraged everyone to give tablets to one another—an allegory for sharing what you knew. 'In big companies, secrets make you special', Jodee would say, 'because you have knowledge that other people lack'. In One.Tel, no secrets were allowed.

The collected wisdom of Jodee's philosophy was inscribed in One.Tel's Beliefs and Values, a mixture of Deepak Chopra, est and New Age management theory, which was all about caring, sharing, positive thinking and peer review. There were to be no hierarchies, no job titles, nor even job descriptions. There would only be missions. That was a One.Tel rule: there must be 'no artificial boundaries that people feel they cannot cross'. Organisational charts were also banned. That was another One.Tel rule: 'We try to do everything as a team'. Email would have been a valuable way of keeping people informed, but that was banned too. Brad believed it was too impersonal to fit in with One.Tel's people culture. 'We're a voicemail company', he never failed to tell people, 'not an email company'. Yet another One.Tel rule.

There was more than an element of a religion or cult about it all. And those who didn't follow the leader risked being challenged on their faith. Paul Fleetwood remembers Jodee coming up to his desk one day when the message light on his phone was blinking. He was led towards the meeting room, where Jodee closed the door and asked him coldly: 'Don't you want to work for this company?'. A puzzled Fleetwood said he did. 'I left you a message half an hour ago', Jodee continued, 'and you haven't answered it. Don't let me ever see that again'.

There were a dozen years between them—Paul had been in high school when Jodee was in nappies—but Fleetwood felt he was being scolded by the headmaster.

Out in the marketplace the company seemed much more relaxed, thanks to One.Tel's public persona: 'the dude'. Young, hip and not too bright, he was the creation of Jodee's brother-in-law, Adam Long, who was an illustrator and interior designer. Long's brief was to design a comic strip featuring two guys who knew nothing about telephones, and the dude was the dumbest character he could come up with.

No one defined exactly what the dude should be like, but his job was to tell customers it was so easy to get a phone from One.Tel that even an idiot could do it, and so cheap that even a layabout could afford it. He emerged as a scruffy surfer who came dressed in bright blue, orange and green, with a goatee beard, long, straw-coloured hair and a green checked beanie. Before long, he had acquired a dog, 'the dude's dog', and a girlfriend called Jennifer, who was smart and sassy and worked at One.Tel. Jennifer, of course, could explain all the company's new products, which was very convenient.

The dude was a massive hit, and vital in making One.Tel an instantly recognisable brand. But inside the company, he was not universally popular, with one older member of the team describing it all witheringly as 'a complete wank'.

Long's colour scheme for the One.Tel offices was also not a hit with everyone. The idea was to cheer the place up, make it more fun, but the bigger and more successful the company became, the brighter and brasher it got. Starting with pastel yellows, pale greens and pinks, it was soon revving up to electric blue, sunflower yellow, lime green and orange, as One.Tel grew and spread to new floors in the building.

The brightly coloured walls also carried huge Adam Long cartoons, illustrating a different theme on each floor. There was an underwater floor, a flying machine floor and a space rocket floor, peppered with motivational messages from One.Tel's Beliefs and Values, such as:

ADD AND CREATE VALUE IN EVERYTHING YOU DO.

MAKE IT BETTER.

GIVE YOUR OPINIONS.

A HAPPY TEAM MEANS HAPPY PLAYERS.

The IT floor featured a Greek mythology theme, with a picture of Theseus and the Minotaur in the famous maze. Underneath was the moral of the story: 'Don't be secretive'. Another cartoon showed the dude swinging his sword at a many-headed hydra, the creature whose heads grew back as fast as anyone could chop them off. Under this, somewhat bizarrely, was an exhortation to 'Minimise Meetings'.

It was daring of Long even to use the word, because it was another One.Tel rule that you could not call a meeting or, to be precise, that you could not call a meeting a meeting. It had to be a 'huddle'. And this was not the only word you had to keep handy. Groups of people, and the benches they sat at, had to be referred to as pods—like dolphins. You could not say desks.

Despite all the rules inside the office, out on the streets it seemed that One.Tel recognised no rules at all—or simply broke them. Every few weeks it would promise to scrap more fees, cut prices further, ease conditions on contracts and deliver more freedom for customers. By September 1996, One.Team had notched up 100,000 connections, which meant that the company had doubled its numbers in only six months. It was like the early days at Imagineering, except the business was growing even faster.

Even those who questioned Rich's choice of Keeling as his business partner now had to admit he had a real flair for marketing. And it wasn't just the dude or One.Tel's snappy brochures that demonstrated it. Realising that One.Tel owned a host of numbers whose last six digits began with a '3', Keeling used Telstra's White Pages on disc to match them against existing six-figure numbers in Sydney's Eastern Suburbs. Soon afterwards, letters were winging their way to residents of Bondi to tell them that One.Tel had specially reserved a matching mobile number for their personal use. It was a brilliant stroke that no fan of the dude could possibly resist.

Sales were going crazy for another reason: the pot of money that Optus had promised to One.Tel for every customer it signed up. Every new mobile number registered brought the company an immediate cash payment of $120—the so-called loyalty bonus—which went straight into the bank. And the more people One.Tel signed, the faster this cash flowed in. One.Tel didn't even need to sell handsets or sign people on to long-term contracts to get these Optus payments. Giving out SIM cards, which counted as new mobile numbers, was more than sufficient.

As a result, One.Team had a powerful incentive to sign up customers that no one else would touch, which is exactly what it did. According to one person who worked at One.Tel from the beginning, 'It was a chronic customer base, full of single mothers, pensioners, and schoolkids'. But with Optus shovelling cash at the company, it hardly mattered.

One.Tel's dealers also got money from the Optus pot for every new punter they pulled in, so they too recruited legions of dodgy customers. Naturally, One.Tel's sales staff were on hefty commissions too, so the process was turbocharged still further.

As an old One.Tel insider tells the story: 'There were dealers who would go and stand on Bondi Beach, or go to Cabramatta and stand on a street corner, with a bunch of application forms and pay people $10 to sign up.

There was no access fee, no minimum call spend, and the contracts had no fixed term, so there was no way of ensuring that these customers would stay with One.Tel and spend money. Dealers would dump the boxes of application forms on us. Often they'd be signing up their friends and family'.

The One.Tel team heard tales of dealers' agents sitting in the park with phone books, filling out forms with people's names and addresses, then knocking on the door to try and get a sale, telling them to, 'Just sign here'. There were frequent complaints from the public about being approached in this way. 'People would ring up and say, "What sort of a business signs people up on a street corner?".

Back at One.Tel it was all they could do to keep ahead of the surge in sales. Everything was being done by hand, so they would stick SIM cards onto photocopied sheets, write down the phone numbers and PIN codes, and send them off. The SIM cards were activated as soon as they left the building, even though there was no guarantee they would fall into the right hands. As soon as this was done, One.Tel could collect its Optus bonus. Optus could claw the money back if the number did not remain active for at least 12 months—and at least half the SIM cards were never used at all—but in the meantime the cash kept flowing. Clawbacks were tomorrow's problem, as were bad debts, which were already running at quite extraordinary levels.

According to a woman who ran One.Tel's collections department in the early days, a staggering 60 to 70 per cent of customers either paid late or did not pay at all, because so few checks were made when they signed on. At parties she heard her young cousins talking about One.Tel and how simple it was to rip the company off. All you needed to get a phone for free was a fake ID—they told her—because One.Tel and its dealers never did proper checks, so they would never be able to find you if you didn't pay the bill.

She reported these conversations to Jodee and suggested they tighten their procedures dramatically. His reply was that it would only stop sales. Thereafter, Jodee often told her that bad debts must be reduced. But One.Tel's sales department was never prepared only way to do this was to toughen credit checks and clamp down on dealers sufficiently to make a difference.

Even when credit checks were tightened—and it happened for short periods at a time—the dealers always found ways to bypass the system. One trick was to ring One.Tel to complain that they couldn't get a customer connected because the computer was down, then persuade someone to process the sale without the normal safeguards. Sales staff at One.Tel who could be relied on to help were rewarded with presents—a new mobile phone, a car charger, or a big bunch of flowers.

The man whose job it was to keep the dealers in line was a 6 foot 5 inch tall ex-Green Beret called Brian

Kirkman, who would pay dealers a visit to give them a warning. His first potential sanction was to get back commissions on non-paying customers. The next was to threaten to banish dealers who did not change their ways. But often Kirkman found his warnings and punishments had been countermanded by the time he got back to the office. George Savva, whose job at One.Tel was to run the dealer network, would tell him: 'You can't do this sort of thing. Dealers are our lifeline'.

Occasionally, the credit department would go head to head with Savva, and persuade Jodee or Brad to back them. They would then receive threats from the dealers, such as: 'I'm gonna kill ya . . . I'm gonna sue ya'. But in most battles with the salespeople at One.Tel, it was sales that won. It had been the same at Imagineering, and it would stay the same at One.Tel right till the end.

It was not just the Optus bonuses that were driving the company to pile on more customers irrespective of whether they would spend money or pay their bills. Even in early 1995, when One.Tel was launched, UK resellers were being valued by the number of customers they had on their books. The going rate back then was $1,000 a head, but the price tag kept rising. It therefore made perfect sense, as a money-making strategy, to grab as many customers as possible and then sell the company. In market slang it was known as 'pump and dump', and there was a common perception that this was exactly what One.Tel's founders were trying to do.

Keeling and Rich denied it constantly—and Jodee still does. But one woman who worked for them in these early years has absolutely no doubt that this was their initial aim. 'It was clear from the start that they weren't in it for the long term, that they were just building a business to sell. All they cared about was jacking the numbers up.'

And if that was their aim, they were certainly succeeding.

6

The Party's Over

Shit, we have a problem.

Optus chief operating officer, Phil Jacobs

The Optus-funded extravaganza at One.Tel could not
last forever, but if the carrier wanted to put the lid
back on the money pot, it was in for a fight.

The man in the front line of any such battle would be
a tough, determined economist called Andrew Bailey,
who was not long out of the public service. In January
1996, eight months after the One.Tel launch, he was put
in charge of Optus's new wholesale division and told to
get a better return on the billions of dollars that had
been spent on the network. In particular, his brief was
to get more out of resellers like One.Tel.

When he first set eyes on the deal that Jodee had won
he was appalled. Not only was it far more generous than
anything the other resellers had been given, but the

contract was so vague and ill-defined that One.Tel could just about dictate its own terms. The agreement had been kept under lock and key since its creation, and even Optus's new chief operating officer, an American called Phil Jacobs who had been flown in from Bell South in Georgia, had not been shown it. His comment when he was told what it contained was blunt and to the point: 'Shit, we have a problem'.

A look at the money flow between the two companies reinforced this view. Optus was pouring millions of dollars into its upstart rival and getting precious little back. The loyalty bonuses alone were costing Optus more than $1 million a month because One.Tel was signing up customers so fast. Worse still, One.Tel appeared to be using the cash to finance cut-price deals and special offers that the carrier could never hope to match. Put bluntly, Optus was paying One.Tel a fortune to pinch its customers.

It was extraordinary that Optus had not twigged that this would happen. A brief look at Imagineering's progress in the 1980s would have shown that Jodee had doubled the size of his company every year, without the help of cash handouts like this. But no one had envisaged him doing the same with One.Tel: they only worried that he would fail again.

Bailey's official declaration of war came in a letter to Rich in March 1996 telling him that the agreement with One.Tel had to be rewritten so Optus could make money too. But hostilities had already broken out months before. As far back as August 1995, there had been a skirmish over ads One.Tel had placed in the *Financial Review* offering cheap STD rates to corporate customers. The company was not supposed to be pursuing this business and an Optus director rang Brad Keeling to tell him to back off.

The same month, One.Tel had taken space in all the Sydney papers to announce a huge sale of mobile phones at knock-down prices. Soon afterwards, Optus had been accused by One.Tel of holding back supplies of SIM cards to slow down the number of new customers it could sign up. Thereafter, fights broke out regularly, with Optus hitting back at almost every One.Tel special offer by slapping on new fees or telling the company to withdraw. On more than one occasion the finance director of One.Tel was hauled over to Optus HQ in North Sydney to explain how the company could offer such incredible deals.

After Bailey took over in January the clashes between these two supposed allies turned into guerrilla warfare. When One.Tel launched a new cheap deal with no minimum spend, Optus shot it down by charging One.Tel a new monthly minimum of $55 a customer. When One.Tel dropped access fees for people taking up new SIM cards, Optus levied a new fee on all existing One.Tel customers who accepted the offer. There was also a running battle over the Optus logo, which some One.Tel dealers were using to fool people into thinking they were getting the Optus service at half price.

Throughout these exchanges, Rich never lost his cool, and never let the disputes get personal. Even though he was at loggerheads with Bailey and his team, he greeted them like long-lost brothers or much-missed friends. When One.Tel reached 100,000 customers, at the height of the conflict, he sent the Optus sales team a cake. One weekend he took them all kayaking on the harbour. On another, he whisked Bailey and Jacobs off for flying lessons at Bankstown Airport. In negotiations, he was charming, street-cunning and sharp, but his instant intimacy left the former bureaucrat unmoved. Bailey had made up his mind to get the relationship back on proper commercial terms, and was determined to see it happen.

Bailey also had other pressures to worry about. He was being bombarded by Optus's retail division—who hated One.Tel—and was facing a similar barrage from One.Tel's rivals, who were desperate to see Brad and Jodee hauled back into line. Barry Roberts-Thompson from Hutchison and Terry Winters from Link Communications were convinced that One.Tel could not afford to sign 10,000 customers a month and offer lower rates unless Jodee was getting far more money from Optus than they were, and they kept complaining about it to the company, and kept being assured they were wrong.

It was not long before matters were brought to a head. In May 1996 Jodee announced he wanted to float

One.Tel on the Australian Stock Exchange before the end of the year so that he could raise money from the public, or even sell the business, lock, stock and barrel.

This was the last thing Optus wanted to see happen, because it would allow One.Tel to grow even faster than before, and would inevitably mean that details of the secret loyalty bonuses would have to be revealed. If the other service providers found out how much One.Tel was being paid, they would all start demanding more, and might well sue. Each had been told they were getting the best deal, and Link even had a clause in its contract guaranteeing it had been given 'Most Favoured Nation' status, so they would be outraged if they discovered that Optus had lied to them.

But as these things happen, One.Tel's rivals soon found out anyway. Out of the ether, a document came through Terry Winters's fax machine, showing all the details of One.Tel's monthly receipts. A flunky in the Optus accounts department had accidentally pressed the wrong button.

Winters admits today that he was 'pretty pissed off and angry' when he discovered the deception, but he laughs about it as he tells the story. At his next meeting with Optus he again asked for assurances that his deal was equal to the best and that One.Tel was not getting a Rolls-Royce ride. Once again, the Optus team ducked the chance to fess up. 'They said no, no, One.Tel hasn't got a better deal. So then we told them we had a copy of their statement to One.Tel. You can imagine the look on their faces. Gotcha. Guilty as charged.'

Bailey's boys were clearly embarrassed at being caught with their pants down, but they did not apologise. Nor did they immediately offer Winters the same deal as One.Tel was getting. So Link threatened to sue, while the other service providers jumped up and down, demanding action. With everyone up in arms, Optus had little choice but to sort things out.

On 1 October 1996 an agreement was reached in which the loyalty bonus was scrapped, Optus agreed to sell its shares, and a large amount of compensation was paid to One.Tel. The terms of this settlement have never been made public, but a close examination of One.Tel's financial records shows that Optus paid a staggering $19.75 million to end the loyalty bonus, and One.Tel handed back $4 million of this money to buy Optus out of its near 30 per cent shareholding. The net result was that Jodee Rich, Brad Keeling, James Packer, FAI and Ted Pretty found themselves proud, sole owners of a company that had another $15.75 million of Optus's money in the bank. It was the second time the carrier had been taken to the cleaners, and years later, Rodney Adler still marvels at how good a deal it was.

Once again, it's anybody's guess why Optus was so generous. And once again, one can only speculate that the Packers were a factor. As a shareholder in Optus Vision and a potential backer of the Optus Group,

James's father Kerry needed to be kept sweet, and it may have been worth paying a few million bucks to do so. According to Jodee, James talked to the new Optus boss, Ziggy Switkowski, a couple of times while the negotiations were in hand.

It probably also made sense to keep Jodee and Brad on side. They had already delivered 100,000 mobile customers to the Optus network, and promised to put more bums on seats—or calls on phones—in the future.

Finally, perhaps, it may have seemed small beer to Optus. Phil Jacobs, who negotiated the payout, was used to the high-spending habits of Bell South in Atlanta, whose headquarters were full of Chinese vases, French antique desks and carpets you could drown in. So a few million Australian dollars may not have bothered him unduly.

But for all that, the torrid 18-month affair with One.Tel had cost the carrier dearly. The prospectus for One.Tel's 1997 public float showed that the young telco had received around $80 million from Optus before the split, and had returned only $69 million of this to its partner. There was little doubt that the folks at Optus were aware of this imbalance, because they now began trying far harder to get their money back, and the fights became even worse than they had been before. Not only did Bailey and his wholesale division take another slice off the bonuses and commissions paid to One.Tel, which raised the company's costs, but Optus's retail division also cut prices in the marketplace, so that margins were squeezed at both ends.

The key battleground now switched to a huge Optus promotion called 'Yes, Today', which was designed to offer the same sort of cheap deals that people had been getting with One.Tel. It had been an immediate, roaring success since its introduction in mid-1996, and was becoming more successful by the day. In Jodee's words, 'They were eating us for breakfast. We could do nothing about it'.

One.Tel's contract was supposed to protect the company from this sort of attack, by guaranteeing extra subsidies so that One.Tel could still compete on level terms—or continue to undercut its rivals, if you preferred to think of it that way—but Bailey told Rich from the start that this support was no longer on offer. And he was not to be budged.

By the middle of 1997, One.Tel was being hurt so badly that it hired a top competition lawyer from Blake Dawson Waldron to draw up a damages claim against Optus for submission to the Australian Competition and Consumer Commission (ACCC). Pages and pages of examples were cited, along with a QC's opinion to say that the company had a case, and before long the carrier had been brought to the negotiating table for another round of haggling.

This time it was far less good-natured. There were two or three screaming matches between Jodee Rich and

Phil Jacobs in front of a team of a dozen lawyers and finance people. And there were a couple of occasions when Brad Keeling really went over the top. Even the team from One.Tel was embarrassed by how rude Jodee and Brad were. According to one of their staunchest supporters, 'It was disgusting'. After one eruption, Brad rang one of the Optus directors to ask whether the guys in the wholesale division would like one of the masseuses who came to One.Tel every fortnight to come round and calm them down. His offer was politely declined.

If the battle was fierce, it was also short-lived. One month after One.Tel's threat to take the case to the ACCC, Optus again took the easy way home and agreed to pay several more million dollars in compensation.

It was the third remarkable victory for Jodee and his team of lawyers in the space of two years. But it had not made them many friends, nor had it won One.Tel the war. In his time at the head of Optus's wholesale division, Bailey had tripled the amount of money collected from service providers like One.Tel and turned it into the carrier's most profitable operation. As a result, there was now virtually no money being made by One.Tel or its rivals.

Over at Hutchison Telecoms, managing director Barry Roberts-Thompson was famous for hoarding paper clips, because he reckoned the only way to make a profit in this business was to cut costs to the bone. But there was no way that Jodee, Brad and One.Tel would ever knuckle down to such discipline, or not for long. And without that, it was going to be very hard to make a profit. So, as the intrepid founders counted the money from the October 1996 Optus payout, they found themselves facing a major strategic problem: what on earth were they going to do next?

Out in the marketplace, mobile phone companies like Vodafone were now valued at anything up to $1,400 a customer, on which basis One.Tel was potentially worth up to $150 million. The obvious answer was to find a buyer—that is, to dump what they had pumped—but the harsh reality was that no one wanted to buy. Analysts who ran the ruler over One.Tel for banks and brokers couldn't see why you would want to pay squillions for a telephone company with no network. And while the UK carriers were busy buying service providers in Britain to get more customers, Optus showed no sign of wanting to do the same with One.Tel here.

The closest the team came to a sale was in mid-1997 when the Packers' family company, Consolidated Press Holdings (CPH), sent a couple of merchant bankers along to kick the tyres. James apparently wanted to put some tens of millions of dollars of the family's money into the business, but Brian Powers, who ran CPH for the Packers, was not keen. He was apparently impressed with One.Tel's energy, but was less than wild about Jodee, and his bankers gave the investment the thumbs-down anyway. They could see no way that One.Tel would ever make a decent profit, because it was spending big to acquire customers and not holding on to them for long enough to get its money back. One banker also took such a strong dislike to Brad Keeling that he wanted to jump across the table and throttle him.

The only other way for the founders to cash in their investment was to float the company on the Australian Stock Exchange, which was what they had wanted to do since mid-1996, even though this looked like falling flat because the market had seen so many similar endeavours flop. A big rival of One.Tel, Digicall, had gone public at the end of 1995 and died an almost immediate death. Another, First Direct, had collapsed around a year later.

In the end, in November 1997, One.Tel had to settle for a 'compliance listing', which required just 500 investors. And even this small number of punters proved hard to find. Part of the problem was the asking price, which had risen dramatically since Jodee and Brad had turned into sellers. Just 13 months earlier, Optus had been persuaded to accept $4 million for 28 per cent of One.Tel, but now the entire company was being valued at $208 million, or 15 times as much, which would make Jodee Rich more than $100 million richer.

These riches would only be paper profits unless One.Tel's founders sold their shares, and they were not planning to do that yet, because only one-200th of the company was being offered in the float. But the prospectus revealed that the original shareholders had already got their hands on some cash by dipping into the Optus money pot. Only months after getting the $19.75 million settlement, Rich, Keeling, Adler's FAI, Packer and Pretty had recovered their initial investment, with a 50 per cent bonus on top. In Jodee and Brad's case this meant more than $3 million. They had also lined up for some big consultancy fees—no doubt for consulting . . . or being consulted—which had seen another $3 million shared out between the lucky five, with almost half going to Jodee.

Even that wasn't the end of it, as Jodee, Brad and the other directors had also written themselves fat cheques in the form of 15 million stock options that could be converted into $2 shares for just 12.6 cents. Jodee and Brad's share of this prize was a healthy $7.5 million apiece, while One.Tel's new chairman, John Greaves, the former finance director of Optus, was in line for $6.25 million. Rodney Adler was next in the pecking order, with $4.4 million, and Mark Silbermann and Kevin Beck—both senior One.Tel executives—were in for $1.25 million each. Two years later, when One.Tel's shares hit an all-time high, you could multiply these rewards 12 times over.

Remarkably, this was not the last of the handouts. Information tucked away at the back of the prospectus showed that two of One.Tel's existing businesses—the valuable internet operation One.Net, which had been launched in April 1997, and the phone card division, One.Card—were not included in the float. For who knew what reason, they were being retained by Rich, Keeling, Packer, Greaves and Adler's FAI, who would collectively receive up to $400,000 a year in royalties from One.Tel until at least 2001.

As it happened, the lucky beneficiaries would choose to sell up before then, and take a lump sum instead. Just seven months later, in July 1998, the two satellites were sold back to One.Tel for a tidy $16.9 million, of which almost $7 million was in cash. Jodee would receive just over half of this, bringing his total cash take-away from all these payouts to around $8 million. His potential reward, of course, was many times larger than that.

The good news for new investors, who had come too late for this payday, was that Rodney Adler was quite certain they were buying into a fantastic business. In mid-1997 he assured a high achievers conference that mobile phones was a business only a fool could go broke in, and that Jodee and Brad were certainly not fools. 'It has to be one of the great growth industries of Australia for the next half decade', he confidently told these future corporate captains. 'Therefore, if you are in that industry, it's virtually impossible to go bankrupt.'

But while Rodney was undoubtedly making a fortune from his One.Tel connections, the company itself was not looking too flash. Even though it claimed to be connecting 10,000 new mobile customers a month, and was now employing 300 people, it was finding it hard to turn a dollar.

Despite the assurances in the prospectus that the company was making a handsome profit and generating oodles of cash, the harsh reality was that the figures were flattered by the $20-million-odd settlement from Optus, the remains of which were still flowing through to earnings. The truth was that One.Tel was now burning through its bank balance at the rate of around $1 million a month.

Whatever the company told the public—and it continued to claim it was cash positive and on its way to even bigger profits—it was no easy task being a service provider. Without the Optus loyalty bonuses, which had made the first two years such a breeze, it was hard to make any money at all.

7

Milking the Customer

It was not a word we wanted to get out.

Jodee Rich

Despite all his public optimism, Jodee had been nervous about the mobile business for more than a year, but he had two ideas for dealing with the problem. The first was to diversify by introducing cheap long-distance and international calls. The second was to find ways of getting more money out of existing One.Tel customers.

This was the purpose of the famous 'milking meetings', which aimed to find ways of 'milking' the customer. It was one of Jodee's great talents to think up names and slogans, and 'milking' was clearly a good one because it left no doubt what the meetings were about. But as he admits today, 'It was not a word we wanted to get out'. It was not in keeping with One.Tel's public image of being fun, friendly and people-focused. Nor did it match the promise that the company was 'in the business of building long-term relationships with our customers'.

The milking meetings were held whenever One.Tel ran short of cash, and since this happened on a regular basis, the meetings were regular too, with Jodee, Brad and a dozen of the brightest team leaders all primed to come up with ideas. The basic strategy was to invent fees that would raise maximum revenue with minimum fuss, but it was hard to find anything that could be slipped in without notice. Those who bothered to look at the details on their phone bill discovered they were suddenly paying $3.95 a month for voicemail, which they had been promised for free, or a $12 access fee on a plan that was supposed to have none. Before long, they would also realise they were being hit with a $5 late fee if they failed to pay on time and a $2 administration fee if they did not agree to pay their account via direct debit. One bright spark joked that One.Tel should charge its customers for the oxygen they breathed while they were on the phone, because it had thought of almost everything else.

Not surprisingly, the new fees caused a huge number of complaints from angry customers, who besieged One.Tel's call centre every time a new impost was introduced, but there was no way they could get satisfaction, however hard they tried, because their contracts contained a clause giving One.Tel the right to do whatever it liked, whenever it wanted. Thousands deserted to rival telephone companies in protest. But the milking continued. One of the cheekiest was for One.Tel to send its mobile customers 'Happy Birthday' messages . . . and then charge them for it.

When team leaders told Jodee they were worried about losing customers or getting them offside, he was happy to explain the economics. 'It's all about bottom line', he told them. 'If you multiply $2 a month by 100,000 customers and then by 12, you get $2.4 million a year. That's the difference between One.Tel making money and not.'

The most successful new fee, charged to those who refused to pay by direct debit, actually produced far more money than this. At one stage it was being paid by around half of One.Tel's customers and contributing a remarkable 35 per cent of the entire group's profit. At that rate, one could afford to lose business or hire more call centre staff to deal with the angry hordes—which was something Jodee often promised to do, but on which he rarely managed to deliver.

It was not only the call centre staff who had to deal with furious customers. The dealers had to hose them down too, and they also complained loudly to One.Tel. When a team leader raised this at milking time, Jodee took him aside to tell him that he needed to start thinking like a businessman. 'Sometimes you have to make decisions that aren't going to make you popular. That's life. Just don't go weak at the knees.' But the lesson some others drew from this was that the bosses of One.Tel 'didn't give a damn about the customer'.

Another of Jodee's strategies for making One.Tel profitable was to sell cheap long-distance and international calls, but he found it impossible to buy STD or ISD capacity at a decent discount because no one was prepared to sell to him. Optus had already warned One.Tel in 1995 to stay out of the long-distance market, and Telstra's wholesale rates were so high it was impossible to make money. As for overseas calls, almost the only way to compete was to get into a cosy club called the Southern Cross consortium, which owned the newest fibre optic cable from Sydney to Los Angeles. One.Tel was politely told it could buy membership for $30 million. But Jodee and Brad were adamant they would not spend money on cable, switches or anything else, since it was still one of One.Tel's core Beliefs and Values not to own its own network.

Then, in mid-1997, thanks to a wave of deregulation in Australia and overseas, the market began to open up, and One.Tel found it had heaps of choice. Three new members of Southern Cross—Primus, Global One and PGE—all had spare national and international cable capacity they wanted to sell, and prices came tumbling down.

This new business certainly looked like a better bet than reselling time on the Optus mobile network, as margins were so much higher. In rough terms, One.Tel could undercut its rivals by selling calls to the UK and

USA at 37 cents a minute and buy time for only 15 cents. However, One.Tel still needed to win customers to make that profit, and its marketing campaign did not get off to a good start. The new service was launched with great fanfare in August 1997, using special One.Tel buses painted lime green and purple, and matching TV ads to tell people: 'Don't miss the bus on One.Tel's great rates'. Shot on video for just $4,000, with the One.Tel team acting as extras and the head of the advertising agency as one of the mugs left behind when the bus drove off, they were an immediate success. But there was a snag: they told people to dial 1478 for access to the new service, and One.Tel's 1478 code was not yet on line. For the next six months, the only way to catch the bus would be to dial the code for Global One, which was 1477.

Not surprisingly, the call centre was again deluged with angry customers, and several weeks of chaos ensued. As a result, One.Tel's new STD and ISD service was slow to get started, and only managed to attract 40,000 customers by mid-1998.

There had also been problems in April with the launch of One.Tel's internet service, One.Net. No one had bothered to brief call centre staff, so thousands of people had rung in to find that no one at One.Tel could tell them how to get connected. This was typical of the way the company was run. There was a saying in One.Tel that it didn't want to forward plan, because it would become too much like Telstra.

Jodee and Brad's aim was to make the call centre 'best in class', just like the billing system, but it was widely regarded as one of the worst in the industry. Its target was to answer 80 per cent of calls within 20 seconds, and to get the abandon rate down below 5 per cent, but in 1997 and 1998 even on good days the wait was often 20 minutes, and 15 per cent of callers gave up or were dumped.

Malcolm Martyn, who worked in the call centre from 1996 to 1998 as a phone jockey, team leader and finally call centre manager, says there were sometimes so many calls backed up that 'the electronic scoreboard in the call centre [showing the number of calls in the queue and the average wait time] looked like it was about to explode. I used to turn it off because it just made staff demoralised'.

Back in the early days, One.Tel's Beliefs and Values had told the team to 'Take time to think' and 'Lie on the grass' (or 'Smoke the grass', as staff liked to joke), but the Castlereagh Street centre was now so frantic that there was rarely time to do either. Eventually, the exhortations to take it easy were cut out of the training given to new employees.

And new employees there were by the hundred, because the attrition rate was appalling. When one new call centre manager arrived in early 1997 she found it was running at 100 per cent a year—which meant the entire staff was changing over every 12 months. Later it got far worse than that.

The reason for the problems was simply bad management. There was no proper planning for new products, like One.Net and 1478, no forecasting of staffing needs, which increased dramatically when bills went out to customers or promotions were launched, and no apparent desire to find solutions. When problems arose, people were shouted at or sacked, but the issues weren't tackled.

At times, the stress was awful for those who worked there. Call centre staff were frequently threatened and constantly abused. They talked about the woman in an American call centre who was sent flowers one day by an unknown customer. She was holding them as she left the building . . . when he shot her.

Malcolm Martyn and the other call centre managers often raised these problems with Jodee and asked for more staff, but Jodee did not want to deal with it and would tell Martyn, 'Don't be a victim', or ask him, 'Why don't you focus on the positives? What wins have you had today?'.

Brad Keeling was no keener to hear the details. According to Martyn, 'They would say, "I want you to get the abandon rate down to under 5 per cent". I'd say, "You can't do that unless you have someone hanging people up, disconnecting them". And they'd say, "We don't care how you do it, just do it"'.

When he prepared figures for the board, Martyn was again instructed not to focus on the negatives. 'If we abandoned 6,500 calls out of 65,000, we'd say, "We have had a 90 per cent success rate in answering calls into the call centre". If board members didn't ask the right question, they wouldn't get the full picture.'

But One.Tel was doing far worse things than hiding its problems in the call centre. According to several team leaders and managers, it was artificially inflating customer numbers to secure bonuses from Optus for hitting its quarterly sales targets (which were different from the loyalty bonuses they had been paid for each customer). One long-serving member of the One.Tel team swears that at the end of 1997 he was asked to do a special job: 'One of Brad Keeling's deputies explained that One.Tel was falling short of its Optus targets and that there was a $500,000 bonus to be earned if we hit it'. Keeling then found the young man 10,000 to 15,000 existing One.Tel customers and told him to mail each a new SIM card, complete with new mobile number.

The young team member hired an army of casuals, including 'Pommie backpackers from Coogee', to stick SIM cards onto slips of paper and put them into envelopes. For several days on end they worked until midnight. The aim of this mail drop was to boost the number of customers on the books, but according to the team leader in charge of the job, and at least two other One.Tel team members, the company did not wait for people to ring in and say they wanted their new number. The backpackers simply activated the SIM cards on the computer before sending them out, which automatically connected each one to the Optus network, thus counting them all as brand new connections.

Fewer than half these cards were actually used, and far fewer than that represented genuine new customers, because they were sent to people who had One.Tel phones already. While some may have ended up with family and friends, a common trick was to slip the new card into an existing One.Tel phone that was on an expensive long-term contract and use it to get cheaper calls. So had it not been for the Optus bonuses, the scheme would have cost One.Tel vast amounts of money.

I put it to Jodee that One.Tel fiddled the customer numbers to get money out of Optus and he denies it absolutely. Even though a number of people swear it happened, he is adamant that they are all mistaken. 'There is no chance in the world that we counted SIM cards as subscribers unless people asked us to connect them', he says. 'We did not do that, and it would be an absolute mischief to suggest we did.'

But the allegation is backed up by people who worked for Optus at the time. They confirm that there were quarterly targets and that the SIM card trick was uncovered. And apart from being sure that this particular story is true, many people at One.Tel say this sort of behaviour was endemic in the company.

Customer numbers were also inflated by refusing to disconnect people who asked to leave the One.Tel family. To ensure that deserters remained on the books as customers—so quarterly targets could be met—the call centre team would be instructed to suspend them instead. This was supposed to be only a temporary measure, but people sometimes found themselves being billed months after they had asked to leave.

According to yet another person, who worked in senior positions in the company between 1997 and 2000, 'Playing with the figures was rife, absolutely huge. It seemed to be what kept One.Tel going sometimes, and while it was done by upper and middle managers, the attitude came from the top'.

One of the reasons why this culture existed, apart from a lack of ethics, was that just about everybody in the company was on commission. Another was that the targets set for people were often absurdly optimistic. Another senior manager, whom Jodee recommended I contact, says he and his colleagues often signed up to business plans they had no faith in. When they protested that the goals were too ambitious, they were told, 'If you can't do it, then you're not the one for the job'. Or, more worryingly, 'You're not a team player . . . you're not a One.Tel person'. Saying no to Jodee, and staying, was not an easy option.

In the second half of 1997, with high hopes that the Australian long-distance business would turn out to be a winner, an international SWAT team was sent off round the world to see whether they might be able to repeat the success overseas. The key in each country would be timing: One.Tel had no desire to be a pioneer, because it would be too expensive to blaze the trail, but neither did it want to arrive so late that all its competitors had already staked their claims.

The easiest way to find out if the moment was right was to get local ad agencies to devise a marketing campaign and do all the groundwork regarding regulations and the state of the market. Soon afterwards, if the SWAT team approved the prospect, Jodee and Brad would fly in for an inspection. For several weeks in late 1997, eight members of One.Team, including the founders, travelled round in a minibus visiting potential rivals. In the beginning, these competitors were surprisingly open about showing One.Tel their business, but eventually a couple baulked at the idea.

Having arranged to see First Direct in Frankfurt, the tourists received a message that the visit had been cancelled. Nevertheless, they turned up, to be greeted by a worried-looking receptionist who asked them why they had come. They were then shut in a windowless room for 45 minutes until an equally worried managing director arrived to explain that they could not tour the facility because his boss in the UK had forbidden it. Jodee and the team had paid the British parent company a visit just a few days earlier.

The Global Strategy, as One.Tel called it, certainly didn't come cheap—the typical cost would be $3 million to $5 million to set up in each country, with a further drain on cash flows for maybe two years after that—and the expansion would take key managers away from the Australian operations. Kerry Packer for one made it clear that he thought it a stupid idea, telling Jodee via James that he had rocks in his head.

But neither the cost nor the warnings stopped Jodee wanting to go for it. In June 1998, One.Tel's first overseas office opened in Los Angeles. The next month the company set up shop in London, and by the end of the year the dude had surfed into Paris, Amsterdam, Zürich and Hong Kong as well.

Naturally, the dude's creator, Adam Long, was dispatched to each of these countries with pots of brightly coloured paint, to decorate the offices in One.Tel style and translate the motivational messages into French, Dutch, German and Cantonese. But the gloss had barely dried on the last of his work before the Los Angeles office was forced to close. It had targeted the Hispanic population, who obviously didn't fall for the scruffy Aussie surfie, el dudo, and weren't too keen on parting with their money. By the time it was shut down, only a year after opening, it had just 20,000 customers and very little money. 'They never paid their bills', says George Savva, who was sent over to close it, 'and we couldn't find them. They would just disappear. They were all transients'.

By comparison, Hong Kong and the Netherlands were both modestly successful, while in the UK the dude was a massive hit. The Brits love a bargain, and most would move to Australia given half a chance, so One.Tel was tailor-made. Before two years were up, more than half a million customers had signed on, and One.Tel was the second-most-recognised Australian brand in Europe. (The Brits also love lager, so Foster's remained number one.) But even in Britain, where the business took off, One.Tel was still losing an enormous amount of money. In fact, by mid-2000, these offshore operations had run up combined losses of more than $120 million, and still had not turned the corner.

As a consequence, the company ate up cash even faster than ever before. At the end of 1997, it had been consuming around $1 million a month. By the end of 1998, it was burning double that amount, and getting through a further $2.5 million a month in investment spending, which worked out at more than $50 million a year in total. And since the banks weren't interested in lending to a telephone company with no hardware, One.Tel was forced to look for more investors—which meant going to the USA, because Australians weren't interested.

In America, the dot-com and telco boom had already taken hold and there was so much money being thrown around that it was hard to miss out. In April 1998 One.Tel raised $17.6 million from an investment fund called Coldstream Partners, run by two friends of Rodney Adler, Stephen Rader and Rudolf Reinfrank.

This cash transfusion meant One.Tel could continue doing things in style. Even though it paid its bills by American Express—so it could collect frequent flyer points—and sent its executives round the world in economy class, it had never thought to economise on office space. In Melbourne it occupied a floor near the top of the Rialto, which was one of the best buildings in town; in Perth it was high up in swanky Central Park; in Brisbane it had a perch in Waterfront Place; and in Sydney it had several floors of the Castlereagh Centre, which was a huge silver building with a rainforest out the front. When it opened its doors in Paris in mid-1998, it was naturally on the Champs Elysées.

From time to time there were ideas of relocating the Sydney call centre to Wollongong or North Ryde, which would have been much cheaper than the CBD, but this never happened. The story within One.Tel was that Jodee and Brad's feng shui master gave the North Ryde building the thumbs down because the pillars were round, not square.

One.Tel's founders certainly were great believers in this ancient Chinese art and let it dictate a number of things in the company's life. In the Castlereagh Street offices, for example, all the desks, or 'pods', were arranged parallel to the lift wells to free the flow of positive energy. At the windows, small golden dragons faced

Craigend, the harbourside mansion Jodee paid $14 million for.

Jodee's powerboat Plus One (right).

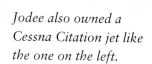

Jodee also owned a Cessna Citation jet like the one on the left.

CHEAP LONG
DISTANCE CALLS!

PROSPECTUS

Welcome to One.Tel. The dude's job was to tell customers it was so easy to get a phone from One.Tel that even an idiot could do it, and so cheap that even a layabout could afford it.

outwards, to ward off evil spirits. Staff were warned not to handle them, in case the spirits broke free again.

There were also fish tanks everywhere—a powerful symbol of wealth, good health and abundance, as well as a reminder of how Jodee had got his start. The first sight to greet visitors as they stepped out of the lift onto the 28th floor was a huge tank with expensive, exotic specimens, including mini-lobsters crawling over rocks. On all the other floors, including the call centre, there were smaller tanks, each close to two metres long. A marine biologist came in regularly to keep them clean and fresh, just as Jodee had done more than 20 years before.

On each floor there was also a heavy object to provide a centre for positive energies. On the 28th floor it was the iconic red phone box; on the 27th a vintage AJS motorbike; and on the eighth, which had the underwater theme, it was a deep-sea diver's suit.

Jodee and Brad took this stuff so seriously that One.Tel flew its feng shui master round the world to 'balance' all its offices. Unlike the company's employees, he liked to fly first class and stay in five-star hotels. It was the master's job to bless any new floors in the Sydney HQ, where One.Tel was still expanding. Naturally, he was also consulted about any significant moves that the company might make, including, so it seems, to potential new call centres. In his spare time, he was happy to suggest lucky numbers for Brad and Jodee and to re-order Jodee's house in Vaucluse to help his children sleep better.

Clearly, the luckiest number was eight. According to One.Tel veterans, there were eight goldfish in the tanks; the collections department was on the eighth floor to increase prosperity; and the company was very careful when it placed ads in newspapers to ensure that the number 88 could be slotted into the copy. The feng shui master may also have been responsible for a ban on red, though this is normally a favoured feng shui colour. On one occasion, 200 folders for a new training manual had to be returned because they were of the offending hue. The master was then asked what colour they should be, and promptly advised on blue. Red was also banned in One.Tel's ads, on Brad Keeling's orders.

These little things aside, the management style at One.Tel was more relaxed than ever. Jodee had taken to walking round in bare feet, and his young South African finance director Mark Silbermann had taken to copying him. Jodee and Mark were also both kayaking into work. Often they would arrive in the morning together, clad in brightly coloured shorts, paddles under their arms, having walked up to the city from Mrs Macquarie's Chair, where they had parked their kayaks under the trees. When asked whether he worried about someone stealing the boats, Jodee replied he could probably afford to lose a couple a year.

There were also stories about Rich's roller-blading habits. On one occasion, after flying to Brisbane with a couple of senior managers, he had supposedly changed out of his suit in the back of the taxi coming in from the airport. Having struggled into his sports gear and laced up his skates, he jumped out at a red light, saying 'I'll race you to the hotel'. One of those with him claimed he had raced the taxi through Brisbane's CBD, running red lights, all the way to the hotel. Later, when they were in the bar having a drink, they heard a 'psst' and looked round to see Jodee peering through the pot plants, asking for his suit.

Despite these eccentricities, or possibly because of them, he was remarkably unpopular in the business community. 'I never saw another businessman create such a sense of loathing', says one lawyer who worked for him, 'and I'm not sure why he did. I suspect it's a bit of the tall poppy thing and some anti-Semitism. It's also the wunderkind stuff: he was happy to appear really clever, and people resented him appearing cleverer than they were'.

This wasn't the only explanation. One.Tel had a reputation in the industry for being arrogant, aggressive and confrontational in its dealings, whether it was with bankers, brokers, suppliers or rivals. And Jodee and Brad both had a talent for putting people offside.

In early 1995, before the company was even launched, Jodee made an indelible impression on a group of software suppliers who were auditioning to build One.Tel's billing system. They had arranged to meet him in a splendid corporate boardroom belonging to one of the suppliers, with a large mahogany table and views of the harbour. Dressed in their city best, they were ready for their pitch at the scheduled time of 4.00pm, but as the minutes ticked by to 4.15, then 4.30, there was no sign of Jodee. Finally, with the clock nudging 4.45, he and his entourage breezed in sucking paddle pops, just like in the good old days at Imagineering. They did not apologise for being late. 'Jodee sat in the middle of the table and put his feet on it. That was his biggest position statement: he was saying "I'm important and you're not"', says one of the software suppliers. The others sat in a huddle at the end of the table, finished their paddle pops and put their sticks in the ashtrays. He was most definitely in charge.

'We were meant to be doing a PowerPoint presentation, so we each introduced ourselves. He said, "I'm interested in you and you, I'm not interested in you, and I might be interested in you".'

When it was all over, the suppliers went for a drink, shaking their heads in wonder. 'We thought it was the height of arrogance, the way Jodee behaved', one of them says today. 'We just couldn't believe it. Someone said, "Did you see that fucking arsehole put his feet on the desk like that?".'

Rich did not endear himself to the press either. Mostly, he ignored them, because he felt it wasn't his job to keep them sweet, but if he read something he disliked he was ready to give the author a free character assessment.

In April 1996, a young reporter called Natalie Apostolou wrote a piece for the industry newsletter *Communications Day*, which reported a rumour that James Packer and Rodney Adler might have resigned as directors, and suggested One.Tel was being sued by a couple of its dealers. The next day she got a call from Jodee, who had been 'unavailable for comment' beforehand. 'Hi Natalie, it's Jodee Rich here', he told her. 'I read your article and I don't know where you're getting these lies from.' He then berated her for what she had written: 'How dare you insinuate that we're unethical? Look at the calibre of the people who are on our board. How can you say they're unethical?'. Finally, he told her: 'Don't you *ever* contact this company again. You're obviously just a gutter journalist, and you should crawl back to where you came from'. Clunk.

It was obvious to many that Jodee did not care what people thought of him. Nor did he appear to know. One acquaintance described him as 'strangely unlikeable'; another called him 'a very odd person'; yet another— whom he regarded as a close friend—told quite unprintable stories about his supposed behaviour.

Those who tried to assess him found the man a puzzle, but on one thing they all agreed: except in business, Jodee made little or no effort to make people like him. Lacking small talk, he preferred to shock instead. According to one of his old schoolfriends, David Bavin, 'He seemed to be amused by making other people feel uncomfortable. He always wanted to be the centre of attention. He could be completely outrageous'. Other friends described him as 'cheeky . . . provocative . . . unfairly dismissive' and said he liked putting people on the spot: 'he had almost no concern for people's reaction'.

One of his closer friends, media mogul Cameron O'Reilly, is famous for describing him as a 'social terrorist'. But a more accurate description, another suggests, is 'social retard'. He would go up to women at parties and say, 'Do you want a threesome?' or 'I'm in a wife-swapping club, do you want to join?'. Another of his favourite chat-up lines with women was 'Show us your tits'. It was all intended as a joke, no doubt, but few found it funny. Another woman who had known him well since university days recounted how he once came up to her at a party to ask: 'When you use toilet paper, do you fold or bunch?'.

All agreed that he abhorred conventionality and acceptability, and had contempt for the establishment. One of his best friends says he would get up in the middle of dinner and announce he was going, or simply leave. There would be no apology or explanation. His wife Maxine would dutifully gather her belongings and follow, saying, 'I guess we're going. Sorry'. Maxine's friends wondered why she put up with it, and some of Jodee's did too.

Some said he was at his worst in restaurants. One fellow diner reported that he was extremely fussy about what he ate and complained continually that nothing was right. Another recalled sitting in a Darlinghurst eatery in 1994, shortly before One.Tel was launched, while Jodee gave one of the waiters an excruciatingly hard time. When the friend begged Jodee to stop, he declined, saying, 'I'm paying him. I own him'.

But there were some who had good things to say about him. He was apparently a wonderful family man, great with his children, and could be generous, caring and emotional with friends. He also had the capacity to focus on people and make them feel special. And he was hard to resist when he turned on the charm, which he never failed to do with One.Tel's most important backer, James Packer.

Jodee's initial dealings with James had all been at arm's length, through Packer's investment adviser, Theo Onisforou. Then, in July 1996, he and Maxine were invited on a cruise of the Greek islands aboard the *Arctic P*, the huge converted icebreaker that served as the Packer family yacht. The service was magnificent, the boat amazing. Only the atmosphere spoiled it for Jodee. It seemed to him like a Roman court, with his fellow passengers, including Liberal Party power broker Michael Kroger and an assortment of James's executives and friends, all vying for the emperor's favour.

Soon afterwards, he and the emperor began to make friends. According to Rodney Adler, they went on skiing trips together and became almost inseparable. 'They were very close', says Adler, 'much closer than James and I ever were'. People who knew them well say they were openly affectionate with each other. One cites an incident at Ellerston, the Packer family spread in the Hunter Valley, as illustration. There were half a dozen of them, he says, with wives and girlfriends, sitting on big leather couches in the Packers' huge private cinema. Without warning, Jodee leapt on top of James, who was stretched out flat, and began a mock fight. 'They were wrestling like two small boys, in front of everyone else.'

Another who saw them together several times at Jodee's property near Airlie Beach says they would lie around for ages in the sun just chatting, like brothers or best friends. 'James thought Jodee was wonderful', this friend says. 'He adored his courage, humour, irreverence and vision. And Jodee really cared for James, too.'

According to Jodee, they talked endlessly—of life, love, women, money and powerful fathers. Jodee says he also advised James how to be his own man, how to stand up to Kerry and deal on equal terms. Knowing this and knowing the Packers, it's not hard to see why James may have seen the One.Tel founder as a guru, or even a visionary. Some who watched the friendship develop felt as though James was under Jodee's spell.

One former insider in the Packer camp, who was never

a great believer in One.Tel, says: 'James had a lot of faith in Jodee, but I think Jodee played him very well. James is a trusting person, he is loyal and he expects loyalty back, and he's a good-natured person. Jodee built up a sense of trust between them. But Jodee knows how to get what he wants. He would have known that the way to get to James was to confide in him and trust him'.

Certainly, the heir to the Packer fortune admired what Jodee had already achieved with One.Tel, and trusted his judgment on where the business should go next. But on this important point, the jury was still out. One.Tel was finding the mobile business tougher by the day; its offshore expansion was costing millions and would not return a profit for two years at least; and the Australian long-distance business was good, but hardly dazzling.

Also, despite the huge prices being paid for mobile phone companies around the world, there were still no buyers for One.Tel. Something had to be done. The only question was what.

8

Big Boys Now

It was a very entrepreneurial decision, a *very* entrepreneurial decision.

Rodney Adler

One.Tel had always vowed it would never own a mobile network. That was for mugs and blokes in grey cardigans. But it was rapidly getting to the point where Optus was squeezing the company so hard, there was no other option. In early 1998, Rich, Packer, Keeling and Adler began to think about scrapping the company's original business plan and challenging the big boys head on. It would cost them around $1 billion to build a full-scale national network and another $500 million to stick around long enough to win some customers. However, if the stakes were huge, so was the prize. They would no longer be at the mercy of the two major carriers, and they could make some serious money.

According to Reg Coutts, Professor of Telecommunications at Adelaide University, who advised the company on its strategy, the pressure to go down this road came from Jodee: 'Jodee was the one driving the national network idea. He could see he could never become one of the boys, one of the carriers, without a network. For too long he'd been beaten up by Optus, and this new network was going to be his entrée to the carrier club. The board seemed to do what he wanted them to do'.

Before One.Tel could build a mobile network, it needed to buy spectrum—which is like a licence from the government to use certain bandwidths—and when the auction came up in May 1998, they were nowhere near ready to bid. Four months later, in September, another auction offered the scraps that Telstra, Optus and Vodafone had left on the table, and One.Tel grabbed a small amount of bandwidth in five Australian capital cities—Sydney, Melbourne, Brisbane, Adelaide and Perth—for $9.5 million.

'It was a very entrepreneurial decision', says Rodney Adler, 'a *very* entrepreneurial decision'.

It was arguably even more than that. It contradicted all of Jodee and Brad's boasting about how smart they were not to own copper wires or dig holes in the ground, and meant a radical change in the nature of One.Tel's business. Up till this point, they had been a marketing company and a packager of other people's products; now they would need the engineering skills to produce their own. And they would have to spend half their life trying to persuade bankers to lend them money.

They did not even have the $9.5 million they had laid on the table, and according to Rodney Adler: 'Jodee and I went everywhere looking for money. We got turned down by an awful lot of people. We must have gone to ten or 20 places. We had no history; they didn't understand about spectrum; we were just too much of a risk'.

Their final port of call in the search for funds was a likeable, fast-talking salesman called Brent Potts, who was a veteran of the 1980s boom and a one-time mate of Alan Bond's. A man of style, who sported monogrammed pink shirts and thick black braces, and wore his hair swept back from his forehead into a big curly wave on his collar, Potts had got them out of trouble before. In 1997, when the float was looking a bit shaky, he had drummed up some extra investors, and in early 1998 he had helped persuade Coldstream Partners to plunge $17 million into the company.

This time, however, not even his contacts, charm and experience could persuade any Australian institutions to come to the party. They told him weakly that it was too close to Christmas. Thankfully, he was able to line up Frank Lowy's son, David, to lend One.Tel $5 million for at least 90 days, on extremely tough terms. And James Packer, as lender of last resort, then agreed to put in another $5 million to get them out of strife.

There was an outside chance that this $10 million might be all that they would need, because Jodee hoped to use the network threat to force Optus to rewrite their existing agreement. Sadly, his bluff was soon called: Optus did not believe that One.Tel was crazy enough to go ahead with such an ambitious plan, or capable of making it work.

At this stage, One.Tel was only contemplating a limited network in Sydney and Brisbane at a cost of $200 million, but even this had no chance of getting up unless One.Tel's rivals were prepared to cooperate, because users would only be able to use their phones outside this area if Optus, Telstra or Vodafone would allow them to 'roam' on their network, or, in simple terms, agree to carry the calls. There was no guarantee any of their competitors would allow them to do this—in fact, there were obvious reasons why they would refuse.

Before laying out the $9.5 million, Jodee, James, Brad and Rodney had hammered this issue back and forth across the boardroom table at FAI, and decided it was probably worth taking the gamble. And a gamble it certainly was. In Adler's words: 'We were taking the ultimate risk that we would get a roaming agreement from Telstra or Optus at a reasonable price. They would fight it. Why on earth would they give it to us? But we felt the ACCC would have to help us. If we were wrong then our $9.5 million of spectrum was going to be worthless'.

No one in the industry had managed to strike a roaming agreement thus far, or even get the nod that it was possible, and there was certainly no guarantee that any agreement would leave room for One.Tel to make a decent profit.

That aside, things were looking pretty good. Two big US network builders, Lucent and Motorola, were offering to finance the cost of a Sydney–Brisbane network, and promising to lend One.Tel even more money so it could acquire customers, which would cost $350 to $500 a head in dealer commissions, marketing and handset subsidies.

Better still, James Packer was determined to forge ahead, and was ready to use his political and financial clout to help overcome any difficulties. He had persuaded his father that the family flagship company, Consolidated Press Holdings, should cruise into the fray and take a 15 per cent shareholding in One.Tel at a cost of $47 million. (Most of these shares were bought from Adler's FAI, which was being taken over by the now-collapsed insurer HIH and did not want them to fall into unfriendly hands.) Simultaneously, James had enlisted an American venture capital fund, run by George Soros's former right-hand man Steve Gilbert, to put in a further $54 million.

With this new, added firepower, the Packers were already thinking in terms of a proper national network, and they wasted no time in planning an ambitious campaign to make it happen. In January 1999, within a month of their decision to invest, James came to Jodee Rich to tell him: 'Dad thinks we should get the Murdochs involved'.

This was a strange invitation, given the families' fierce rivalry down the years, and even stranger if Rupert and Kerry loathed each other, as some reported. But on a business level it made perfect sense. The Murdochs' financial strength would make it far less risky to pick a fight with Telstra and Optus, and the support of Rupert's newspapers, combined with the Packers' TV and magazines, would give One.Tel unmatchable muscle in the battle for customers. The families were also sharing a bed at Foxtel already, so they appreciated the advantages of coupling up.

It was James who extended the invitation, and Rupert's eldest son Lachlan who received it. Towards the end of January 1999 they talked about the idea over dinner, and Lachlan was an immediate enthusiast. At the tender age of 27, the Murdoch heir presumptive was a bit of a dude himself, although he preferred a shaved head to scruffy, long blond locks. He rode a big Ducati motorbike, listed Greek philosophy and ancient history as two of his recreations, and had built a rock-climbing wall in the garage of his Elizabeth Bay mansion to indulge in the third.

Not surprisingly, young Lachlan liked the style of the company, loved its marketing approach, and was busting to get into this sort of new-technology invest-ment. The following morning, he arrived at News Ltd's Sydney offices on fire with the idea. 'He went in with guns blazing', says one Murdoch executive. 'He was so hot on it that people were reluctant to stick their necks out.'

The next step was for James and Jodee to give Lachlan and the numbers men a more detailed presentation, and for Lachlan to 'talk to Dad'. A few days later, Jodee, Brad, Lachlan and James found themselves on a plane to New York to see Rupert. Thus far, the septuagenarian Murdoch had largely resisted the siren call of telecom-munications and internet companies, and had pointed to the radio and automobile boom of the 1920s as a warning of how fortunes would be lost. But as the share price of dot-coms and telcos continued skywards, he had clearly begun to wonder whether he should go along for the ride, joking that it would put a billion dollars on News Ltd's value overnight if they were to add '.com' to the company name.

Rupert and Kerry were acutely aware, as were James and Lachlan, that the new-economy pioneers, such as Jeff Bezos of Amazon.com, were rapidly winning the race for riches. According to one Sydney banker who knew the Packers and Murdochs well, this galled them both. 'Rupert and Kerry had worked for close to 50 years to amass a fortune', says the banker. 'Then they read Forbes 400 and find some pipsqueak dot-com guy is worth ten times what they are, after just six months, for doing nothing. Suddenly they are looking like piss-ants, and they want to have a piece of it.'

In any case, Rupert could hardly have resisted the pitch if it was anything like as gripping as Sue Lecky and Emiliya Mychasuk made it sound in the *Sydney Morning Herald*.

> Deep inside the Avenue of Americas engine room of Rupert Murdoch's global media empire, Rich—accompanied by business partners Brad Keeling and, more importantly, James Packer—made the presentation of a lifetime.
>
> Murdoch listened as the trio pitched their vision to transform the fledgling mobile phone group One.Tel into a major player on the Australian and, eventually, world telecommunications stage.
>
> What they needed were backers with deep pockets. Murdoch's great rival Kerry Packer was already on board. And the News Corp chief's son, Lachlan, who had been introduced to One.Tel by the younger Packer, was sold on the idea.
>
> The bare bones of a deal for News to sink capital into One.Tel was on the table. But it needed the senior Murdoch's imprimatur.

Those who have been inside the News Ltd bunker in New York report that it's actually unremarkable. There are no huge metal doors or acres of carpet, such as one has to cross in the fictional world of Evelyn Waugh's famous press baron, Lord Copper. And on this occasion, Rupert, Lachlan and their finance chief, David Devoe, were not in the least frightening.

For the first half-hour Jodee and Brad waited outside while James made the pitch, which went something like this: Australia's phone companies were capitalised at around $50 billion and One.Tel could grab $10 billion of this if it could run second or third in the race. It had already proved a master at winning customers, and with the marketing muscle of the Packers and Murdochs behind the company there would be no holding it back.

Jodee and Brad then went in for a two-hour grilling. According to Jodee, Rupert loved the thought of a $10 billion prize and relished the idea of taking on Telstra, whom he clearly disliked as much as everybody else did. There was a lot of talk about details, and some concern from Rupert that it would take too much of Lachlan's time, and then it was done. They shook hands on the deal and left.

Less than two weeks later, on 16 February 1999, news that Packer and Murdoch were sinking $710 million into One.Tel, for 40 per cent of the shares, was on the front page of almost every Australian newspaper. Few in the press or the stock market could believe it. There was now the prospect of a whole new future opening up. The company that hardly anyone had taken seriously, the duo that so many people disliked, had won the acclaim and backing of Australia's two most powerful business dynasties.

Strangely enough, only one journalist had been invited to One.Tel the previous afternoon to be given the news. The IT Editor of the *Australian Financial Review*, Grant Butler, was called to the One.Tel offices for a 3.00pm announcement, but arrived to find that he was the only one there. Having no idea what was going on, he was curious to see Jodee and Brad talking to James Packer and Lachlan Murdoch at the far end of the office. Before long, the big four ambled over to shake hands and say hello. Then, they posed rather sheepishly for a photograph, jumped into the lift and left.

Butler was still not sure what was happening, but eventually he was shown a draft press release outlining the deal and told he had to stay put till the official announcement was made. There had apparently been a stuff-up. Packer, Murdoch, Keeling and Rich had not yet signed all the necessary documents.

Three hours later, the news was made public and Lachlan issued a statement to say how confident he was that One.Tel had 'the quality and depth of management' to be a major player in the industry. One could only guess how he had arrived at this conclusion, but clearly it wasn't based on Jodee's track record at Imagineering, or on a good hard look at how One.Tel had been run.

It was just the PR guff that people utter in such circumstances.

Most of the financial press were thrilled by the excitement of it all. According to Terry McCrann, writing in the finance pages of the Murdoch tabloids, the deal offered:

> A fascinating view into the future. Of media. Of telephony. Of Packer and Murdoch. This is James's second big deal after running the negotiations to buy Crown casino. It marks Lachlan's entry into the big deal time ... It is also a powerful signal about the entrepreneurial dynamics of the latest generation of Murdochs and Packers.

Elizabeth Knight in the *Sydney Morning Herald* provided a rather more sober view, questioning whether the two young pretenders had actually lost their marbles:

> Thanks to the internet, the market is becoming increasingly familiar with cash-flow-negative companies trading at ridiculous prices but this move would be shocking to even the greatest optimist ... There is so much blue sky in the current trading price—and even in the $7.14 issue price to News and PBL—that this investment enters the league of the completely mind-boggling.

Emiliya Mychasuk and Sue Lecky, also writing in the *Sydney Morning Herald*, found it hard to wrap their brains around it, observing that it was 'unfathomable that a company that has existed for less than four years, and is chewing up money faster than it is coming through the door, could rank among Australia's top 50 publicly listed companies'.

But the investing public had no trouble swallowing it at all. If the Packers and Murdochs thought it was good enough to risk several hundred million dollars, then it was certainly good enough for them. Within a week of the deal being announced, the share price had rocketed to $13, which was nearly twice what Murdoch and Packer had paid, and more than four times what James and Kerry had spent two months earlier. On this basis, the two families were already sitting on a paper profit of $900 million and gaining fast on the dot-com kings. Poor old Optus's parcel, which the carrier had given up two years earlier for just $4 million, was now worth more than $500 million. One imagined that somewhere in North Sydney, a few Optus executives were probably kicking themselves—or, indeed, being kicked.

At this price, One.Tel was worth more than $2 billion, which was quite frankly ridiculous. Had it been valued by the market on the same basis as Telstra, which was trading on a Price–Earnings ratio of around 20, it would have needed to be earning $100 million profit a year. But if you looked at the figures, it was actually losing money, and burning cash from its day-to-day operations at the rate of more than $2 million a month.

Clearly, Murdoch and Packer had not bothered about such details, being far too interested in the future. More strangely, they had not insisted on having their own finance director in One.Tel to look after their $710 million investment. It appeared they were too dazzled by the dream.

One Packer executive, who knew Jodee's style of old, warned his young boss about the need to keep a closer eye on it all. 'My only counsel to James was: "Jodee is super bright, he's right about his vision of the market, but you need to put strong management in there".' His advice was ignored. 'It was very hard to warn James about One.Tel', he adds, 'because he was such a believer'.

Some of the top people at News Ltd also had doubts, but kept them to themselves. Soon after the deal was announced, Lachlan took a team down to One.Tel's offices to discuss synergies between the two companies. Jodee and Brad were exuberant, in full flight, and Lachlan was clearly excited. 'Those of us who had been around for a while', says one executive, 'weren't too impressed'.

Few at News Ltd were surprised at Lachlan's passion for it all as he made no secret of the fact that it was his mission to drag the family business into the 21st century. But many of his managers, who were old-fashioned newsmen, remained unenthusiastic. Col Allan, the editor in chief of the *Daily Telegraph*, for example, was famous for his scepticism about the internet and other new-fangled technology. It was well known in News Ltd that he insisted on having his emails printed out and brought to him so he could write his response on paper and have his secretary key in the reply.

Over at Packer HQ, the family's investment decisions were also being driven by the younger generation, led by James and his new chief executive at Consolidated Press Holdings, a young Indian-born Australian, Ashok Jacob. Thanks to these two young guns, the Packers were staking more on One.Tel than they had ever risked on Pay TV, and almost as much as they were paying for the hugely profitable Crown Casino.

This was a sign of where James and Ashok wanted to take the company and how fast they wanted to do it, but it was a far bigger gamble than the Packers were used to taking.

For all Kerry's wildness on the racecourse and at the casino, he had never been a big punter in business—aside from some huge, wild plays on the foreign exchange and money markets in which he had lost hundreds of millions of dollars. In the more normal course of building the family business he liked to buy cheap and sell at the top. And he never fell in love with his assets. Everything was for sale if the price was right—even the TV stations. The key to success, he believed, was to stick to what you knew, to own companies that put cash in the bank, and to grind down costs to the minimum.

You could see Kerry's philosophy in action as soon as you set foot inside the Park Street offices. Even on the third floor, where Packer Senior had his bunker, the decor was dour and old-fashioned, with not the faintest sign of luxury or display. The carpet was a thick, deep Wilton, but the walls were plain, the wood panelling was pure public service and the potted palm in the waiting area an obvious plastic replica. There was an air of somnolence about the place, like a long-established shipping company. And there was an unmistakable sense of history. The walls by the lift were peppered with black-and-white photos of Sir Frank Packer—challenging for the America's Cup in the 1960s, holding forth at dinner, or standing in his suit and hat at the races. There were pictures, too, of ancient presses at the *Telegraph*. And one of Channel 9's earliest studio cameras was parked in a corner.

The receptionists also harked back to another age. There were no little black suits or oblong glasses, no Prada, Armani or Scanlan & Theodore. Nor was there an ounce of flashiness in the offices of the company's most senior executives. They were small, modest and disconcertingly open to view from their neighbours—of a type and size that would normally be occupied by accounts clerks rather than executives charting the course of a $6 billion company.

Here, perhaps, was the crux of it. With Kerry in charge, Packer executives had rarely been asked to peer too far into the future. There was no grand plan like Murdoch always appeared to have, nor any heroic vision of where the company was headed. There were just businesses to be run, pitfalls to be avoided, and recessions to look out for.

James, Ashok and their advisers wanted to change all that. They were convinced that the TV and information business was on the brink of a new era, in which free-to-air TV and magazines would be overtaken by technology, and they believed that the Packer empire needed to transform itself to survive. They were also sure that the new economy—telecommunications and the internet—was where they had to be.

For them, the future lay in buzzwords like 'digital', 'interactive', 'convergence' and 'delivery platforms'. They talked of TV pictures coming to computers over the internet, or to televisions down the phone line, and even being beamed to mobiles. They said they had to get involved or get left behind, and they believed there were fortunes to be made if they got it right. James even saw a time when they could deal on equal terms with Telstra and carve up a market for free-to-air TV, Pay TV and telephony between them—especially now that they had One.Tel.

How reluctant Kerry was to share this vision, one can only guess, but the investment in One.Tel broke all his old rules. It was expensive, cash negative, speculative, and in a hi-tech industry that the Packers knew very little about. On the other hand, he could not argue too vigorously against it while the share price kept rising and the dude continued to conquer all in the market-place. And James was constantly reminding him that he had missed out on a golden opportunity in the mid-1990s to own 25 per cent of Optus, which would have brought the Packer family several billion dollars. In sum, Kerry was a supporter as long as money was being made, but if anything went wrong the stage was set for a confrontation.

There were certainly others at Park Street who doubted it was a smart move to commit hundreds of millions of dollars to building a fourth or fifth Australian mobile network. Ted Pretty's partner, Peter O'Connell, now director of operations at Consolidated Press Holdings, who had been an early investor in One.Tel, was extremely sceptical about the prospect and told Ashok Jacob he thought it was madness. 'Jodee was convinced Australia was big enough to have five mobile networks and he was absolutely wrong', says O'Connell. 'In Germany, where they can support four networks, you have a million people going up and down the autobahn every day, passing city after city with a million plus people in them. In Australia you just don't have critical mass: 100,000 people going up the Hume Highway and it's 800 kilometres between the only two big cities.'

O'Connell parted company with the Packers soon afterwards, amid rumours that Jodee had told James to

sack him because he had been so negative about
One.Tel's plans and prospects. Jodee denies doing this,
although he admits that he and O'Connell had a huge
fight about it at the time.

Nick Falloon, the chief executive of the Packers' public
company, PBL, who had risen to the top during Kerry's
more conservative reign and had earned a reputation as
a tough, cost-conscious manager, was also unenthusiastic. He had met Jodee aboard the *Arctic P* in 1996
and had apparently taken an instant dislike to him. He
also seemed to resent the fact that Jodee had so much
influence over James. Most of all, he did not share the
vision of a world in which dot-coms and telcos would
consign all other businesses to the scrapheap.

It is not clear how loudly Falloon objected to the
One.Tel deal, but several people report he was kept out
of the loop when the decision was made. His views on
Jodee, and on the merits of believing in hi-tech dreams,
would remain a constant source of friction between
him and the young Packer heir until he was sacked in
March 2001.

But worries about One.Tel failing or going bust were
still a world away. The only concern was about One.Tel's
soaring share price, which had risen by almost 300 per
cent in the two-month lead-up to the Packer–Murdoch
deal being announced, and by 36 per cent on the day
the news had broken. It looked like several people had
got wind of the Packer–Murdoch investment and made

money from it, and the Australian Securities and Investments Commission (ASIC) wanted to know how. In early March, with the ink barely dry on the documents, 30 Australian Federal Police and ASIC investigators raided One.Tel's offices and took away files. In the weeks that followed they called in James, Lachlan, Jodee, Brad and others. Several suspicious trades had already been highlighted by the Australian Stock Exchange, who had sought in-house telephone directories from News Ltd and PBL to check whether the names of any senior managers correlated with the trades.

The spotlight eventually fell on Brad Keeling's father, who had apparently made a quick $20,000 profit on the shares. Three years on, with Keeling's father dead, ASIC has still not laid charges nor closed its investigation.

Inquiries into the other main players never went anywhere, and it is hard to believe that any of them would have been so stupid as to break the insider trading laws themselves, because they were all making a mint from the deal already. Back in December, One.Tel's chairman, John Greaves, had picked up almost $4 million by selling some of his shares to the Packers—a handsome reward for a year in the job. Rodney Adler's FAI had collected more than $43 million by doing the same thing, which represented a 75-fold profit on what it had paid for them.

But this was nothing compared to the bonanza for Jodee, James and Brad. As part of the deal with News

Ltd and PBL, all existing shareholders in One.Tel enjoyed a 'return of capital', in which one in every ten of the shares they held was bought back for $8.50 apiece. As a result of this arrangement, Rich and Keeling picked up $62 million between them, while James Packer collected $6.5 million for his private company, Dorigad, and another $14 million for the family company, Consolidated Press Holdings. Rodney Adler and John Greaves received a further $1.7 million each on top of the money they had made in December. The buyback was funded, of course, from the money that the shareholders of News Ltd and PBL were putting into the company.

The explanatory memorandum told One.Tel shareholders that this device was necessary to ensure that the two new investors could get their holdings up to 20 per cent. This would allow Jodee and Brad to get money out of the company without actually selling shares on the stock market. And both needed the cash urgently because they were already busy spending it.

During 1998 Brad had splashed out almost $5 million on a lovely waterfront home in Mosman called Harston House. A famous 100-year-old landmark with fine gardens, tall trees and big verandahs overlooking the harbour, it was like a small country estate in the middle of the North Shore. He had plans to expand it. Since it lacked a tennis court, or the space to build one, he was soon trying to buy the house next door so he could knock it down. His neighbours, who had lived there for 20 years, were not prepared to move.

Meanwhile, Jodee was playing in an even bigger league. In May 1999, just days after the share buyback was approved, he laid out $14 million for a house called Craigend, setting the record for the most expensive Australian residential purchase of the year.

Built on a vast block, right on the tip of Darling Point, it had a huge flagstone terrace with views of the Harbour Bridge, and green lawns that stepped down to the water's edge. There was a pool, a tennis court and deep-water moorings, and had it not looked onto the back of the naval dockyard at Woolloomooloo and been overshadowed by a large block of flats, it would have been perfect.

The house itself was built in 1935 in a style that was half Moorish palace, half art-deco-meets-P&O. At the time of purchase it was in a sad state (as it still is today), having been derelict for years, and was more construction site than stately home. But it had long served as the US consulate, and one could easily imagine it regaining its former glory. By the time Jodee spent a few million dollars on it, as he planned to do, it would be sensational. The summer parties overlooking the harbour would do the Great Gatsby proud.

Jodee already had a beautiful house in Vaucluse with lovely, but distant, views of the city, and in August 2001 he was asked by *Good Weekend*'s Jane Cadzow why he wanted another. She reported him lost for an answer:

'I completely agree with you', he says after a moment's reflection. 'I'm totally happy in the house that we built ten years ago. So why do you need a bigger house?' he asks himself. 'Why do you need a house on the water?' Silence. 'I don't have a good answer . . . I was indifferent about the purchase of it', he says. 'And it's not that I have a greedy wife either.'

Jodee told Cadzow he had rowed past the house many times as a boy and thought it would be fun to own it, and perhaps that was the real reason. But another answer was probably: why not? When you are worth several hundred million dollars, as Rich now was, you have to find something to do with your money. Kerry Packer wagers tens of millions at baccarat and gives $50,000 tips to cocktail waitresses. Others spend it on racehorses or vintage cars.

Rich had also bought a fabulous property in the Whitsundays called Woodwark Bay. It was private, secluded, and 'a gorgeous piece of real estate' according to those who went there. Nestled between two headlands and surrounded by national park, it had wild oyster beds on the beach and a couple of kilometres of white sand, with rainforest behind. It was truly amazing. It was also huge, spanning about 1,200 hectares, or 3,000 acres, yet Jodee had picked it up for a song. It had been owned by the Japanese property company Kumagai

Gumi, who had planned to turn it into a big resort. After they struck trouble back home Jodee had landed it for a bargain $2.5 million—which was around one-20th of what Kumagai had spent.

Jodee's plan was to build several separate 'mansions', each with its own theme, and turn it into an eco-friendly hideaway for the super-rich. There was going to be a beach house, a house on the headland, a rainforest house, and a dream home for him and Maxine, none of which had been started by the end of 2001.

To get there, he could fly his private Cessna Citation jet to Proserpine Airport and take a helicopter out to the property. He could be in Sydney for breakfast and the Whitsundays for lunch. And if he went to Thredbo in the hope of snow, and found the skiing was no good, he could just swing the plane round and go north instead.

There were plenty of toys at the Whitsundays retreat for Jodee and his guests when they arrrived: several motorbikes, a few AWD buggies and a big speedboat to take them to Hayman Island or Hamilton Island for lunch. Most of the time he kept a huge powerboat called *Plus One* there. This had been custom-built in the mid-1980s for another fast entrepreneur called Pat Burke, who ran the Hartogen Group until it collapsed. *Plus One* had been commissioned for a crack at the Sydney-to-Brisbane waterskiing record, no less, but Burke and his companies went belly up before the attempt could be made.

By the time Jodee bought the boat, she was in need of repair and refitting, so he had ripped out her two enormous engines and slotted in three big MerCruiser V8s to make her go even faster. This new incarnation was tested for the boating magazine *Club Marine* by a freelance journalist, Graham Lloyd, who took the helm off Sydney Heads and was blown away by the experience. 'On more than one occasion the boat was totally clear of the water', wrote Lloyd, 'soaring across the valleys between the crests, before cleaving back amidst a swelter of spray and foam'.

Jodee did not have only one such runabout. He also had a 9-metre Scarab Thunder, worth around $200,000 new, and a far more ritzy Riviera 4000, described by its Australian manufacturer as 'the offshore masterpiece for achievers'. At around $450,000, or more than $10,000 a foot, the Riviera was similar in design to offshore racers like *Plus One*, but came complete with double bed, teak decking, leather trim and a cocktail cabinet. As the sales pitch made clear, it was ideal for a man who had two huge houses but wasn't sure why. 'Achievement has always been your goal', it crooned. 'Now, with the Riviera 4000 you truly have a performance cruiser that reflects your need to outperform those who choose to compete with you at work and at play . . . The Riviera 4000 offers your whole family the opportunity to share the privilege of achievement and the respect of your friends and associates.'

The powerboats were by no means the end of it. Back in 1997 Jodee had been looking at buying a plum- and gold-coloured Mooney Ovation jet plane for $560,000. And he would soon be buying a brand new Eurocopter Squirrel helicopter for around $2 million, which cost the best part of $100,000 a year to insure and was popular with the armies and police forces of Europe.

For a man who often claimed that money did not turn him on, he seemed to love the trappings that came with it, but when I ask him about this at one of our many meetings after the One.Tel collapse, he repeats the mantra: 'Money's not important, it's not what drives me, it's not what brings me happiness. I ride a $100 bike, I don't drive a Porsche, neither Maxine nor I wears any jewellery, the kids go to public schools'.

I ask him why he bought Craigend if his millions were so trivial to him. Having failed to find an answer for *Good Weekend*, he has another shot: the house in Vaucluse was too small, they needed a fourth bedroom, and Craigend was going for a decent price, he says. I suggest to him that the rest of the world will think this laughable, that this huge house in the middle of Sydney is a 'look at me' statement. 'I can tell you completely from the bottom of my heart that that's not true', he says.

So what about Maxine's Porsche, the three power-boats, the $6 million jet, the $2 million helicopter, the Whitsundays resort, the fish tank business he started at the age of 12, his share trading at school, the fact that he has spent most of his life making large amounts of money—how does a man to whom it apparently means so little end up with so much?

He likes creating, he says, he likes building things. The money is a by-product. And why shouldn't he spend it, he asks, on doing the things he likes?

I agree that he's not Kerry Packer or Alan Bond, that money is not his God. But beyond that, I'm not sure what he's trying to prove by protesting. He does not give money away on a grand scale, and after the collapse of One.Tel he will engage in some pretty serious asset shuffling to protect his fortune. It's disingenuous, I suggest, to claim that money is not important to him, to say he could lose it all and not give a damn. He's shocked when I challenge his explanation, angry that I can question his integrity. 'Are you suggesting I'm not being truthful with you?' he asks. 'No', I reply, 'I just think you're kidding yourself'.

But whether money was important to him or not, the deal with Packer and Murdoch, and the accompanying lift in One.Tel's share price, now made Jodee extraordinarily rich. By May 1999, he had been propelled to number 12 on the *BRW Rich 200*, that ever-faithful scorer in Australia's money game. Thirteen years earlier, at the tender age of 26, he had been the youngest member on the list. Now he was back at the top, with 30 times as much to his name, and this time, according to the *BRW* scribes, he was undoubtedly here to stay:

The lessons from his early days are helping to shape
One.Tel as a force to be reckoned with. Rich and
marketing whiz Brad Keeling have made One.Tel
one of the few profitable telcos in Australia.
Recognising the sector's potential, media scions
Lachlan Murdoch and James Packer have climbed
aboard. One.Tel's share price has rocketed as a
result, making Rich worth more than $700 million
on paper. Last year, he was barely on the radar
screen.

Keeling had also shot onto the list from nowhere to clock
up $150 million, in a style that *BRW* said was indica-
tive of the new wealth of the 1990s. 'Technology is
changing the way people interact, and will ultimately
change the whole business model', *BRW* reported breath-
lessly, 'and it is where the money is'. It went on:

> Thirteen of the people who have entered the list
> this year are paper millionaires and have seen the
> value of their shares soar as investors chase a piece
> of a winning internet or telecommunications stock.
> The so-called millennium kids tend to run in packs.
> Jodee and Brad at One.Tel; Chris, Penny and Tony
> at Computershare; Graham, Bill and Geoff at Flight
> Centre. With a few exceptions, they are young and
> university-educated. They do not flaunt their
> wealth and, more importantly, are keeping their
> businesses pared to the bone.

Those who penned this glowing write-up doubtless meant it to be hugely complimentary, but even at this stage there were those who warned that the frantic boom in telco and dot-com stocks was something that could only end in tears.

9

Market Madness

I can calculate the motions of the heavenly
bodies, but not the madness of people.

Sir Isaac Newton, 1720

At the height of the tulip boom in Holland in 1640 the most-prized bulbs changed hands for 10,000 guilders apiece, which was 50 times what the average worker earned in a year. For the same price, you could have bought six Rembrandt paintings or the fanciest mansion in Amsterdam. Crazier still, you could have rebuilt the *Batavia*, the magnificent Dutch warship that was wrecked on the west coast of Australia in 1629 and whose replica was moored at Sydney's Darling Harbour during much of 2000. Such is the madness of markets.

When the first tulip bulbs arrived in Antwerp from Turkey in the mid-16th century, a merchant mistook them for onions and cooked half of them for dinner, or so legend has it. Not liking the taste, he planted the rest in his vegetable garden and was delighted with the result. As to why prices then took off nearly 70 years later, who can say? But after massive fortunes had been made and lost, sanity returned, and the bulbs went back to their rightful place as kings of the flowerbed.

In the 360 years since tulips had their brief day in the sun, no boom has quite matched the frenzy of that one, but some have run close. In 1720, in the greatest financial fraud in British history, half of London's gentry were ruined in the famous South Sea Bubble. In the space of nine months, worthless stock in the South Sea Company rose tenfold in price, even though the company was not actually trading. Even the cleverest were caught in the crash. The brilliant scientist and philosopher Sir Isaac Newton lost £20,000, which was then a considerable fortune. 'I can calculate the motions of the heavenly bodies', he reflected ruefully, 'but not the madness of people'. A pamphlet written in Boston a few months later described the collapse:

> All on a sudden the Scale is turned ... none cares
> to buy; all are for Selling, and where one hath
> Gained by this Evil Trade, many poor Families have
> been ruined, brought to Poverty, and turned
> beggars.

In the late 1960s, the lunacy resurfaced in Australian mining stocks. A little-known exploration company called Poseidon saw its shares rocket from $1 to $280 in just four months after it struck nickel at Windarra in Western Australia. While the boom raged, according to Trevor Sykes, the author of *The Money Miners*, 'Every rag tag and bobtail stock was swept along with it, on any sort of sniff and wild rumour'. Then, almost as fast as prices had risen, they fell back again, and the biggest gambling spree of modern times came to an end. Poseidon's little nickel mine ended up losing money and by 1975 the company was bust. Meanwhile, thousands of people in Australia and London had lost millions.

In the late 1980s it was the Japanese stock market that took leave of its senses, becoming so overvalued that it was worth almost as much as the rest of the world's stock exchanges put together. The Tokyo property market was even crazier. For the price of a small block in the Ginza, Tokyo's prime shopping district, one could have bought half of Australia's Gold Coast, while the land on which the Imperial Palace was built would have fetched more than all the property in California. Over a decade later, share prices and property values in Japan are well below where they were, and Japan's banks are still suffering from the bad loans they made to fund it all.

In the late 1990s, the great boom was in dot-coms and telcos. And if ever the tulips were given a run for their money, it was here. According to the American economist David Hale, the last two years of the 20th century saw twice as much money punted in venture capital—almost entirely on dot-coms and telcos—as in all the previous 18 years put together. From an annual average of US$5 billion in the mid-1990s the flow of funds suddenly surged to more than US$110 billion in 2000. On the stock market, where these companies were passed on to the public, the gambles and losses were far larger.

It would be impossible to put a figure on how much money was won and lost in this period, but when dot-com mania hit its peak in early 2000, the online bookseller Amazon.com was worth US$41 billion, which was about the same as the car giant General Motors, while the internet portal Yahoo! was worth US$125 billion, or more than three times as much. The entire US Nasdaq market, where most of these companies were quoted, weighed in at US$6,250 billion dollars.

None of these dot-coms was ever worth billions because of the profits it made, as they all made a loss and ate cash at the most alarming rate. But then none was really worth billions in the first place. Two years on, even blue chips like Yahoo! and Amazon.com sell for around one-tenth of what they sold for at the peak, while most of their stellar companions have burnt up on their descent from the heavens.

In booms like this buyers typically abandon reason, which is why even poor Newton failed to see that gravity applies to soaring prices, just as it does to apples. Investors paid crazy prizes for dot-com shares because they believed in a dream. And perhaps the best illustration of this is a company called NetJ.com.

This dot-com, which never got past the wannabe stage, was capitalised on the US Over-The-Counter market in March 2000 at US$107 million, even though it had no money, no income and no profits. Good old NetJ.com did nothing at all, and had no immediate plans to change its ways. According to filings with the US Securities and Exchange Commission, it was looking for a business to acquire but was not anticipating 'any substantial activity' in the foreseeable future.

NetJ.com was what is known as a 'Blank Check' or a 'Blind Pool' company, which meant that no one knew what it might become—or whether, indeed, it would become anything at all. But this was what made the shares such a terrific bet, because it might soon have a new technology business in its empty box. As Michael Lewis, Bloomberg columnist and author of *Liar's Poker*, so elegantly described it, it was 'pure possibility'. All the other shares you could buy on the market—like mining companies, grocery stores, oil giants and dull old industrials—had finite, identifiable roles that you could put a price on. With NetJ.com, and many other internet companies, the sky was the limit. No one knew how high the company could rise, or what it might not do— and in late 2001 they still did not know, because NetJ.com was still doing nothing. It was pure hope, or pure hype. The greater the mystery the better it was.

Did anyone really know what the leading Australian internet companies, such as Liberty One, Sausage, Solution 6 and Eisa, did for a living? Almost certainly not. Nor did they care. It was enough to be told that they were at the cutting edge of a technological revolution that was going to change the world.

Within a year of becoming the first home-grown Australian internet stock in late 1998, Liberty One was worth almost $1 billion. Another year later, it was being put to sleep by the corporate doctor after losing $58 million in its last six months of business, which, for the record, included web design, music retailing, an online Chinese bookstore and the internet rights to images of Greg Norman and Pat Rafter. Its creditors lost $20 million and its 16,000 shareholders lost the lot.

The e-tailer dstore was an even crazier example of how greed and hope fuelled the boom in Australia. Billed as a web department store that would put David Jones and Myers out of business, it was valued at $200 million in early 2000. Yet its total lifetime sales barely matched what either of those groups ring up in a day—and it managed to run out of cash in the middle of the Christmas rush less than a year after it set up shop.

Several million dollars of the Packers' money went down with dstore, just to show that even the smartest investors can get it wrong more than once. But, to their credit, they did a whole lot better with their own internet business ecorp—which comprises eBay, ninemsn and

Ticketek—because they created the concept and sold it to others. In June 1999, a few months after their punt on One.Tel, the Packers' company, PBL, reaped $160 million by offloading 20 per cent of ecorp's shares to the public. At the time it was floated, ecorp had hardly begun doing business, and obviously wasn't making a profit, so it was hard to decide what price should be asked. A suitable rule was probably to think of a figure and double it, but the Packers' advisers were more ambitious than that. Eventually, they stuck a price tag of $804 million on the company, which they justified as being 15 times its projected *sales* for the first year.

If this doesn't immediately strike you as mad, then just consider this comparison. In the mid-1980s, Imagineering was floated on the stock market for $12 million, which was 12 times its earnings, or profits. Had it been floated at 15 times sales, it would have been sold to the public for $390 million.

Yet Australian investors in ecorp bought and bought and bought. In the 18 months following the float, the share price rocketed from $1.20 to $8.60, making the company worth almost $6 billion. And at this even more absurd price, the brilliant analysts at investment bank Goldman Sachs reckoned it was such good value that people should buy more. Unlike most Australian internet companies, ecorp is still in business, and set to record its first-ever profit, but it's now worth only one-20th of what it was at the peak.

One.Tel, of course, was never a dot-com, but like all the other telcos it was swept along in the same surge of hope and hype. Back in 1995 when the dude set up in business, mobile phone companies were valued at around $1,000 a customer. By early 2000, when Vodafone bought Orange in the UK, those same customers were changing hands at around $20,000 a head, or 20 times more. There was no way in the world that such valuations could ever be justified by profits that Vodafone, or any other mobile phone company, could make.

One.Tel's stock market value at the peak was almost as wild. Having been floated in November 1997 for $208 million (at which price no one wanted to buy), in late 1999 its shares were selling like hot cakes at prices that valued the company at more than $5 billion. This was around 700 times One.Tel's annual earnings and 15 times its sales revenue, just like ecorp. It was also considerably more than the value of Australia's national airline, Qantas, and almost as much as the entire Packer business empire, which had taken 80 years to build up. As with the dot-coms, there was no way One.Tel could ever make enough profit to justify this price. It only made sense because there was a bigger fool prepared to pay more. Which there was . . . until there wasn't . . . and the price came tumbling down.

Once again, a comparison with Imagineering is revealing, because if One.Tel had been selling at 12 times earnings, as Imagineering did in 1985, it would have been valued at only $84 million, or roughly one-60th of what people were paying on the stock market.

If you looked at One.Tel's so-called 'earnings', you might have had doubts about whether it would be wise to pay even that, because the small print in the accounts for 1998-99, which were published shortly before the shares hit their peak in November 1999, made it clear that the company was losing money. You could see instantly from the cash flow that things were not well: One.Tel had chewed through more than $61 million in the year to June 1999, of which almost half had been eaten up by the company's day-to-day operations.

Naturally, this was not something that was advertised in the official press release in August, which was relentlessly positive, as always. The One.Tel Story was that revenue was soaring, subscribers and profits had more than doubled, and blue skies were ahead.

Nor could you tell there was trouble from some of the newspaper stories, thanks to One.Tel's skill in keeping such things out of the press. To ensure that only good news was reported, One.Tel's head of investor relations, Sandy Slessar, had been asked to take the unusual step of ringing financial journalists to offer them a sneak preview of the accounts. This was extremely unorthodox, because results have to be released to the Australian Stock Exchange before anybody else is allowed to see them, but Slessar said she would mask the actual figures, and journalists could slip them into their copy at the last minute.

Deadlines are always tight on a Friday night because newspapers have to print twice the normal number of papers and weekend editions are huge, so several journalists were grateful for the offer. Aaron Patrick, whose deadline at the *Australian Financial Review* was 5.45pm, grabbed the chance with both hands, and told the world the glad tidings that One.Tel's profit had increased commendably:

> Discount telephone company One.Tel Ltd showed on Friday its share market success was more than marketing hype, reporting a large increase in full-year earnings and a huge jump in customers.

But others weren't so sure that One.Tel's motives were pure, and held off until the official ASX statement arrived at 6.00pm. By luck or good judgment on Slessar's part, this was after most broking analysts had gone home for the weekend and just as most editors were shouting for copy that hadn't been filed. But the wait was rewarded, because the fine brush strokes showed that One.Tel had only avoided going deep into the red by 'deferring', or not counting, $32.4 million in costs incurred in the company's new European and Australian ventures. This was one of the things Imagineering had done so successfully in 1989 to disguise its losses.

Consequently, *The Australian*'s Geoff Elliott was able to tell an entirely different story, which went like this:

> A change in accounting policies has saved junior telecoms group One.Tel from posting a $25.4 million loss for the year to June 30.

In fact, the $25 million loss still underestimated the company's problems, because it became clear three days later that One.Tel's sleight of hand had covered up an even larger hole. The full accounts, filed with the Australian Securities and Investments Commission (ASIC) revealed that $48 million of expenditure had been deferred, and a loss of more than $40 million concealed.

One.Tel had often boasted that it did not engage in such naughtiness, but it now defended the practice, claiming that it was only doing what everyone else in the industry was doing. 'It would have been irresponsible for us *not* to defer these costs', One.Tel's chairman, John Greaves, told the *Australian Financial Review*'s Neil Chenoweth. 'If what we were doing was unacceptable, the auditors wouldn't sign the accounts.'

In fact, the auditors may soon have wished they hadn't, because the Institute of Chartered Accountants of Australia (ICAA) looked at the accounts closely and identified 48 items of concern, which they listed in a letter to Steven La Greca, who had performed the audit for BDO Nelson Parkhill. La Greca and BDO were subsequently reprimanded by the ICAA's disciplinary committee and ordered to pay $1,000 costs apiece. The committee's judgment stated that they had 'failed to observe a proper standard of professional care, skill or competence in the course of carrying out their professional duties'. It also concluded that BDO's audit report was in breach of the Corporations Law, Australian accounting standards and Australian auditing standards.

The Australian Securities and Investments Commission conducted its own separate investigation into One.Tel's 1999 accounts and persuaded, or perhaps forced, the company to change its accounting policies, which it believed were also in breach of the law. In September 2000, possibly as a result of this kerfuffle, BDO Nelson Parkhill was replaced by Ernst & Young as One.Tel's auditor.

Shortly after this strange episode with Sandy Slessar, *The Australian*'s Geoff Elliott wrote a piece suggesting that One.Tel had some explaining to do. He also accused the company of 'highly questionable' behaviour and reported that the ASX was investigating. His reward was an angry two-page letter from Rodney Adler telling him that his attack on Slessar was 'repugnant'. She had only been trying to help, said Adler.

Despite all the adverse comment in the press about One.Tel's accounting practices and its mounting losses, the company's shares continued their merry climb on the ASX. Those who were buying the new technology dream weren't interested in dull stuff like deferred expenditure or last year's cash flow.

In fact, they weren't much interested in the past or the present. Like the other dreamers, their eyes were focused firmly on the future, where the skies were looking bluer than ever.

10

Boom, Boom, Bust

I can't tell you how many times Kerry told me:
'Jodee, you fucked up. You paid too much
for spectrum'.

Jodee Rich, 2001

Unlike its dot-com cousins, One.Tel had a reason-able chance of making profits—even if it would never make enough to justify its absurd share price—but everything rested on the company's ability to make its 'Next Generation' mobile network pay, and there were plenty of experts who doubted it could.

It had cost Optus several billion dollars more than expected to lay out its cables and mobile network during the 1990s, and it had been almost a decade before the carrier made a profit. Worse still, Optus had almost gone bust along the way, despite having two hugely rich and hugely experienced telephone companies—Bell South and Cable & Wireless—behind it.

Even with the Packers' and Murdochs' money, One.Tel had neither the funds nor the expertise to match such heavyweights. And it was not clear that they knew how big a gamble they were taking. According to Professor Reg Coutts, who had been advising them since 1996: 'They never really analysed anything. They convinced themselves it was sustainable. That's the intoxication that happens when you're doing that well. There was an element of, "We'll show you guys". There was some personality stuff happening'.

Or, as Bob Mansfield, now chairman of Telstra, puts it: 'I guess ego took over, they reckoned they could cut the legs off Telstra'.

To survive in the telecommunications business, you need immensely deep pockets, extremely strong nerves and a fair bit of luck—and it is perfectly possible to fail, even if you have all three. But One.Tel's dynamic duo clearly had no doubts that they would succeed. During 1999, Brad Keeling told fund managers and stockbrokers' analysts that One.Tel planned to be No 2 in the Australian mobile market. The company's investor relations manager, Sandy Slessar, was even more bullish. In a report headed 'Frequently Asked Questions' prepared in March 1999, just after the Packers and Murdochs invested $710 million, she anticipated the following exchange:

Q: What does One.Tel propose to do with the funds?

A: The sky's the limit . . . [The money] gives
One.Tel the ability to compete as No 1 or No 2
mobile operator in Australia.

There's an old saying in life: 'Be realistic, demand the
impossible', but if Jodee, Brad, James, Lachlan and the
other directors really believed that their company could
oust Telstra from top spot in the Australian mobile market,
they were even more cracked than their critics believed.

There was far more likelihood that they would send
One.Tel broke in the effort, because the market was
already looking dangerously overcrowded. In the UK,
there were four mobile phone carriers servicing 56 million
people. In Australia, thanks to One.Tel and Hutchison
Telecoms, there would soon be five chasing a population one-quarter of the size. There was a very good
chance there would not be enough business to go round.

One.Tel's publicly declared target was to win 2 million
customers by 2005, which was extraordinarily ambitious by any measure. The company would have to
recruit eight times as many people as it had managed to
sign for its Optus reseller service since 1995. It would
also have to capture twice the number of customers that
Vodafone had secured in the 1990s, in half the time.
Toughest of all, it would need to sign up almost one-
third of all the existing mobile users in Australia.

On the positive side, it was almost certain that the
market would keep growing rapidly so One.Tel would

not have to rely on stealing all its customers from its rivals, and the network could probably make money with only half the number of customers One.Tel was aiming at.

However, there were also plenty of things that could go wrong. It wasn't hard to imagine that other carriers would be doing the same sums, and it didn't take a genius to see that the scramble for customers could drive prices down. The chances were that precious little money would be made by any of the networks, especially the new ones, until a couple of players had gone to the wall. So unless One.Tel's other businesses turned profitable pretty quickly, it looked like the company would find it hard to stay in the game. Nor were its rivals likely to give up quickly. Apart from Telstra and Optus, its two key opponents were Vodafone and Hutchison Telecoms (operating under the Orange brand name), both of which were backed by huge multinational mobile phone companies with massive resources.

If One.Tel were to succeed, it would be because of its products and its marketing. The Next Generation mobile network would be the first in Australia to offer a whole range of exciting new features, from traffic reports to stock prices, sports results, cinema bookings, TV guide, horoscopes, weather forecasts and even the lottery results. It would also have the backing of two huge media empires that controlled more than half of the country's TV, papers and magazines between them, and who had unmatchable marketing muscle. Best of all, it would be cheap because One.Tel had landed an amazing deal with Lucent (once the electronics division of the US telephone giant AT&T) to build its new national network in Sydney, Melbourne, Brisbane, Adelaide and Perth almost for nix.

Not only had Lucent promised to put up all the $1.15 billion in finance that was needed, but it was so keen to get One.Tel's business that it was even throwing in $20 million to help meet the costs of acquiring new customers. One.Tel would not have to pay a cent in interest or anything else until 2003, and would not even begin repaying the capital until 2005. Better still, the clock would not start ticking on the loans until every-thing was performing properly, so if the network didn't work, Lucent would get nothing until it did. Finally, if the One.Tel subsidiary that operated the network went bust, there would be no recourse to, or recovery from, One.Tel's existing businesses. In other words, Lucent and its lenders were wearing all the risk.

The One.Tel team, led by Jodee's acolyte at Imagineering, Kevin Beck, who had negotiated this bril-liant deal, reckoned it was the best the industry had ever seen, and they were probably right. Lucent and Motorola had both been so eager to win the contract—to stop themselves falling further behind Nokia and Ericsson in the race to build digital networks—that One.Tel had been able to conduct a bidding war. Beck had run parallel negotiations, jumping from one to the other as each new offer was made, to extract even more concessions.

But in its rush to get the business, Lucent had possibly been too optimistic about what it could do. Back in 1998, the American company had promised it could build a new network with only 2.5 MHz of spectrum, which was all that was then on offer from the government. One.Tel had snapped this up at the September auction, but soon realised that it would not be enough.

With such a small amount of bandwidth, one could only have 1,000 people on One.Tel mobiles in Sydney's CBD at any one time; and each mobile tower would only be able to carry eight simultaneous calls. As the boss of Sun Microsystems, Scott McNealy, famously remarked, it would be 'like trying to put a pig down a python'. Technically, one could ease the problem by building more towers and making the cells smaller, but this was expensive and difficult. And since One.Tel and its new shareholders were determined to win 2 million customers, the only option was to buy more spectrum. The problem was that none was available, and no auction was planned.

The Packer–Murdoch team had known about this when they pumped in their millions back in February 1999 and obviously felt that it wouldn't be too hard to fix. And sure enough, it wasn't. The Packers' Canberra lobbyists were wheeled into action to argue the need for greater competition in the mobile market. Meanwhile,

James dined with the Minister for Communications, Senator Richard Alston, a couple of times, and Lachlan and James both talked to the Prime Minister's office. Before long, to no one's great surprise, the government agreed to sell more. In June 1999 Alston announced that another 30 MHz would be released in all of the capitals, which would be enough for One.Tel and another player to have 15 MHz each, the amount that Optus, Telstra and Vodafone had already bought for themselves. It would be dubbed 'the One.Tel auction' by the rest of the industry—for obvious reasons.

With this problem sorted, Jodee, Brad and James now began to think about global conquest . . . as you do. Undaunted by the huge task ahead of the company in Australia, One.Tel announced in November 1999 that it would roll out a hi-tech '3G'—or Third Generation— network in the UK, where it would bid for a mobile licence at the next auction in early 2000. This scheme was several times more ambitious than the plan to carve up Australia, because it would mean risking tens of billions of dollars and going head to head with companies like Vodafone Airtouch and British Telecom, which were more than 100 times One.Tel's size.

At least one of James Packer's advisers tackled him about the wisdom of getting into a fight with these people, but James's reply was: 'You're being too cautious'. He was convinced that the future of media and telephone companies would increasingly converge, and he was adamant that little One.Tel could become a world-class player with the Packers' and Murdochs' support.

Lachlan and Rupert were also hot to trot, and one look at their UK businesses told you why. With 4 million subscribers to their Pay TV service BSkyB and more than 5 million readers of their newspapers—*The Sun, The Times, The Sunday Times* and the *News of the World*— they already had a huge target market and a massive promotional machine. Since the new UK network would be 3G technology, which allowed TV pictures and the internet to be beamed at lightning speed through to people's mobile phones, News Ltd's media resources would give them an extra competitive edge. The Murdochs would be able to provide all the news stories and TV pictures that the most demanding customer could ask for.

Lucent was also thrilled at the prospect because it would bring billions of dollars of new business and boost its own share price still further. In late 1999, Jodee and Brad flew to New York a couple of times to talk to Rupert and Lachlan, and to spend a day at the Bell Labs research facility in New Jersey, which Lucent owned. It seemed like a fantastic idea, and everyone took comfort from the fact that everyone else thought it was great. Lucent, which was 100 times the size of One.Tel, told Rupert how impressed they were with Jodee's team, while Jodee told Lucent that the Murdochs' support made the UK venture an odds-on winner.

Back in Sydney, on 23 November the press were called in to hear about the glorious future that this alliance would deliver. Gung ho as ever, Jodee made it clear that the One.Tel army would not be stopping at Dover. Germany and Italy would be the next to fall, with Lucent putting up the entire $30 billion needed to build the One.Tel network across Europe. This time, Lucent had been so keen to lead the charge it had secretly promised to throw in a few hundred million pounds extra to be used in the UK licence bid.

It was heady stuff. The UK auction was still several months away, and sales of the German and Italian licences were even further down the track. They were about to march into battle against the biggest, richest, toughest telephone operators in the world, whose financial muscle and experience far outweighed their own. Yet everyone was talking as though Europe had already been won.

To kick off the campaign, the Murdochs now announced they would sink another $200 million into One.Tel shares, so the company could pay the £125 million deposit that all UK bidders had to provide. This new show of faith in the company, along with talk of victory, was enough to send One.Tel's stock into orbit again. The day after the press conference, the share price rocketed 42 per cent, adding $900 million to the company's value, and firing it into the ranks of Australia's Top 30.

The financial press could scarcely believe it. Even in this hi-tech bubble it was hard to credit such blind optimism. Here was a company, remember, that did not make money, had not secured a UK licence and still needed to buy spectrum in Australia to build its network—which might, or might not, make a profit. As John Durie's *Chanticleer* column in the *Australian Financial Review* scathingly summed it up: 'One.Tel's stock price has long since parted with reality, but yesterday's 42 per cent increase can only be described as a joke'.

Durie's colleague, Aaron Patrick, who had unwittingly been so kind about One.Tel's 1999 results, was almost as savage. A few days earlier he had described the company as fragile, reminded readers it had generated no cash for two years, and suggested that the share price was artificially high because supply was so limited. He had also chosen to remind readers:

> This is Rich's second incarnation as a technology entrepreneur. In the 1980s he founded Imagineering, and was prominent in Australia's PC industry for eight years. Despite a promising listing in 1985, Imagineering overextended itself, fell into financial trouble and Rich sold out, humiliated.

Patrick's comments were not well received by One.Tel, and he was promptly banned from the next press conference. When he turned up anyway he was taken into one of the glass-walled meeting rooms by Jodee and told he had problems with his personal life that he was taking out on the company. 'You young guys just write what you like', said Rich, 'and the bizarre thing is that people believe you'. The article also prompted a letter from One.Tel's solicitors to say they had been instructed to sue for defamation, and another three-page complaint from Rodney Adler, who was angry that his favourite company kept flying into so much flak.

> You denigrate the achievements of two great Australian entrepreneurs, Jodee Rich and Brad Keeling, you underestimate and under-represent the extent of their achievements and surprisingly you misunderstand what One.Tel is and where it is going.
>
> As you can appreciate, it is because of comments and articles like the one you wrote that Jodee Rich and Brad Keeling do not talk to the press, because it revolts them how their comments are manipulated. In America, they would be held up as examples of what can be achieved. In Australia they are insulted.
>
> Finally, if I may add, watch One.Tel. We are proud of the company, and if you believe a $2.5 billion market capitalisation is high, I look forward to talking to you in a year's time, as it is certainly my opinion, and I have 20 million plus personal shares behind the forthcoming statement, that it will be much higher in 12 months.

In the short term, of course, Adler was absolutely right because One.Tel's share price doubled within the week. On 26 November, just two days after the announcement that One.Tel would march on Europe, the price hit a new high of $2.84 (the equivalent of $28.40, because each share had been split into ten new shares in May 1999). This made the company worth $5.3 billion, which was almost as much as all the Packers' businesses put together. At this moment, on this day, Jodee Rich was worth close to $2 billion.

It did not take much nous to realise that this would be a good time to sell. But the trouble with hype is that people believe it. Sadly, for Jodee, selling even a few shares was not an option because the Packers and Murdochs had put their faith in him. The major share-holders had agreed to give each other notice when they wanted to sell, so Kerry Packer would have to hear about it. As one market insider put it, 'I would not have wanted to tell Kerry I was going to sell. That's not a conversation I would have wanted to have'.

By this time, there were only two months to the start of the Australian spectrum auctions, which were due to begin in January 2001, and One.Tel was in an awkward position. Lucent was already going hammer and tongs to get the network ready, building it on the assumption that the company would have at least 7.5 MHz of spectrum to work with, so unless Jodee and Brad wanted to shove the pig down the python, they had to win at any cost. Unfortunately for them, their rivals knew this too.

There had already been several meetings between the Packers and One.Tel's two founders to figure out how high the bidding might go. Jodee, Brad and James were all confident it would be manageable. They were convinced that Hutchison Telecoms, which was also planning a new mobile network, would stay out of the Australian auction because they were committed to 3G technology, which needed a wider spectrum than the one on offer. Kerry Packer was equally sure they were wrong. 'These people are big gorillas and they will try to fuck you', is how Jodee recalls him putting it.

This was not the only warning that they might be in for a rough ride. Just before the auction began, Canning Fok, managing director of Hutchison's parent, the huge Hong Kong conglomerate Hutchison Whampoa, ran into Rupert Murdoch and assured him that his company certainly would be bidding. Jodee, James and Brad chose to believe he was bluffing.

As the auction began, One.Tel's worst-case scenario was that it would have to pay $200 million to get what it wanted, but it rapidly became clear that this was way off the mark. Hutchison came into the bidding hard, along with another of One.Tel's rivals, Primus Australia, and it soon became obvious that they would need to find a couple of hundred million dollars more just to stay in the game.

Once again, the company's broker, Brent Potts, was asked to ring round Australia's institutions to see if they would kick the tin, and once again the answer came back 'No'. They were not prepared to cough up unless they knew how much One.Tel was going to have to pay for the Australian licences. They were also worried that the UK auctions, where prices would go even higher, were still to come.

Quite what would have happened if this had been the final answer one can only guess, but Bankers Trust, which had pumped millions into Imagineering at the top of the market in 1988, fortunately agreed to come to the party again. It was said that the bank kept a white board in its investment department reminding fund managers to steer clear of companies run by Jodee Rich, but if this was so, it was now wiped clean. Bankers Trust's analyst, Victor Gomes, loved the One.Tel Story and could see Jodee and Brad trouncing their older, duller rivals in the battle for customers.

The bank's decision involved a lot of number crunching, a couple of visits to James Packer at Park Street and, apparently, a talk with Rupert Murdoch. Gomes and his boss Rohan Hedley finally agreed to put $140 million into One.Tel at $1.50 a share, which was an 18 per cent discount on the market price. Once Bankers Trust was in place, the other institutions, such as AMP and Mercantile Mutual, meekly fell in behind. Brent Potts and his team raised another $140 million over the phone in 45 minutes after the market closed, and even had to turn money away.

Bankers Trust's condition for stumping up the funds was that News Ltd and PBL would also pump in $140 million apiece, at least one year earlier than they had promised back in February 1999. Rumours soon spread that they were unhappy about this, and before long these were being written up in *The Australian* by Geoff Elliott, who also reported Rodney Adler's admission that One.Tel had already blown its auction budget by $200 million.

The article prompted yet another angry letter from Adler to say: 'Business is about relationships, and the board of One.Tel thought that if we spoke to you in an open and friendly way, you would reciprocate'. After that, it became more personal:

> There is little doubt that for several reasons you have boxed yourself in a corner, and you are so negative towards One.Tel that you have forgotten to be a dispassionate, factual journalist. The public would prefer the facts rather than your opinion, and from One.Tel's perspective we consider it a waste of time to talk to you, as we do not believe we get a fair go.

> We received incredible institutional support last week, and we have one of the best management teams in Australia. We are cashed up, no debt, have a market capitalisation of approximately $4 billion

and we are expanding globally. This is obviously all mundane, pedestrian stuff for you. Eventually you will learn that life is about give and take—not just take!

Back at the auction, which was taking place over the internet and being recorded on computers in a drab windowless office in Canberra, the price was now climbing so high that even the Reserve Bank and Treasury had started to take an interest. Obviously, it was not only One.Tel that was shocked by how much the sale was raising.

Finally, on 26 March, some two months after bidding began, One.Tel secured the spectrum it needed, but only by agreeing to pay $523 million, which was ten times what Telstra, Optus and Vodafone had laid out at the first auction in May 1998. To meet the extra cost, Jodee and Brad were forced to go back to Bankers Trust again and persuade the bank to stump up another $60 million. It was some consolation that Hutchison was paying even more.

When news of the victory broke at the One.Tel offices—and victory was how Jodee and his team regarded it—there was much back slapping and high fiving. But the harsh reality was that the network would now cost 50 per cent more than they had budgeted for, which would make it even harder to turn a profit, and increased the likelihood that they would need to raise extra cash somewhere down the line. And within a week, One.Tel's chances of doing that were hit for six.

On Monday, 3 April 2000, while Australia slept, shares on the US Nasdaq market went into free fall. In Australia the next day, dot-com and telco stocks lost almost a fifth of their value. The following week in the US, capped by Black Friday, 14 April, the world saw the biggest wealth meltdown it had ever seen. Black Friday alone wiped US$11 billion from the fortune of the world's richest man, Bill Gates, and sliced US$113 billion off the market value of the world's most expensive company, Cisco Systems, which supplied switches to companies such as One.Tel.

'We are moving from greed to fear', said one American commentator. 'The Nasdaq is the roach motel of Wall Street', said another. 'You can check in, folks, but you can't check out.'

When the stock exchange opened in Australia on Monday, 17 April, fear had no rivals. By the end of the day the average dot-com stock had lost another third of its value. Ecorp, Spike and eisa were down by a half, and the company that had kicked off the Australian internet boom, Liberty One, was showing an 80 per cent loss from its recent highs.

Most of the telcos suffered just as badly. The April tech-wreck wiped 70 per cent off the value of Open Telecom, the company that had made its founder Wayne Passlow a billionaire and one of the ten richest men in

Australia. It also sliced 75 per cent off the worth of Davnet, which had briefly given its managing director, Stephen Moignard, a $350 million paper fortune, and knocked 50 per cent off the value of Hutchison.

By comparison, One.Tel got off lightly, losing only a third of its value. And things could easily have been worse. If the crash had come two weeks earlier, the institutions would have been in panic mode and One.Tel would have had no chance of raising money. Murdoch and Packer would have been required to dig even deeper into their pockets if they wanted the new Australian mobile network to go ahead.

The company could still pull back in Europe, where prices in the UK licence auction were also going berserk. On 6 April, three days after the first wave of dot-com carnage, as the bidding raced past £2.2 billion, Jodee and his team decided to give up the chase. They had already exceeded their limit by £300 million and had neither the money nor the inclination to go on. Others did continue driving the price up, and by the time the auction finished three weeks later, Hutchison Whampoa's Canning Fok had agreed to pay more than £4 billion for the licence that One.Tel had wanted. Remarkably, he found himself being hailed, briefly, as a genius.

Interviewed by *Business Week*, Fok was happy to explain what a great deal he had done. 'We are very safe', he purred. 'Even using the most conservative figures, we are very safe.' Two months earlier, Vodafone had bought his old UK network, Orange, for £32 billion, or roughly £8,000 pounds per customer. His new network, he boasted, would be able to deliver customers for a third of this price, so he could not possibly lose.

But two months was a world away, because the new technology bubble had burst. One year later, most telco share prices would be down by 75–85 per cent, and the banks that had lent money to buy 3G mobile licences would be worrying about how much they had lost. In December 2000, the Bank of England would issue grave warnings about the risk of banks going bust because they had lent too much.

Not surprisingly, Kerry Packer now became openly concerned that One.Tel might run out of money, if only because, in this timid new world, he and Rupert would be the only ones who could save the company. Kerry and James also started to argue over the $340 million that they had committed to the investment. The tensions that had always been there started coming to the surface.

Poor Jodee was even less popular with Australia's richest man. Kerry had already criticised him for buying Craigend, and he now warned Rich he was in danger of losing it because One.Tel had overpaid for the Australian licence. 'From that point on, I can't tell you how many times Kerry told me: "Jodee, you fucked up. You paid too much for spectrum"', Jodee says today. James also relayed his father's opinion at regular intervals, with comments like: 'Dad really thinks you've fucked up'.

Kerry was right, of course, as he usually was. But by the time One.Tel got to the auction in March 2000, it had already begun building the network that would cut the legs off Telstra, so there was little choice but to pay the price.

And since James and Lachlan—and Kerry and Rupert—had been backing the plan from the start, they must take a share of the blame for getting the company into this position.

Relations between Jodee and Brad also took a knock around this time, because of something that Keeling let slip to a Sydney journalist. The rules of the UK licence auction prevented bidders talking to each other while the sale was on and also stopped them telling tales about the auction process. It is not clear exactly what Keeling said to Christine Lacy of the *Australian Financial Review*, since neither wants to talk about it, but his comments clearly raised the possibility that One.Tel had broken the auction rules, thus exposing the company to the risk of losing the £50 million deposit it had put down.

When Lacy rang One.Tel in Sydney to check her story, shortly before her deadline, there was panic. A series of angry phone calls followed between Jodee in Paris, Brad in Sydney and One.Tel's lawyers in London, in which Jodee left Brad in no doubt that he was furious at what had happened. It seems that ultimately the *Australian Financial Review* was persuaded not to run the article, so the danger was averted, but Rich and Keeling's relationship clearly suffered. And from this point on it seems to have got steadily worse.

To outsiders, One.Tel had always been 'Jodee and Brad's company', but the two men had never been personally close, and many in the company sensed a deep rivalry between them. Very few of One.Tel's senior staff ever managed to be friends with both, and those who liked one often disliked the other. It was as if they vied with each other to be most popular.

Brad had never been as passionate as Jodee about the One.Tel 'vision' but his interest now began to wane further, and it was probably this that created the tension between them. He was there in body but not in mind, according to one woman who was close to him. He also kept milkman's hours: in at 5.30am, out by 3.00pm, and off to the snow in winter by lunchtime on Friday. He had other investments to look after, other projects to work on, and was said to be keen to get out.

He had always played second fiddle to Jodee, anyway, and there had never been much doubt about who was boss. 'Brad was a nice man, a charming man, but in the four years I was there, he never made any contribution to anything', says one senior One.Tel manager witheringly. He had rarely challenged Jodee on anything and, as time went by, he stood up to him less and less. Even if he clearly disagreed, he would say 'fine' and walk away.

He also appeared to avoid Jodee as much as he could. It may just have been coincidence, but from here on they were rarely on the same side of the world. By the time One.Tel collapsed in May 2001 they were even cooler. Since then, they have hardly spoken to each other at all.

11

Warning Signs

I have been treated so badly by your company
that I am absolutely without words to
understand why you people are in business.

One.Tel customer, July 2000

One.Tel was increasingly in chaos. In just five years,
it had grown from nothing to a business that
spanned seven countries, employed 3,000 staff and had
annual sales close to $1 billion. And neither its managers
nor its systems had been able to keep pace with this
incredible growth. According to one senior accountant,
'It was the perfect example of how not to manage a
company. It was run like a family business or a fish and
chip shop. It had 3,000 employees, but it was still more
like a company with ten'. Or as another put it, 'The place
was a joke. There were no structures, no accounting
systems, no processes, and no controls'.

New managers who were hired from outside were
horrified at what greeted them on arrival. According to

one senior executive who joined from a rival carrier in mid-2000, 'There was only one way to fix One.Tel's problems, and that was to frogmarch the top two layers of management out the door—Rich and Keeling included'.

The flat management structure had been fine when there were only 30 people in the company, because everybody could muck in and help, but with 100 times that number it was a recipe for disaster. Finding the person responsible for doing a particular job could be a nightmare. The telephone list didn't tell you who did what, and no one had offices, so new managers found themselves wandering down the rows of pods, asking for people by name. The lack of job titles made it easy for people to claim it was not their job to do what was needed.

The ban on email added to the problems, because there was often no written record of requests to get things done. Staff were told to keep diaries so they could preserve important voicemail messages, but rewinding and transcribing these messages wasted a huge amount of time, and staff, particularly in the call centre, were often too busy on the phone even to listen to them.

As to whose fault it all was, there was really only one answer. As an experienced manager who was brought into One.Tel in 2000 puts it: 'The buck stops at the top. Jodee and Brad were responsible for the state of the company. It was obvious it was heading for a crash, and if they couldn't see it coming, I'm just astounded'.

The dynamic duo had been perfect for One.Tel in the early days because they had been brilliant at selling the vision and brave enough to take risks, in spite of all the dangers. But neither was suited to the tedious, daily grind of managing the multimillion-dollar enterprise that One.Tel had become. According to one colleague in the top echelon of the company: 'Brad was out of his depth when it went past marketing', where he surrounded himself with an ever-expanding team of gorgeous young women, whom he looked after in avuncular fashion. When he wasn't concentrating on sales campaigns, he spent much of his time on One.Tel's sponsorship of the Australian ski team (who wore One.Tel's purple logo on their lime-green suits and received thousands of dollars in financial support). Jodee, meanwhile, had his eyes on the big picture.

Below this top level, experience was in desperately short supply. As one management consultant put it, 'There weren't enough boring people in the company. There weren't enough men in grey cardigans'. Jodee and Brad always employed young people at One.Tel because they were cheap, had no commitments and worked hard. They then pitched them into positions for which they were not remotely qualified, hoping that they would shine. Some rose to the challenge spectacularly well, but others cracked under the pressure or were simply not up to the job.

In the first half of 2000, with One.Tel still growing at a crazy pace, this dearth of decent managers became a more serious problem, because Jodee and his finance director Mark Silbermann were overseas. Both were living in Paris, commuting around Europe and trying to get One.Tel's businesses in the UK, France, Germany and the Netherlands up and running. They were also still trying to turn One.Tel into a major European mobile operator. Even though the company had been forced to pull out of the UK licence auction because prices had gone too high, there were more licences up for grabs in Italy and Germany, and there was also the option of setting up a so-called Virtual Mobile Network, which was a sophisticated way of being a reseller. This involved piggybacking on someone else's network, therefore Rich and Silbermann were looking for a European telco to act as a big brother so that One.Tel could keep chasing the dream.

Consequently, between February and September 2000, the mounting chaos back home had to be tackled by One.Tel's joint general managers, George Savva and Steve Hodgson, who shared responsibility for running the company's Australian operations—itself a potentially chaotic situation.

The two could hardly have been more different. Savva was a short, plump, emotional salesman, known as the 'Galloping Greek' because he was always rushing around trying to fix things. Hodgson was a tall, thin, reserved accountant of British origin, who sat in meetings and stared out the window. The joke in the office was that

Steve was never wrong, because he made no decisions, and George was never right, even though he made lots of them.

Almost everyone agreed that George Savva was a lovely man, but most also added that he was a hopeless manager. In less than five years he had gone from selling phones at Strathfield Car Radio to being joint head of One.Tel's Australian operations, so it was hardly a surprise if the job was beyond him. 'He should have been running a One.Tel shop', says a senior manager brought in from one of the big carriers during 2000.

Savva had been with One.Tel since 1995 and done well out of his years with the company. A lover of fast cars, he drove a Porsche, an Alfa Romeo and a Range Rover at different times, and rode a $38,000 Ducati. An engaging man with a round face, big straight nose and soft brown eyes, he wore the uniform favoured by most One.Tel executives: a Ralph Lauren Polo shirt, jeans and loafers, with a chunky gold watch on his wrist.

When I met him just after the collapse he was quick to admit that he was sometimes overwhelmed by his responsibilities, and out of his depth on billing and IT. He was a salesman and a good one, he told me, looking me straight in the eye and using my name, as all good salesmen do. I asked him if there was anything he regretted about his time with One.Tel and he answered ruefully: 'If there's one thing I could change, I would never have gone into local calls'.

One.Tel made the decision to offer local calls in November 1999, while everyone was focusing much harder on the new mobile network, and it was quite possibly the most stupid thing the company ever did. It involved buying calls from Telstra for 22 cents and reselling them for 17.5 cents, which not only ensured One.Tel would lose money on every call but also attracted an army of unprofitable customers who put a massive strain on the company's finances and billing systems. Ultimately, it also led to so many complaints about One.Tel's service that the Sydney call centre became a nightmare to deal with and customers deserted in droves.

The rationale behind selling local calls at a loss was that people would switch their phones to One.Tel and then make lots of long-distance calls, which were extremely profitable. Typically, the move was ill-conceived and unplanned. According to one team member who helped run this new business from the beginning: 'The decision was made in a day. There was no information, no training, and everyone in the company was thinking mobile phones, so basically nobody knew anything about it'.

Despite the fact that nothing was ready, Jodee and Brad launched the usual advertising blitz, telling people to 'Switch to One.Tel', and customers were soon signing up at around 40,000 a month. Within a year, there were almost 500,000 extra people on One.Tel's books, or roughly double the number of mobile customers, all of whom had to have their phones transferred from Telstra and Optus. This took up a huge amount of time and resources, and put a fantastic strain on everyone, customers included.

In mid-2000, One.Tel hired a top executive from Telstra at a much-increased salary to get the business working better. It had looked bad from the outside, but it was far worse when he got there. He had wondered how the hell the company could make money on local calls, and he now discovered it didn't. There was no business plan to support what the company was doing, and no way of knowing if it would ever make money. One.Tel didn't even know how many customers it had. The only way to find out was to ring up Telstra.

In his old job this executive had worked on an 80:20 rule, which assumed that 80 per cent of the people and processes were good and 20 per cent were bad. He applied the same figures at One.Tel, but with the proportions reversed. He was dumbfounded by the incompetence of the company, and thought Jodee the worst of all.

One.Tel could not even transfer its customers correctly. One in four attempts to bring people across from Telstra, Optus or AAPT failed because paperwork went missing or procedures weren't followed. Often, customers were disconnected and lost their phone service altogether. Even more frequently, they were barred from making long-distance calls. There was a mass of complaints.

But the real catastrophe was with One.Tel's poor billing system, which simply couldn't cope with the huge number of extra customers that it now had to process. One.Bill1, as it was called, had been built in absolute record time back in 1995, and had once been the best in the industry. However, the software had only been designed to handle tens of thousands of customers and was now trying to cope with 750,000. What's more, it was being forced to deal with 1,000 different products and tariff plans—for mobile phones, local calls, long-distance and the internet—which were constantly being changed at a moment's notice. The strain on the system was intolerable. 'It was horrendous', says the former Telstra manager, 'It just couldn't do the job'.

The obvious answer was to scrap One.Bill1 and start again, but nobody in the IT department, who would be responsible for building a new system, dared suggest such a radical step. According to Toby Billington, a senior software developer: 'No one had the guts to say to Brad or Jodee, "We can't make it work". Everyone was completely spineless in saying we can put a patch here or a patch there, when what was really required was to throw it out the window'.

Thanks to Jodee and Brad, One.Tel's computer experts were already working on far more urgent tasks in any case. Their highest priority was to develop a billing system for the Next Generation mobile network, which had to link into One.Bill1, but they were also writing new software for the GST, which was to be introduced on 1 July 2000. Aside from that, they were busy writing billing code for new plans that One.Tel was promising its customers. Typically, they were doing this with hardly any warning, so there was rarely time to test the modifications. According to one senior programmer: 'Sometimes it was not until the change went live that we found out it wasn't working. Then we would have to stop the whole billing system, and it would take a couple of days to fix it'.

By mid-2000, the system was crashing constantly. Then it got worse. For about six weeks from mid-August onwards, One.Tel was unable to send out any bills at all because the new GST instructions would not work properly. This put considerable strain on the company's finances because cash stopped coming in. When bills did start going out again in October, there was a tidal wave of complaints. Customers were hit with huge demands for money and asked to pay for calls made up to three months earlier. Not surprisingly, many were furious and refused to pay.

In one of my many interviews with Jodee in 2001, I tackle him about these problems with billing and the GST, and ask how One.Tel could have failed to test such changes properly. He tells me that he does not know the answer because he was in Europe at the time, but he agrees that, in hindsight, his managers should have allowed more time. I put it to him that One.Tel's software developers say they were never given long enough to test anything, that companies like Optus and Telstra take six months to trial their systems but One.Tel only ever gave its IT people days or weeks. 'They would say that, wouldn't they?' he replies, 'but they all had schedules which they agreed to'.

In fact, dozens of people in One.Tel have told me that Jodee was always pushing to introduce things before they were ready, so I put this to him, too. He is 'amazed' that people say this. Things go wrong in any business, he says, and it is management's job to fix them. And it was not the problems with the billing system that brought the company down.

However, problems with billing *were* important in the demise of One.Tel, and not just because they made it hard for the company to collect its money. They also caused thousands of angry customers to ring the company's Sydney call centre, which was already under siege from people whose home phones had been disconnected, or who had been barred from making long-distance calls. And this experience was guaranteed to send even the most loyal One.Tel fan into an even greater fury.

Back in 1998, the company had aimed to answer 80 per cent of callers within 20 seconds. Now it often took more than an hour to reach the front of the queue.

At the end of this marathon wait you had to deal with over-stressed, overworked, underpaid telephone jockeys who spent their days being snarled at.

Most callers did not even last the distance. By mid-2000 the Sydney call centre was failing to answer 70–80 per cent of callers, who were hanging up or being disconnected. Those who took up One.Tel's offer to leave their number typically waited four or five days for someone to call them back, gave up and rang the call centre again in an even fouler mood.

If One.Tel had set out to drive these people mad, it could not have done a better job. Even those who had the patience and luck to get through often found that the customer service reps did not know enough to help them. An internal One.Tel memo from July 2000 identified 30 different varieties of error that the call centre was making—from customers being given wrong information, to SIM cards and phones going missing, to faults not being recorded and people being signed up on the wrong plan. The cause of these problems was said to be: 'Too little training. Too much info. Not enough time in training. Little if any training after initial introduction'.

The stress on employees was possibly just as bad as it was for customers because there was no way to escape the angry hordes, except leave. And this people did by the score. At the worst point, in late 2000, staff turnover was running at 300 per cent a year, which meant that the average call centre employee lasted only four months in the job.

New recruits were hired in batches and trained for three weeks to master One.Tel's systems, products and plans—and learn the One.Tel Story. But sometimes the number of callers was so high that they were snatched from the classroom after a few days and thrown into the fray. George Savva was deaf to all protests about their lack of readiness. 'I don't care', he would say, 'just get a voice on the end of the phone'. Often, the shock of battle was so traumatic for this half-trained army that they deserted immediately, so the solution just made the problem worse.

Other efforts to stem the flood of calls were no better. Savva would regularly come down to the seventh floor of the Castlereagh Street HQ, where the call centre was based, and abuse people for not doing enough. 'He would shout and scream and rant and rave', says one. Another manager used to go round the room pasting little yellow Post-Its on everyone's desk, with the helpful message: 'Please answer more calls'. In the words of a senior executive, hired from Optus in late 2000 to improve the quality of One.Tel's service, it was 'an absolute shambles'.

For those who could not get satisfaction out of the call centre—and many did not—the only recourse was to complain to the Telecommunications Industry Ombudsman, or TIO, which involved getting into another long queue of angry One.Tel customers. Those who had enough rage or stamina to reach the front of this one were given a special 1800 number by the TIO. This number connected them directly to the 26th floor at One.Tel's Sydney offices, where a ten-strong 'Managing Director's Team' was supposed to deal with their complaint.

By mid-2000, this small outfit was dealing with 800 furious customers every month. By September the numbers had swelled to 1,200 a month, and by December the tide had risen yet again to 1,600, at which point One.Tel accounted for roughly a quarter of all the industry's complaints, beating its competitors hands down in the race to be Australia's most unpopular carrier. One can imagine that many thousands more customers lacked the determination needed to get into the statistics.

The TIO's rules required One.Tel to record all these incoming calls so it could listen to them if complaints weren't settled—and the tapes make great listening—but the easiest way to gauge the depth of people's animosity to the company is to dip into some of the letters and emails it received at the time.

In July 2000, for example, a businessman employing 90 people emailed senior management to tell them:

> I have been treated so badly by your company that I am absolutely without words to understand why you people are in business. There should be laws against you people for trading. I will be contacting

as many people as possible and letting them know of the shabby treatment you give. I have notified my bank not to allow any more funds to go to you. Perhaps you need a lesson in customer service. A 30-cent return call would have saved you probably $5,000 this quarter.

In May 2000, another wrote direct to Jodee, complaining:

I still have not received a written response from anyone in your organisation. Very, very poor effort for such a young company wanting patronage. Not likely in this area, if I have anything to do with it, after the lack of service I have received from you.

Yet another wrote to Steve Hodgson in October 2000 to say that she had written personal letters to Brad Keeling and Jodee Rich in April and August:

As yet, I have had no response from either managing director to any of my letters. I am totally disgusted by the lack of response, which is a true reflection of the appalling service I received during my nine-month ordeal while I held an account with your organisation.

One business couple went so far as to send Rich a letter by registered mail to his home address in Vaucluse. One.Tel, they said, had supplied them with a heap of services on their mobile phones, such as voicemail and call waiting, which had failed to work. The company had not only failed to fix the problem, it had compounded it:

> We have found your staff RUDE, ABUSIVE, UNHELPFUL, NON-CARING, NO CUSTOMER SERVICE AT ALL. If there was a prize for this, your company would win hands down. We have never been treated like this by anyone. If any employee of mine treated any of my customers in this manner, they would be looking for another job. One.Tel is now suing us. It should be us suing for loss of income, plus pain and suffering. How could a director of such a company hold his head high?

Nor was it only small companies who blew their stack. Singapore Airlines terminated its dealings with One.Tel in mid-2000, shortly after the airline's Australian finance manager faxed the telco to complain:

> We have repeatedly been in receipt of reminders and threats of legal action or credit status downgrading . . . for invoices we have never received. We are not impressed by such lack of communication.

One month later, the problem still remained, so the finance manager wrote again:

> Despite many phone calls to One.Tel's accounts managers, I have not received any written reply to

date. Instead, all we have received is a fresh reprint of some outstanding debts . . . we regret to inform you that we are left with no alternative but to cancel all Singapore Airlines accounts with One.Tel.

Another businessman wrote to George Savva and Steve Hodgson to say: 'In a world where most businesses are investing heavily in customer retention, for obvious reasons, it is my perception that One.Tel has a churn and burn mentality'. This irate client claimed to have suffered a catalogue of misfortune and ill-treatment at the hands of the company and its customer service reps. He had been without his mobile for two weeks because they had sent him the wrong SIM card, then was barred from using another phone because they cut it off, and finally pushed from pillar to post as he tried to sort things out. As a result, he was switching his company's five mobile accounts to Orange, adding as his parting shot:

> All I want at this stage is to be rid of One.Tel forever, as quickly as possible. I can honestly say that I have never in 30 years of business dealt with a company which has a more blatant and transparent disregard for customer service.

It wasn't only these customers who One.Tel risked losing. The company's favourite slogan was: 'Tell your friends about One.Tel', and many of these unhappy punters were

Rich kids: James Packer and Lachlan Murdoch with Jodee Rich and Brad
Keeling in February 1999. The Packers and Murdochs, or their
shareholders, lost nearly $1 billion in One.Tel.

Jodee and the dude announce they want to build a European mobile
network costing $20 billion, November 1999.

Brad Keeling launching One.Tel's $1.15 billion Next Generation mobile network in Sydney, May 2000.

George Savva, One.Tel's joint general manager. 'He should have been running a One.Tel shop', says an ex-colleague.

Noster culpa. *Rupert Murdoch told News Ltd shareholders he accepted his share of the blame for the $575 million loss on One.Tel.*

Jodee tells the press on 24 September 2001 that he has done nothing wrong. He denies that Packer and Murdoch were misled.

And then there was TeleOne. The dude's creator, Adam Long, formerly married to Jodee Rich's sister Nici, shows off the company's mascot. Jodee says he would like to be involved in TeleOne if his name is cleared.

Kevin Beck (on the left) and Mark Silbermann, former One.Tel directors, pose for the photographer at the launch of Tele.One.

planning to do exactly that. 'We will never, nor will our family and friends, ever use any company associated with One.Tel again', wrote one.

A telecommunications consultant, who was a rather more serious person to offend, also vowed to warn his clients. 'I have corporate customers asking me for my expertise regularly, and I guarantee that I will definitely be steering them in a different direction.'

By the end of 2000, the TIO was becoming increasingly angry with One.Tel about the way in which it was dealing with these disgruntled customers. Finally, the Ombudsman himself, John Pinnock, wrote a stiff letter to One.Tel deriding the company's performance and attitude, and calling for a meeting. 'It is clear', wrote Pinnock, 'that there are systemic problems in dealing with customer complaints. I am also most concerned that recent letters and emails from various employees of One.Tel show a complete lack of understanding and acceptance of One.Tel's obligations to the TIO and to its customers'.

In February 2001, Pinnock and a couple of his senior staff flew up to Sydney from Melbourne for a showdown with the company. Jodee attended the meeting and was conciliatory and almost apologetic, promising that One.Tel would cooperate fully in future, but Pinnock was obviously not impressed. Later, he told the press that he had tried to persuade the company that it had serious problems with the way it treated its customers, but 'They did not seem to care'.

Soon after Pinnock's visit, a pow-wow was held in One.Tel to think of ways to deal with the crisis. Jodee's answer, according to one of those present, was to invite the TIO staff for a picnic. 'I know', he said, 'we'll organise a day out in Melbourne and get them to come along'.

Complaints from One.Tel customers kept rising, and the amount that the company was required to pay to the TIO for investigating them kept growing. By the time One.Tel collapsed in June 2001, the TIO was owed $400,000 in unpaid fees, which it would only be able to recover by lining up alongside all the other unsecured creditors.

The TIO was not the only watchdog to have a bite at One.Tel. In September 2000 the company was also attacked by the Australian Competition and Consumer Commission (the ACCC) and then by the Australian Communications Authority (the ACA) over complaints that it was hijacking its rivals' customers by transferring their phones over to One.Tel without consent.

Sometimes these unwilling customers were being 'slammed', as the industry jargon put it, through sheer incompetence, but more often it appeared to be deliberate. The door-to-door sales teams that One.Tel used worked on commission, and some were simply claiming sales that had not been made. A common trick, when turned away from a house, was to ask for a signature to prove that the salesperson had called. Most householders were too polite to say no, and did not realise that they were signing a request to switch their phones to One.Tel.

It was only when these hapless recruits got their first bill, weeks or months later, that they twigged what had happened. Then, when they tried to complain, they found themselves waiting an hour in the queue at One.Tel's call centre. Those who asked to be switched back to Telstra or Optus courted yet more trouble. According to the watchdogs, it often took weeks to get the old service back again, in which time they were frequently unable to make STD or ISD calls. Sometimes they lost their phone access altogether, because it was disconnected without warning.

By September 2000, when the ACCC took One.Tel to court, these 'slamming' complaints against the company were running at 200 to 300 a month. One.Tel was fined $500,000 and forced to write to 100,000 customers offering them the option of having their services transferred back to their original carrier.

It was a miracle that none of the company's problems with its customers was ever picked up by the media. One senior regulator still can't quite believe it: 'They wrote all this bullshit about Packer and Murdoch and how brilliant it all was. I was just astounded. If they had chosen to look at the way the business was run they would never have written such crap. The way One.Tel treated its customers was appalling'.

The problem with One.Tel's Sydney call centre should have been obvious to journalists, as it was an open secret that it was the worst in the industry. The head-hunters knew it, the job agencies knew it, the company's staff and customers knew it, and so did those rivals who hired ex-One.Tel employees.

But it was not just the press who were kept in the dark. One.Tel appears to have been able to conceal the situation from its major shareholders and non-executive directors. James Packer, for example, continued to boast that One.Tel was exceptionally well run, and described Jodee and Brad as 'great managers' who were streets ahead of their rivals at Telstra and Optus. This was strange, since some people at PBL, who were forced to use One.Tel's mobile service, complained bitterly. One former executive reports: 'When PBL started to use One.Tel it was a disaster. All our accounts were moved over. It was a nightmare for all the PAs here. You'd mention it to James, that there were lots of problems, and you'd have Jodee on the phone and he'd be abusive. He'd say you guys are being unrealistic and unfair'.

One might have thought that One.Tel's troubles would also have been obvious to anyone who entered the company's Sydney headquarters, because there were electronic scoreboards throughout the building that showed how many customers were stacked up in the call centre queue and how long they had been waiting. The boards went red when the wait time rose above three minutes, and flashed red soon after that. Since they were displayed where all could see, there was not much chance of the warnings being missed, but there were ways to fool the system and One.Tel's managers became masters of the art of making the lights turn green.

One of the simplest ways to achieve this tranquillity was to have the call traffickers divert customers to the other call centres in Brisbane, Melbourne and Perth. But this could be detected by anyone who looked at what was happening in those cities, so a better ruse was to pick up callers from the front of the Sydney queue and just dump them down at the back again. An experienced dumper could get rid of 5,000 calls a day by answering the phone on mute, hitting the transfer button and pressing autodial, which brought the caller back into the One.Tel switchboard as a new call. The trick worked wonders with the figures. The system scored the dumping as 5,000 calls answered and 5,000 fresh calls received— so there was a huge increase in productivity and a corresponding fall in average wait times.

The drawback was that most calls weren't really answered, and One.Tel's customers went ballistic. Having gritted their teeth for an hour to get through to a service rep, they heard the line go quiet for a moment, then encountered the 'Welcome to One.Tel' message all over again, at which point they realised they had waited in vain. No doubt this helped explain why four out of five callers gave up in disgust.

These little tricks of the trade were part of every call manager's repertoire, because their bonuses and reputations were greatly increased by making the figures look better than they were. But the scams were encouraged by One.Tel's senior managers to make the figures look better for the directors. 'There was absolutely huge pressure on us to get the calls off the board', says one call centre manager, 'but it was a statistical thing not a customer service thing. It didn't matter how, it was, "Just get them off the board"'.

The deception was also valuable in ensuring that visitors to One.Tel never discovered what an awful time customers were having. Whenever analysts, investors or shareholders were brought round the building, the call centre manager was warned to have the boards on green by the time they arrived. And here they had yet another dodge to fall back on. By pushing a button on the PABX, one could 'busy out' the line, so that customers received the engaged signal. This rapidly reduced the number of calls waiting, because it stopped any new callers getting through. 'We would do this if there was someone important in the building', says one call manager, 'for purely aesthetic reasons'. Or simply to mislead.

On one infamous occasion, in late 2000, with 200 customers on hold, an average wait time of an hour, and all the boards flashing red, there was a panicked instruction from George Savva that Kerry Packer was about to tour the building. 'Get those calls off the board', staff were told. Before long, the queue had been hacked back to a handful of callers and wait times had fallen to 45 seconds.

Unaware of this triumph, One.Tel's poor customers vowed to tell their friends about this nightmare, as they found themselves transferred to the busy signal, or spinning in an endless queue. Meanwhile, the company's most important, and probably most observant, shareholder did not even know he had been fooled.

12

Fat Rewards

Jodee, Bradley and their team have achieved
enviable results in a very short time.

John Greaves, One.Tel chairman

Concealing the chaos inside One.Tel was one thing. Hiding the fact that its finances were in a mess was much harder. Every six months, the company was required to report its results to the Australian Stock Exchange, and every year it had to publish a full set of accounts. As time went on, the financial press became increasingly keen to pull these figures apart, but in August 2000, their work was done for them when the Australian Securities and Investments Commission (ASIC) insisted that One.Tel deduct millions of dollars worth of advertising and customer acquisition costs it had previously been deferring.

ASIC had told One.Tel several months earlier that the practice was a rort that breached Australian accounting standards and the Corporations Law, so the company was forced to declare an extra $173 million of costs that it had previously been burying in its balance sheet. As a result, the company plummeted to a shocking $291 million loss, or almost 50 cents for every dollar it collected. Even without ASIC's intervention, the company was deep into the red.

One.Tel's spin doctors explained to the press that losses were to be expected because the company was growing fast in Europe and Australia, and spending heavily to set up offices and acquire hundreds of thousands of new customers. But the obvious question was whether it would ever get its money back. The Dutch operation had lost $34 million, the UK business had lost $39 million, and the French venture had lost $40 million. Finally, the Australian operations, including the new local call business, had managed to lose more than all three foreign ventures put together.

Nor was the cash flow any prettier. In the year to June 2000, One.Tel had ripped through $169 million in its day-to-day operations, or six times as much as in 1999. If you added what it had spent on spectrum and hardware, it had consumed almost $800 million. This meant that it had eaten up all the money it had raised from PBL, News Ltd and the other investors during the year.

Worse still, as Keeling admitted to journalists when the results were announced, there would be another massive loss in 2001 and a third in 2002, because

One.Tel's new mobile network was about to start haemorrhaging cash.

Needless to say, none of this was highlighted in the glossy annual report that One.Tel sent to its shareholders in September, which managed to avoid using the word 'loss' in the first 37 pages. There was nothing about the $291 million loss in the chairman's letter or the personal missive from Jodee. Nor was there any mention of it in an entire page of 'Key Financial Information' about the company. Strangely enough, the directors also felt it too trivial to talk about in their review of operations. It was in the accounts, of course, as it had to be. And there was one solitary line in the directors' report, in the boring grey pages at the back, which reported blandly that: 'The consolidated loss of the Consolidated Entity after providing for income tax amounted to $291.1 million'.

As always, the rest of the One.Tel Story was about 'success', 'achievement', 'growth', 'the future', 'exciting opportunities' and a whole range of businesses that were going to become profitable very, very soon.

The losses were not the only topic that One.Tel's annual report glossed over. Deep in the financial statement, where companies have a statutory duty to disclose what they have paid their directors, was the extraordinary revelation that Brad and Jodee had helped themselves to bonuses of $6.9 million apiece—on top of annual salaries of $560,000—despite the company's shocking performance.

Amazingly, only one journalist was alert enough to spot it. A couple of hours after One.Tel had finished an extremely positive press conference, Christine Lacy of the *Australian Financial Review* rang the company's new head of investor relations, Tracy Cutting, to say she had been leafing through the figures and wanted to know what Rich and Keeling's bonuses were for. Alas, poor Tracy couldn't tell her, because no one had warned her that Jodee and Brad had been given an extra sack of money—even though she was effectively the company's PR manager. And neither Rich nor Keeling could even be raised for a comment.

The next morning it was front-page news in the *Australian Financial Review* and the talk of the town. The company's chairman, John Greaves, tried his best to justify the bonanza by telling the public: 'Jodee, Bradley and their team have achieved enviable results in a very short time, and One.Tel has always adopted the policy of rewarding its employees for success'. He was drowned by a chorus of outrage.

Bankers Trust and the other institutions that had stumped up $340 million only six months earlier—after which the share price had fallen steeply—were probably the angriest of all, because they had been kept completely in the dark about the payments. But they were hardly alone, as every man and his dog joined in the attack: on talkback radio, in the letters columns, in the press and in parliament. Jodee and Brad had taken home more than any other executive in Australia except Frank Lowy, the founder of Westfield, whilst presiding over one of the biggest corporate losses of the year. To many, it seemed like the 1980s were back, and greed was good all over again.

One.Tel provided no detail as to why the bonuses were paid, but it was presumably connected with the company's share price, which had briefly pushed Rich's fortune towards the magic $2 billion mark before heading down-wards. Two weeks later, after more pressure from ASIC, this was confirmed by One.Tel. The first payment of US$1 million apiece had been made to Jodee and Brad when the company's market capitalisation went above $1 billion. A further US$2.5 million each had been paid when it topped $2.4 billion, and yet another US$1 million each when it rose above $3.4 billion. Sportingly, Jodee and Brad had agreed not to collect another US$1 million each for the few hours in which the market capitalisation topped $5.4 billion in November 1999. All the payments had been made between August 1999 and February 2000.

Typically, Jodee was keen to imply that these huge handouts had been someone else's idea. 'Just after we listed', he told the *Australian Financial Review*'s Christine Lacy, 'we were a little company with just over 300,000 subscribers. The board said to us, "Gee wouldn't it be great if some day we were a $1 billion company and maybe a $2 billion company one day"'.

Followed no doubt by: 'Please, Jodee and Brad, have some more money'.

Meanwhile, without any trace of irony, Brad Keeling told Lacy: 'We have been very open about it'. There had just been some 'shareholder association types' and 'the stock exchange' asking a few questions, he explained.

It clearly did not occur to either man that One.Tel's millions rightly belonged to all its shareholders, who should have been told about such payments and asked to approve them. After all, it was a public company, not Brad and Jodee's private money box.

But Bradley—as he insisted on being called in print because it was better feng shui than Brad—had badly misjudged the whole affair. On the day the news of the bonuses broke he assured a distressed Tracy Cutting that there was no need to worry because the story would soon be wrapping fish and chips, and the fuss would die down. Dead fish would have been a better analogy, because the bad smell from this affair would never go away.

Almost a year later I asked Jodee whether he regretted taking the money and he said: 'In retrospect, of course'. Then he pondered silently for 20 seconds. I waited, expecting words of contrition, but he offered justification instead. 'When the bonuses were paid, shareholders were making heaps of money, seven or eight times their investment, and the press were writing that we were gods, for creating all this wealth. I do regret that we didn't disclose the agreement to the market when it was signed.'

I told Jodee that these huge bonuses were how most people remembered him, and that some thought him no better than Skase or Bond. I also asked him whether he had considered giving the money back. 'I don't think it would make any difference', he said, looking pained. 'The company has gone down, and I have been painted as a villain.'

Even if the bonus payments could be justified, they were not Rich and Keeling's only reward. Anyone who looked at the company's full accounts, rather than the bowdlerised version sent to shareholders and the press, could see that Jodee and Brad had amassed a load of booty since the One.Tel train had left the station in 1995. Prior to the float in November 1997 they had shared consultancy fees, dividends and royalties worth around $12 million in cash. On top of that they had picked up stock options worth many tens of millions of dollars.

Eight months later they had split the lion's share of $16.9 million from the sale of One.Net and One.Card, of which almost $7 million was in cash. And eight months after that, in February 1999, they had shared some $62 million of the money the Packers and Murdochs had put into One.Tel.

More prosaically, they had paid themselves salaries of almost $1 million each in 1999, on top of which they had also collected dividends, which in Jodee's case were worth more than $1.3 million. Better still, they had picked up royalties from One.Net and One.Card in 1999 and 2000, even though they had sold these businesses back to One.Tel. In Jodee's case these came to another $2.1 million. And finally, they still had hundreds of millions of dollars worth of shares.

In cash terms, Jodee and Brad had pocketed almost $115 million from the company between them in three years, and since One.Tel had not made any money in that time, almost all of this had been provided by the Packers and Murdochs (and their shareholders). Quite what they felt about footing the bill for all this largesse one can only guess, but since James had himself lined up for some of these benefits, such as the consultancy fees, dividends, royalties and return of capital, he was in no position to criticise.

As for the bonuses, it was agreed that they were a publicity nightmare. At the News Ltd annual general meeting in October, Rupert Murdoch said he still had faith in One.Tel but wished it had better PR. A month later, James Packer told One.Tel's shareholders that it was 'a mistake' not to have disclosed the bonus agreement in 1998 and that the timing was, 'to say the least, unfortunate'. But James emphasised that he and the Murdochs still supported the company and its founders, despite the blizzard of bad publicity and the $291 million loss. 'The opportunity for this company is an enormous opportunity', he said. 'It is growing very quickly. From our perspective and News's perspective, that is indeed what we wanted.'

In private, James was an even more ardent believer. In mid-October 2000, with the bonus storm still raging and the shares down 40 per cent since the news had broken, he went into the *Sydney Morning Herald* at Darling Park to lunch with its editor Paul McGeough and a clutch of senior journalists. Normally, those who don't work in the building have to wait at security till someone escorts them upstairs, but as James's family were part owners of the paper he was able to sign himself in and go straight to the executive level on the 19th floor.

There's no doubt he impressed the *Herald* journalists. He was poised, self-confident, and clearly on top of the detail of his businesses. Ranged against his ten examiners, if that's the right word, he gave at least as good as he got. Unlike most high-profile businessmen at such lunches, he was on his own, with no finance people or PR flunkies to hold his hand. When someone suggested this was brave of him he joked that it was a good tactic: if he said anything stupid that was reported in the paper he would be able to claim that the journalist had misquoted him.

He drank orange juice throughout the lunch, left his glass of wine untouched and hardly looked at the food on his plate. While others ate, he talked about Telstra, which he clearly disliked; the internet, which he raved about; and Fairfax Newspapers, publishers of the *Herald*, which his family still wanted to buy. When asked why the Packers were so keen to acquire it, he told the journalists passionately that it was because the *National Times* had treated his father so disgracefully in the mid-1980s, by outing him as the Goanna. In short, it was revenge. 'If any company had done that to your father', he told them, 'you would feel the same'.

When it came to One.Tel, he was just as straightforward. The *Sydney Morning Herald*, and other journalists, had got it wrong. The company was not in trouble, Rich was a visionary, he and Keeling were brilliant managers, and the business would be a huge success. What's more, the shares would soon climb again. Just to show those present that he was prepared to back his judgment, he suggested they each take a piece of paper and write down where they thought the One.Tel share price would be in a year's time. He was sure he would be closer than they were. No one wrote down zero, but only because no one took him up on the offer.

Few people in the market shared James's ebullient optimism. Indeed, one of the company's bigger shareholders, the American venture capitalist Steve Gilbert, was about to fold his tent and leave. He resigned from the board in November 2000 and, shortly afterwards, it was revealed that he had been selling his One.Tel shares for almost a year. Having paid around $54 million for his 5 per cent stake in the company in December 1998, he had cashed in most of it by April 2000 at almost three times the price, thereby escaping the worst of the tech wreck. He was famous for having earned his investors a return of 38 per cent a year for many years, and now one could see how he managed it: he knew when to get out.

Remarkably, news that he was selling had not reached the market, even though the law required him, as a director of One.Tel, to notify the Australian Stock Exchange within 14 days of any sale. His lawyers apologised for the oversight, but only after details of his dealings had been revealed by the *Sydney Morning Herald*. Neither the ASX nor ASIC saw fit to punish him.

A couple of analysts and journalists had also taken a hard look at One.Tel's future prospects and concluded that it faced serious problems, and they began to warn publicly that the company would run out of cash by mid-2001 unless more money was raised. The stock watchers at Merrill Lynch even dared to suggest, after emerging from a briefing Jodee gave to analysts a few days before Packer's Fairfax lunch, that One.Tel might be prepared to solve its cash problems by selling its Next Generation mobile network to someone else. The *Herald* picked up Merrill Lynch's report and gave it a run in the business pages.

Shortly after the article appeared, Brad Keeling rang Merrill Lynch and spoke to one of the analysts, Alice Begun, whose name appeared on the report. According to a couple of people, he abused her for ten minutes, threatened to 'ruin her career', and called her a range of unsavoury names, including 'little cunt', for not checking her story with the company. When she tried to point out that the report was quoting, or interpreting, remarks made by Jodee Rich, who was One.Tel's founder and joint managing director, he continued cursing her. Soon afterwards, he angrily told *The Australian* that the Merrill Lynch report was 'grossly inaccurate'.

A few days later, with the shares still sinking, Brad was in New York for a telecommunications conference. He assured Michael Pascoe of Channel 9's 'Business Sunday' that the stories about One.Tel needing more money were complete nonsense: 'It's not a question of us requiring an injection of cash, because the European businesses are becoming and, in fact, now are cash flow positive and about to explode into earnings. This company is going to be very, very profitable over the next few years'.

Keeling assured Sunday viewers that One.Tel still had several hundred million dollars in the bank and would have $75 million left at the end of the financial year, 30 June 2001. After that, he said, the company would be coining money. It was a claim he had already made in September to coincide with the release of the annual report, and it would be repeated by One.Tel's chairman, John Greaves, at the company's annual general meeting in November then reaffirmed twice by Jodee Rich, in February and April 2001.

It was the first time in its history that One.Tel had nailed its colours to the mast like this, and it was not a particularly smart thing to do, but, according to Jodee, there was little alternative: 'I was being called by analysts every day, Brad was being called, James was being called, and we were all being asked how much cash we would have by June 2001. There was enormous pressure on us'.

The aim was clearly to reassure investors that the company would not go bust despite its $291 million loss in 1999–2000, but after the bonus row and One.Tel's frighteningly bad performance, the promise was now seen as a test of Jodee and Brad's credibility. It became a forecast they absolutely could not afford to miss. The company's internal budgets suggested it would have $105 million cash left by June 2001, so Rich and Keeling felt sure they had a buffer. But it wasn't hard to see that things might go wrong. If the Next Gen network ate more cash than it was supposed to, or if the European and Australian businesses continued to lose money, they would be in trouble. And regardless of Brad's assurances to Channel 9 viewers, One.Tel's European ventures were certainly not yet cash flow positive. Nor were they just about to become so.

Unfortunately for One.Tel's two founders, the company had just missed out on a deal that would have made it safe. Back in May 2000, Jodee had asked the bankers at

ABN Amro in London to find a 'Big Brother' for One.Tel, to give it more financial muscle and support in Europe, and before long, the Finnish telephone company Sonera had tentatively agreed to invest $1.1 billion for a 30 per cent share. Teams of bankers and lawyers had then looked at the books, done their investigations and blessed the deal. By September, a memorandum of understanding had been signed, and everything was ready to go.

On the 28th floor of One.Tel's Sydney headquarters, the chairs in the meeting room had even been set out for a press conference to announce the linkup. Then, with less than 24 hours to go till the sounding of the trumpets, Jodee was told it had all fallen through. The investment had been vetoed by bankers acting for the UK mobile giant Vodafone, which was trying to buy Sonera and did not want to pick up One.Tel as well.

Naturally, Jodee was hugely disappointed. He knew perfectly well that the injection of another $1.1 billion would make One.Tel far more robust and remove any worries the market had about the company running out of cash. He also knew the deal would be one in the eye for One.Tel's growing band of critics. According to Jodee, James Packer was also upset because he was counting on the deal helping him win his battle with Kerry over One.Tel. 'James must have told me half a dozen times that Sonera's investment would give great credibility to the business', says Jodee, 'and it would put to rest all the shit he was taking from his dad'.

Unbeknown to Jodee and the Packers, or anyone else at One.Tel, Merrill Lynch in London had investigated One.Tel's finances on behalf of Sonera, and come to a disturbing conclusion. By their calculations, the company was likely to run out of cash in early 2001 if it didn't get help from Sonera. This was the verdict that the same bank's Australian analysts had also reached quite independently, for which they had been so roundly abused by Brad Keeling.

Poor Bradley was clearly finding the pressure hard to take. His father was dying, there was the row over the bonuses, the share price was diving and the company was losing more money than ever before. According to one of his close colleagues, in September he was forced to pass up seats at the opening ceremony of the Olympics in September, as a guest of James Packer, because he had a rash of cold sores.

In November, he lost his temper with a journalist from the *Sydney Morning Herald* in spectacular fashion. The paper's telecommunications correspondent, Kevin Morrison, had emailed him to ask about rumours that One.Tel's chairman John Greaves was planning to step down. Morrison was keen to know whether the company had lined up anyone to take Greaves's place, or whether Brad might take the chair himself. It was a perfectly reasonable enquiry about the direction of one of Australia's largest public companies, but it was enough to send Keeling ballistic. He went off like this:

I get enough flak from you, that I think I'll just keep my head down, tail up, and work to build an even greater business than the great business we already have. If John resigns we won't be in any hurry to find a replacement. If someone shows up, fine; if not, so be it. It's not essential. One day we will find a new chair if we need one.

Keeling then turned his attack on the man, who happened to be one of the mildest-mannered journalists on the paper:

I am the parent of a teenager. If you were a student in her schoolyard you would be classed as a bully. Were you a bully at school? Do you ever feel pride in anything anyone else ever does? Or do you only feel pride when you hurt someone else and their families? I think I know.

Finally, the chief of Australia's fun and friendly telephone company called another great warrior to his aid:

It is said that one night at a dinner party Winston Churchill, having had a little too much to drink, was spoken to by a lady guest who said: 'Sir, you're drunk', to which Churchill replied: 'Madam, you are ugly, and yet tomorrow morning I will be sober'. In the morning, following this long correction in the telco sector, this long night, the dawn will reveal a robust, bright, brilliant, great company, One.Tel. What is it, exactly, that you will still be?

13

Free Time

We were in growth, growth, growth mode.
It was buy, buy, buy. We were trying to acquire
customers as quickly as possible.

George Savva, One.Tel joint general manager

When One.Tel started out in 1995 it had needed less than $5 million to set up business. With its own mobile network, it would have to risk $2 billion— or 400 times that amount—and there was no guarantee that the company's shareholders would ever see a cent in return.

However, even this was not the full measure of the gamble that Jodee and Brad had persuaded the Packers and Murdochs to take. By boasting that One.Tel could be No 1 in the Australian market, the dynamic duo had raised the stakes even higher, virtually ensuring that Telstra and Optus would try to king-hit the company before it became too big. If that did happen, far more ammunition would be needed, greatly reducing the chance that the $2 billion bet would pay off.

These were not the only hazards, because One.Tel was relying on its loss-making European and Australian businesses to become profitable so they could pour hundreds of millions of dollars into the new network over the first few years. If these operations did not start making money soon, Jodee and Brad would have to go back to the Packers and Murdochs and beg for more.

They were also in a race against time. By 2003 they would have to start shelling out millions of dollars in interest to Lucent. Two years after that the capital repayments would kick in, and by 2006, they would be paying back the $1.15 billion network cost at the rate of $250 million a year. If they did not have at least 1 million paying customers on the network by then, they would have precious little chance of making the payments.

As always, Jodee was supremely confident that One.Tel could do it. 'Next Gen was a fantastic product', he says today. 'We listened to our customers, and our great strength was that we could be fast and nimble, so we could give them what they wanted.' He was sure the new voicemail service would be a winner. It allowed you to answer messages one by one, as you listened to them, and you could whiz through any that annoyed you. 'If you had a long message from your mother-in-law speaking slowly', says Jodee, 'all you had to do was press the 6 and 8 buttons and it would speed up. So you could listen to her three-minute message in 30 seconds. People loved that'. The dial-up movie guide was also a great attraction, and One.Tel was sure its technology was snappier than anything Optus or Telstra had to offer. But would the network be available in time?

The original plan was to launch Next Gen in Sydney and follow with Brisbane, Adelaide, Perth and Melbourne, when those networks were ready. This is how the situation stood in May 2000 when the first Next Gen TV ads were launched. But when Jodee returned from Europe in August, where he had been working since January, he was aghast at the delays and promptly decreed they should go national immediately.

He would soon be telling the public that the network was 'six months ahead of schedule' and 'one of the fastest build-outs in the world', but in reality construction was running six months behind and nothing was ready at all. It had proved incredibly hard to find sites for base stations, because Telstra, Optus and Vodafone refused to share towers. There were also local communities to pacify. In Melbourne, a plan to put the transmitter behind the cross of a Greek Orthodox church caused uproar. In Adelaide, there was an outcry over proposals to use an Anglican steeple. In Sydney's northern beaches, it looked like they might have to use the roof of Keeling's weekender on Scotland Island because local residents were up in arms about all the other sites that had been proposed. In Queensland, they solved the problem by building fake palm trees to house the transmitters and plonking them in parks.

Even in Sydney, coverage was still patchy at best. Calls would drop out and there were buildings in the CBD where you couldn't get a signal at all. In the harbourside suburbs, nearest the city, the coverage was poor—and further out it was even worse. It became a habit for the directors of the company to ring in and complain that they kept losing calls while driving to work.

In the four other cities the network was not even supposed to be finished till January or March 2002—another five to seven months away. And as they were also running six months late, networks in these cities might not be ready for another year or more.

Fortunately for One.Tel's customers, it was still possible to make calls on Telstra's network in all these cities, thanks to a 'roaming' agreement which allowed their phones to switch automatically to Telstra whenever they couldn't get a proper signal. On the face of it, this was a fantastic deal because it gave One.Tel national coverage without having to build towers in every paddock in Australia, but it did not come cheap. Every time One.Tel's customers used Telstra's network to make or receive a call, the company was slugged for the retail price.

Given One.Tel's lack of cash, it was vital that roaming was kept to a minimum. But going national with only half a network raised it to the maximum. Had One.Tel recruited an army of people to run up bills with its rival it could not have spent more money. In the second half of 2000 at least 75 per cent of Next Gen traffic was roaming on Telstra's network at vast expense. Even in mid-2001, when the Next Gen network was supposedly complete, One.Tel was still paying Telstra $5 million a month for roaming—or more than half what it was collecting from customers.

It was not just the network that was not ready. According to an internal company memo in August 2000, there were a host of other problems. Customers could not send text messages to other networks or use their phones abroad, and the voicemail service was also causing trouble. One of its undesirable features was that you could get into other people's mailboxes by accident. Lachlan Murdoch discovered this for himself when he tried to leave a message for his supermodel wife Sarah O'Hare and found he was listening to messages that others had left for her. He complained to Jodee, and there was a great hue and cry in the company as they desperately tried to fix the problem. Teething problems were inevitable, Lachlan was told.

More worryingly, one in six new connections to the Next Gen network was simply failing to work. Disappointed and angry customers rang the Sydney call centre and experienced the full nightmare. Even though Next Gen had been launched three months earlier, call centre staff had still not received training on the product.

Nor could they access customers' records because these were stored in a new information system, One.Sys4, which they had not been taught to use. Worst of all, as the memo admitted, Next Gen billing was still not up and running. It was expected to be ready some time in the second week of August, but there was no guarantee this would happen, and in the meantime, several thousand customers had not been billed for three months. Some would end up not being billed for six months or, indeed, at all.

Despite the chaos, Jodee was not prepared to wait. His attitude had always been to get customers first and fix problems later. So the national launch went ahead. One senior manager describes it as a suicidal decision, and says it should have been delayed six months. Another says, 'Everything in Next Gen was released before it was ready, so nothing ever worked properly, and nothing ever satisfied the customer'. But Jodee is adamant that he made the right decision, and does not recall anyone advising him against it.

Most likely Jodee just wasn't listening. Arrogance, stress, or the sheer enormity of the operation, made him far less inclined to involve people and hear people out. Increasingly, his managers found him intimidating, and declined to tell him bad news. 'Everyone tried to make him happy by puffing it up', says one.

Despite its supposedly democratic nature, One.Tel had always been a thinly disguised autocracy in which Jodee made all the key decisions, and it was getting more like that as time went on. 'It was a company of managers who did exactly what they were told', says one woman who worked there from the start. 'Even his top executives were frightened of him. I sat with them in meetings for years, and I know they had no say. It was, "Yes, Jodee, yes Jodee, yes Jodee".'

Many felt Jodee liked it this way—despite his philosophy of empowering people—and some observed that he promoted those people who did not stand up to him. 'There's no doubt he surrounded himself with yes men', says a senior member of One.Tel's finance team. 'If you have good managers, you give away decision making. If you have yes men, you keep control. And he was a control freak.'

'His whole style was to intimidate', says one accountant who tried to argue with him. 'He wondered why no one told him the truth. That's because when they did he would just tear shreds off them.'

Keeling was clearly no better. 'Brad managed by fear and intimidation', says one woman who worked closely with him throughout the company's life. 'They were both tyrants. They had unrealistic expectations. It was one thing after another. If you said you couldn't do it, you were cut off at the knees.'

By several accounts, One.Tel was no longer as 'fun and friendly' as it had been at the start. Many of the company's senior staff say that, as the business grew and the pressure increased, a culture of bullying emerged, with Jodee setting a pattern that his deputies followed. 'He was despotic, a complete and utter egomaniac', says one 20-something lawyer who held several important positions in the company.

'He never yelled, but he loved getting into you', says a senior member of the Next Gen team. 'One of his favourite expressions was, "This is going to affect your bonus". Another was, "Why do I employ you?".'

'He was really creepy', says a successful young woman who worked closely with him. 'He was quiet, calm and controlled, but he made you feel bad. He played on people's weaknesses.'

On one occasion, One.Tel's young head of marketing was summoned up to the so-called 'power pod' on the 28th floor to show Jodee a stack of new phone card samples. The offices being open plan, there was the usual audience, with six or seven senior people sitting close enough to witness what went on. According to two of them, the phone cards she brought were not quite what Jodee wanted, so he either threw them at her or threw them into the air, scattering them all over the floor. The young woman got down on her hands and knees and dutifully picked them up, placing them in a neat pile on the desk in front of him.

In one of my conversations with Jodee, I raise this incident, because he won't believe that people have told me he was intimidating and a bully. His response to the story is as sure and straightforward as it could possibly be. 'It's absolute crap', he says. 'I would never throw anything at anyone.' When I ask him whether he might have thrown the cards into the air, rather than *at* her, he says, equally dismissively but not quite so definitely, 'I don't recall ever doing so'.

I tell him that I haven't yet checked the anecdote, so it may not be true, but I ask him how two people who claim to be eyewitnesses could possibly have got it so wrong, and how so many people in One.Tel could have formed the view that he was a despot. He shakes his head and tells me, 'I am not an aggressive, threatening manager, and if you've got people saying these things, then I don't get it'.

Afterwards, I check the phone card story with the alleged victim, who confirms it, and tells me that Jodee has phoned her since our talk. She is keen to point out that she loved her time at One.Tel and misses it. Her only regret, she says, is that she picked up the cards.

One.Tel's promise to be the No 1 mobile network undoubtedly put pressure on the company to deliver results with Next Gen in double-quick time. The Packers and Murdochs were pushing hard, as was anyone else with money on the line. According to the company's master salesman, George Savva, 'Bankers Trust was on the phone all the time. The banks were always in our ear, too, saying: "We've lent you a billion dollars, why haven't you got more customers?"'.

The promises that One.Tel had made to the banks were almost twice as ambitious as the ones it was now making to the public. In May 2000, it had told the consortium lending $1.15 billion to Lucent that the Next Gen network would have 420,000 customers by June 2001, almost 900,000 by mid-2002, and more than 1.3 million by June 2003. To hit these targets, the sales team would have needed to sign up 40,000 people a month in the first year, rising to almost 60,000 a month in the third year (one in four customers was expected to desert every year). With its old network, One.Tel had rarely managed to sign up more than 10,000 people a month.

There was no hope of this fairy tale coming true, but George Savva was clearly told to get as close as he could. 'We were in growth, growth, growth mode', he says. 'It was buy, buy, buy. We were trying to acquire customers as quickly as possible.'

The quickest way to drum up business was to set up an in-house sales team supported by a barrage of ads in the Murdoch newspapers, which News Ltd was providing for free as part of the February 1999 deal. According to Savva, One.Tel could only recruit customers this way by offering super-cheap deals that undercut its rivals. So the company was soon giving away $250 phones for free on plans that had a minimum spend of only $9 a month.

Not surprisingly, Telstra and Optus replied with deals that were almost as generous, and began to match One.Tel ad for ad in the newspapers—and giveaway for giveaway. In Jodee's mind, there was no doubt about what One.Tel's biggest rivals were trying to do: 'It wasn't that they decided to take us on, they decided to kill us'.

The price war made it harder for One.Tel to round up the customers it needed, but one way or another, it still managed to hit the targets it had given the market. By December 2000 it had around 100,000 subscribers. By mid-2001 it was claiming to be on track for 265,000. Whether all these customers spent money or paid their bills was another matter.

According to Ian Richardson, joint owner of the big national mobile telephone dealer Rigi Digi: 'We could sell Next Gen to low users or to people who wanted cheap calls, but not to business people or anyone who used the phone a lot'. One.Tel's corporate sales department even stopped offering Next Gen to its customers because it knew they would be unhappy with the service. It gave a batch to Jodee's father, Steven Rich, in the early days, and apparently he complained bitterly about them.

In the early days, One.Tel's corporate sales team also supplied free phones to Peter Ritchie, the ex-Imagineering director who had tried to slow Jodee down in the 1980s. All 28 employees of his water purification company received free, top-of-the-range Nokia 8210s, no bigger than a cigarette packet. Better still, they were told they could use them to call each other for nothing, 24 hours a day, 7 days a week. 'I knew then that One.Tel was a goner', he says.

Free Time 24×7, which allowed One.Tel customers to call other Next Gen customers for free any time of the day or night for a year, was introduced by One.Tel in November 2000 and ran right through to the end. It was a George Savva idea, sanctioned by Jodee, which Savva believes 'really hurt' the company. Jodee, on the other hand, maintains that it 'worked unbelievably', even though it led to One.Tel carrying at least a third of the calls on its new network free of charge.

Not surprisingly, Free Time was immensely popular, but at considerable cost. A group of 300 Melbourne taxi drivers used One.Tel phones as their own private network, on which they called each other for free. This produced no revenue for One.Tel but incurred big costs because there was no coverage at all in Melbourne until January 2001, so all calls were carried on the Telstra network. Even at the finish, when the Next Gen network was supposedly complete, One.Tel customers in Melbourne were roaming much of the time, so 20-minute calls frequently produced $10 bills that the company had to pay.

Nor was it just a few Melbourne taxi drivers who cottoned on to the idea. According to one senior Next Gen team member: 'One dealer in the heavily Arabic suburbs around Auburn in Sydney's west described hordes of black-dressed women wandering in together and signing up for Free Time. Another described packs of 18-year-old schoolgirls in the Northern Suburbs, giggling and laughing their way into a dealer's store, all clambering to get on the One.Tel deal'.

The theory was that when a customer bought a One.Tel phone, they would recruit all their friends to the network so they could talk to them for nothing. Ultimately, it was hoped, they would become paying customers too. Consequently, those who signed contracts were often given a free BYO SIM card—meaning, 'bring your own phone'—to give to a boyfriend, girlfriend, wife or husband. This meant that these friends could take advantage of Free Time without even signing a contract or buying a One.Tel phone. According to Rigi Digi's Ian Richardson, the promotion could not possibly have made money for One.Tel: 'It was all about connections, connections, connections. They were doing it to get connections, whatever the cost'. Dealers like Rigi Digi scored a $35 commission for every SIM card used, so Richardson always asked his customers to make at least one call.

The free BYO SIMs—which anyone could get if they wanted—came with no contract period, no connection fee and no access fee, and offered calls at a bargain 13 cents for 30 seconds. Not surprisingly, they were by far the most popular plan in the marketplace, accounting for roughly one-third of all One.Tel's customers. They were also one of the biggest loss makers, collecting an average revenue of just $26 a month per user—*before* any of the costs of running the network were taken into account, before Telstra was paid for roaming charges, and before anything was paid to Lucent.

The BYO SIM cards also allowed existing One.Tel customers to abandon plans that locked them into higher call rates. One ex-employee, Mark Stibbard, obtained two brand new free Nokia 3310s for himself and his wife on $9 per month minimum spend plans, then fitted two free BYO SIM cards so they could make calls at less than one-third of the price. Shortly afterwards, he was rung by One.Tel's Sydney sales staff and sent a free Alcatel phone worth $200 or more, with yet another SIM card. By the time the company crashed, he had three new One.Tel mobiles and five different phone numbers, all of which could be used to call other people on the network for free. He was almost certainly showing up as five separate One.Tel customers.

BYO SIM cards could also be used in old 900 MHz phones which did not work on One.Tel's new 1800 MHz network, but they automatically roamed on Telstra every time a customer made a call. In an attempt to cut its losses, the company compiled a list of people who were roaming 100 per cent of the time and identified those who were using 900 MHz phones. It then warned them they would be charged for Free Time unless they bought an 1800 MHz handset. Naturally, these people were promised cheap phones and more great deals if they stayed with the network—which cost One.Tel yet more money.

Others roamed 100 per cent of the time because they had set up their mobiles to preselect the Telstra network, where coverage was better. University students were wise to this simple trick, and several dealers also showed their customers how to do it because they were embarrassed by One.Tel's performance. 'The network was shit', says Rigi Digi's Ian Richardson, who eventually told all his customers to do it. 'I drove into Sydney from the southern suburbs in March 2001 and I couldn't get a line the whole way. So I gave up using my Next Gen SIM card altogether.' This, remember, was almost a year after the Sydney launch. When asked if the network got better as time went on, Richardson agrees it did: 'Yeah, it went from absolutely shithouse to shithouse'.

Jodee was aware of the high cost of Free Time and roaming and was constantly trying to reduce it. On one occasion, he even phoned the biggest 'abuser' himself. Introducing himself as 'Peter, from One.Tel', Jodee told the man that he was the highest user of Free Time among One.Tel's many thousands of customers. The man replied: 'Does that mean I win a prize?'.

From January 2001 the Free Time rules were tightened, but the new limit of 500 minutes a month and 20 minutes per free call did not stop One.Tel's army of freeloaders, who soon discovered that the 20-minute cap could be avoided by hanging up after 18 minutes and dialling again.

Another way One.Tel hoped to get connections, and boost subscriber numbers was to sell prepaid mobiles. As Jodee had seen at first hand, these were all the rage in Europe, where they were driving 50 to 80 per cent of the market's growth. But One.Tel was handicapped here because its own product, which was called Lime City, was not allowed to roam on Telstra's network. The national carrier had refused to give permission, because it did not want One.Tel competing with its own prepaid product.

As Telstra well knew, without roaming, it would be almost impossible to sell Lime City at any price, because One.Tel's coverage was still so bad. Even when the Next Gen network was finished, the phone would still not work in the Blue Mountains, the Whitsundays, Uluru or 100 other places that tourists like to visit, so it would be hopeless for backpackers and visiting businessmen, who typically bought such products.

Undaunted, Jodee told his staff to find a way of getting Lime City phones to roam on Telstra, without authorisation, and in direct breach of One.Tel's contract with the carrier. He admits he did not tell Telstra he was doing this, but claims they would have found out anyway had One.Tel succeeded, so the two sides would have been forced to come to a commercial settlement. He clearly sees nothing wrong with this way of doing business. In any case, a large team of people spent almost three months trying to achieve it, even though the technicians assured Jodee at the start that it was not possible. At one big meeting, he told them impatiently, 'I cannot believe something so simple could take you so long'.

When the woman responsible for implementing Lime City, Vicky Broszon, told Jodee it simply could not be done, there was a stand-up row in the middle of the office. Afterwards, Jodee went across to one of his managers, who had watched the fight, and told her: 'I'm concerned that Vicky isn't a One.Tel person. Make her a One.Tel person or get rid of her'. Days later Broszon was sacked.

Eventually, Lime City was launched without the ability to roam on Telstra, despite protests that the customer would hate it. Jodee's answer to this, according to one member of the Next Gen team, was to say: 'I don't care about the customer. I *want* a prepaid package'.

The task of shifting this unattractive product was given to Paul Fleetwood, who had joined One.Tel on its first day back in 1995 and was in charge of selling phone cards to a similar market. 'I want 15,000 connections to Lime City in December', Jodee told him. When Paul replied that this could not be done, Jodee smiled sweetly and insisted: 'I want you to be a hero and do 15,000 in December'.

Fleetwood's team flooded Sydney's Eastern Suburbs with the phones, offering free calls, discounts and cheap

phone cards in ,an attempt to get them moving, but
One.Tel still managed to sell only a few thousand of
them by the end of May 2001. Often, those who did
buy them came back to complain. Shop keepers told
stories of people throwing their Lime City phones on
the counter and demanding their money back, or even
throwing them through windows. Many of the convenience stores that stocked the phones and their prepaid
cards decided they didn't need that sort of inconvenience
and gave them back to One.Tel.

But as was so often the case with One.Tel, none of
these problems with Lime City, Free Time or BYO SIM
cards hit the headlines. Nor did they shake Jodee's public
confidence. In April 2001 he told a telecommunications
conference organised by Merrill Lynch that the Next
Generation business was signing up customers faster
than ever, and exceeding its targets. Even the doubters
in the audience were impressed by his optimism and
enthusiasm, and by the figures he could muster to
support his case.

But a more sober look made you wonder whether it
was really going so well. In late 2000 the company had
removed credit checks on new Next Gen customers so
that nothing would stand in the way of sales, and this
was bound to lead to big problems with bad debts. More
recently, Jodee had insisted on sending out SIM cards
already activated—so that new customers would not
have to ring the call centre to get themselves connected—

even though there was a major risk of One.Tel losing out from fraud if cards went astray.

More broadly, if you took all the freebies and free-loaders into account, it was hard to see how One.Tel could be earning anything from Next Gen at all. Even towards the end, in April 2001, one-third of calls were being carried for free, almost half were still roaming on Telstra, and a good proportion of the rest were being charged at uncommercial rates. For much of the time, the company was either collecting no money from calls or giving the revenue away to its biggest rival. Meanwhile, it was paying out millions of dollars on dealer commissions, advertising, marketing, sales, handset subsidies and administration—before it even began to think about paying the interest and repayments on the $1.15 billion cost of the network and the $523 million it had spent on spectrum.

According to the One.Tel liquidator's calculations in July 2001, the total amount of revenue earned by the new network in the nine months prior to the collapse was only $52 million, which compared with a cash outflow of more than four times that amount.

In the short term, of course, all the special offers and Free Time promotions made One.Tel's figures look great because they pushed up the number of customers and kept down the cost of acquiring them: giving away BYO SIM cards meant One.Tel avoided paying $350 handset subsidies and big dealer commissions. But whether these customers were worth having in the long run was entirely another matter.

Back in November 1999, when One.Tel's number crunchers had sat down to write the business plan for Lucent's bankers, they had discovered to their horror that the numbers just did not add up. Using assumptions they thought were reasonable, the new network made massive losses in the early years and only small profits later, which were swamped by the need to pay back Lucent.

One.Tel's answer back then had been to change the assumptions, by pumping up the customer numbers, cutting the cost of acquiring them, slashing dealer commissions and increasing the amount that customers spent. Hey presto, the sums had come right—but in the real world, as One.Tel was finding, it was not so easy to conjure up profits or revenue.

Whether Next Generation would have succeeded in the long run, we will never know. Telstra's chairman, Bob Mansfield, is one of many who believes that One.Tel's strategy was bound to fail. 'Giving shit away is easy', he told me after the collapse. 'Giving shit away and making money, that's hard. The big guys won't let you cream them forever. If you get into a price war, you are going to drive down margins and drive yourself out of business. The only guys who will win are Telstra.' And, of course, they did.

14

A Crock of Shit

We were travelling blind, totally blind.

One.Tel accountant

At One.Tel you never had to dig far to find trouble. It was in Next Gen, it was in the call centres, it was in the fixed-wire business. But most of all it was in the finances, where the controls were woefully inadequate for a company with sales of $1 billion a year.

The responsibility for ensuring that One.Tel had the accounting systems it needed to stay on track fell to Mark Silbermann, the company's young South African finance director. Dark-haired and good-looking, with a taste for Armani trousers, Silbermann was extraordinarily sure of himself, but he was not the most popular of One.Tel's bosses, nor the most respected. In fact, many of the people who worked in the finance area felt that he was just not up to the job, despite his arrogance.

'He was totally out of his depth. He didn't know much about accounting, and he had no interest in finance', says one of his deputies.

Silbermann's supporters said he was smart, dedicated and worked harder than anyone else in the company, but even they admitted that finance might not be his strongest suit. And they accept the common view that he was incapable of standing up to Jodee in a dispute.

When One.Tel was floated in 1997 its prospectus claimed that Silbermann was a member of the Institute of Chartered Accountants of South Africa. In fact he had passed the necessary exams but had not been admitted, because he had gone to London straight afterwards. When challenged about this little white lie by a journalist in 2001, Silbermann claimed it was an honest mistake made by the person who compiled the brochure. Yet somehow it slipped into his biography year after year.

Silbermann was certainly inexperienced to be running a complex business like One.Tel even if he was technically qualified to do so. But it was hardly surprising if he had been outpaced by the company's meteoric rise, because One.Tel had grown 20-fold since he had joined back in 1996, at the tender age of 29. To make life harder still, he had other duties weighing him down: he spent as much time on operations as he did on finance, and for most of 2000 he was busy setting up One.Tel's European ventures.

His deputy, Steve Hodgson, who was a few years older than Silbermann and liked Armani shirts, was thought to have a far better grasp of accounting principles, but he gave colleagues the strong impression that he wanted to be elsewhere. One accountant who reported to him says, 'He was very smart, very good with numbers, and knew how they related to the business, but he did absolutely nothing with it'. Others say he was good, but never pushed hard enough. He was another yes man who couldn't, or wouldn't, stand up to Jodee.

Like all of One.Tel's top managers, Hodgson was paid a large amount of money, and some felt he stayed only because he didn't want to lose it. In his previous life he had worked for One.Tel's auditors, BDO Nelson Parkhill, where he would have earned around $80,000 a year. Now he was pulling in almost four times that amount, and sitting on stock options worth $3 million. Silbermann, for his part, was clocking $400,000 a year, and had nearly 5 million One.Tel shares, worth $11 million at the top of the market. In his short time with the company he had graduated from a rented property in North Bondi to a $1 million house, to a $3 million home in ritzy Rose Bay.

With Silbermann and Rich both in Europe during much of 2000 and Kevin Beck also there till July, there is not the slightest doubt that One.Tel was short of decent managers, especially in the finance area. It is also clear that Jodee realised this, although probably too late. By the end of the year, the company was trying to recruit a whole range of people, including a billing specialist, a credit specialist and a chief financial officer for the Australian business. It was also looking, without success, for a new finance director to replace Silbermann so that he could concentrate on running the company's operations. Unfortunately, One.Tel's reputation was so bad that no one at Telstra or Optus was likely to be interested in the job. The head-hunters recommended other people, but they either got the thumbs-down from One.Tel or decided they didn't want to join.

A highly respected candidate who had been finance director of one of Australia's top 50 companies was taken on a quick tour of One.Tel in late 2000, and could see immediately he did not want to be involved: 'It wasn't hard to see that the business was out of control. If you talked to the right people, it was plain that the back office wasn't working—the processes they used weren't supported by proper systems. And billing was in a mess'.

Another top finance man, who turned down the chance to run One.Net, which also needed a new boss, had a similar reaction: 'It was run by kids. They didn't know what their business was, what its costs were or how much money it was making. I asked for management accounts, business plans and so on, and I was told, "That's not the way we do things". I walked away feeling I had no answers to anything. I was horrified.

There were none of the disciplines needed to run a business'.

Yet another, who accepted a senior position in One.Tel in 2001, against the advice of almost everyone he consulted, only found out how bad it was after he arrived: 'I was really shocked. There were no policies, no processes and no procedures. No one knew what the human resources role cost, or the finance department or the call centres. In fact, no one knew what anything cost. There were four businesses in One.Tel and you couldn't do a proper profit and loss account or balance sheet for any of them.

'I tried to set up a formal budgeting process, and it was almost as if Jodee wasn't interested. He told me: "Go talk to Mark Silbermann, he's the finance director". Jodee was only interested in the big picture, the sexy parts of the business, like Next Gen. But Mark wasn't interested either. He didn't want profit and loss accounts and balance sheets. He said: "We manage cash flow".'

Most companies with sales of $10 million have departmental budgets and profit centres so that management can keep costs under control and know which parts of the business are making money. One.Tel had nothing of the sort, even though it was 100 times the size.

Most companies have business analysts to tell them which product lines are profitable, but One.Tel rarely bothered with them either. It launched new tariff plans at a moment's notice, and typically set prices to undercut its rivals. Sales were paramount.

Most companies also have accounting systems that can tell them whether or not they are heading for the rocks, but One.Tel was short of these as well, and in the second half of 2000 the ones it did have were crippled by the collapse of One.Tel's billing system.

Normally, One.Tel's top managers relied on two key measures of where the company was headed. The first was the monthly 'flash report', which came out two or three days after the end of each month. The second, and far more reliable, was the management accounts, which normally arrived a couple of weeks later.

The flash reports were intended to be a very rough assessment of sales and profit for the previous 30 days, a quick back-of-the-envelope calculation based on key numbers such as average revenue per user, the total number of customers and the estimated profit margins of each division. They were so rough that no one was quite sure whether or not the figures included GST, so on that basis alone they could be out by ten per cent.

The management accounts, on the other hand, were designed to give an accurate picture of what was happening. But in the second half of 2000, bills were going out six to eight weeks late, and often going out wrong, so the figures were two months out of date. The accounts for October had to be prepared in November with figures for August. In the words of one of the company's senior accountants: 'We were travelling blind, totally blind'.

With the rough and ready flash reports now the only instrument that the management and board had to steer by, the accountants spent more time preparing them so they could be sure they were accurate. Instead of just scribbling the figures on a few scraps of paper, they gathered as much information as they could, talked to people within each business unit, and tried their best to work out how each was travelling. Disturbingly, their enquiries told them that One.Tel's Australian businesses were making less money, or losing more, than forecast. But this was something that Jodee and his acolytes simply refused to believe.

In the last quarter of 2000 there were running battles between the group financial controller, David Barnes, and his immediate boss, Steve Hodgson. Every month, it was Hodgson who won: Barnes presented his careful and cautious estimates of how much profit the business was making, and Hodgson revised them upwards to show that One.Tel was on budget and going well. There was no evidence to support this, and plenty of indications to the contrary, but Jodee, Brad and Mark desperately wanted to believe that everything was fine because they had staked their future on hitting the forecasts for 2000–2001. And if the company missed them it would be a disaster.

For three months, no one knew for sure whether the optimists or the pessimists were right. But by December

2000, the billing system was back on track, the systems were working again and it was possible to prepare proper figures. These confirmed that One.Tel's Australian operations were way off budget, and making big losses, just as the accountants had thought. This would make it extremely hard for Jodee and Brad to keep the promises they had made to the market.

Publicly, the results for the six months to December 2000 proclaimed that One.Tel had lost only $5 million more than expected, but according to senior members of One.Tel's finance team, the accounts had been heavily massaged to achieve this result. Between $10 million and $15 million of 'adjustments' had been made to bring the figures nearer to the target.

According to the finance team, this was necessary because One.Tel had run some $20 million behind budget in the first half of the year, just as David Barnes and his number crunchers had believed. The flash reports, which had been sent to One.Tel's board of directors—after being upgraded by Steve Hodgson to show that all was well—had been $4 million a month too optimistic.

The board was not informed of this $20 million shortfall—and it must be said that Mark Silbermann denies there was one. They were assured that everything was fine.

On 25 January 2001, at a regular bi-monthly board meeting, the non-executive directors—Lachlan Murdoch,

James Packer, Rodney Adler and John Greaves—were told that One.Tel would finish the financial year in better shape than the market had been promised, with 'a significant cash buffer'. They were also given a copy of the company's PR strategy for its first-half results, due for release seven days later, which listed One.Tel's 'Key Messages' as:

- Do not need cash
- Businesses turning EBITDA positive
- Company continues to deliver on forecasts

The use of the phrase 'turning EBITDA positive', which is loosely translated as 'just about to make a profit', was interesting given that Keeling had assured Channel 9 viewers three months earlier that the European ventures were already producing cash.

The recommendation of One.Tel's PR company, Hawker Britton, for dealing with any critics was also worth noting. Hired after the bonus fiasco, the new spin doctors suggested that the company should 'flag with journalists that they are being monitored and need to be accountable'. As if journalists were the company's main problem.

A week later, One.Tel hired a suite at Sydney's swish new Radisson Hotel near Circular Quay to tell analysts and the press how well things were going. Marshalling his bar charts, which showed subscriber numbers and revenues leaping ahead, Jodee was at his persuasive best.

The business was fantastic, the future was rosy, every-thing was on track. There would be $75 million in the bank at the end of June 2001, as promised, and One.Tel would be minting money thereafter.

You did not have to be the greatest sceptic to wonder whether these predictions could really come true. One.Tel had already consumed more than $230 million of its $336 million cash reserve in the six months to December, and had gobbled up another $27 million in January, so it was already $2 million short of what it was supposed to have in five months' time.

One.Tel would have to spin on a sixpence if Jodee's promises were to be kept. The $101 million loss in the first half would have to turn into a $10 million profit in the second. But Mr Positive was adamant that this would happen. According to Jodee, the UK and European businesses would improve in cash terms by $57 million in the second half, while the Australian oper-ations, led by fixed-wire (local and long-distance calls from home telephones), would perform an incredible $89 million turnaround.

Some of One.Tel's second-line managers had already been fed this story. Gathered in the meeting room on the 28th floor at Castlereagh Street, they had been shown graphs of the company's operations around the world, which plunged deep into the red before suddenly flip-ping up and roaring skywards. In business, they call these hockey-stick companies, which have a brilliant future just around the corner. The charts showed that all the company's businesses apart from Next Gen were about to leap into profit at exactly the same moment, and provide a steady stream of cash to fund the company's new mobile network. One of the more cynical members of the audience could not hide his disdain and coughed the word 'bullshit' into his hand so that those around him could hear.

There was no doubt these forecasts looked great. There was also no doubt that One.Tel's directors swallowed them. But in the opinion of several senior finance people, there was no chance they would come true: the numbers they were based on were 'a crock of shit'.

David Barnes, the group financial controller, who had been sitting with Jodee on the 28th floor all the previous week preparing the presentation, was clearly of this mind, and was concerned about what to do. A small, slight man who always wore a suit to work—even at One.Tel, where most people dressed in jeans—Barnes was the classic, conservative accountant. There was a joke in the company that Jodee had cut his nuts off long ago and put them in a jar. But he now found the balls to resign. Barnes told two of his closest colleagues that he was not prepared to do what his bosses were asking, and that he considered it completely unethical. He had a wife and children and a future to think about, he told one of them as they walked to the Customs House Hotel for a farewell drink; he could not afford to be the chief financial officer of a company that was producing misleading data.

In one of my meetings with Jodee, I suggest to him that Barnes quit for this reason, and he shakes his head, looking exasperated. It is completely untrue, he says: he left One.Tel because he was working too hard and wanted to be in a smaller company. Barnes himself, who could clear up the mystery, has refused to elaborate.

Before leaving, Barnes handed a blue file to one of his colleagues. It was several inches thick, full of computer print-outs and other documents with Barnes's hand-written notes on them. He had been keeping a meticulous record of the changes he had been asked to make to flash reports and forecasts, and who had asked him to make them. The colleague locked it away in a drawer, having been told by Barnes to keep it safe.

The sudden departure of Barnes left his 30-year-old deputy, Tim Holmes, in the hot seat as the new group financial controller. It was now his job to ensure that the One.Tel board and the market were given numbers that reflected what was really happening in the company, rather than what the management wanted to believe. He told several colleagues that he was also thinking of leaving because he was appalled by the battles that they had been fighting since late 2000. But he had only been with One.Tel a few months, so for the moment he resolved to fight on.

By the end of February, the management accounts for January 2001 were finalised. These showed that the figures given to the board at the 25 January board meeting were wrong. Far from being on target, as the ever-optimistic flash reports had promised, the Australian operations had fallen another $5 million short of their profit forecast. When combined with the admitted $5 million shortfall for the six months to December, it meant One.Tel was running $10 million behind budget, even after the adjustments. By the end of March, the management accounts for February would show this gap opening up to $20 million. By the end of April it would be clear that the company had fallen even further behind.

Given how little margin there was for error—if One.Tel was to keep the promises that Jodee, Brad and the chairman, John Greaves, had all made to the market—these management accounts spelt Danger with a capital D. So you might think it was vital for One.Tel's directors to be kept fully informed about the figures. In December 2001, six months after One.Tel's collapse, I asked Jodee whether these management accounts were ever shown to the board, and whether One.Tel's directors were told in clear and unequivocal terms that the company was running $20 million or more behind budget. During a ten-minute exchange, which ended with me shouting at him, Jodee repeatedly refused to answer the question. We both knew how important it was.

In fact, the management accounts for January, February and March were never shown to One.Tel's directors, who continued to be fed a diet of flash reports

and optimistic forecasts, and told that the company was
still on track. Nor was news of any shortfall relayed to
analysts, journalists or the Australian Stock Exchange,
who were all told by Jodee in the official February
briefing that everything was tickety-boo.

Stranger still, the management accounts were not
shown to Geoff Kleemann, finance director of the
Packers' public company, PBL, who had been deputed
to keep an eye on One.Tel for the company's two biggest
shareholders. We will come to the reasons why Kleemann
and the board did not see them, but, for the moment,
let's just say Rich and Silbermann are adamant that
One.Tel's directors were properly informed.

Geoff Kleemann had been given the job of watching
over One.Tel in October 2000. Jodee and Brad had been
called into News Ltd's Sydney HQ to brief Rupert
Murdoch on the state of the business. After the chat,
Lachlan and James took the dynamic duo aside and
told them it was time the Packers and Murdochs had
their own finance man to look after their $1 billion
investment.

It is a matter of debate what Kleemann was told to
look for and how closely he was told to look, but he
never had an office at One.Tel, did not visit regularly,
and did not conduct a full-scale investigation of the
company's finances. In fact, hardly anyone remembers
seeing him there or knows what he looks like.
Nevertheless, many accountants find it amazing that

anyone who is so highly thought of could spend any time in the company and not see that things were amiss.

Undoubtedly, one of Kleemann's jobs was to discover whether One.Tel had enough cash to survive until 2003, when the Next Gen network was supposed to start making money. According to Jodee, James Packer and Geoff Kleemann came into One.Tel's offices on 19 January 2001 and spent the morning looking at forecasts for the European businesses—which Keeling had promised were about to 'explode into earnings'. They also went through the business plan for the Next Gen network, focusing on how many subscribers it had and how much cash it would use. Within days, they were also receiving daily emails showing key subscriber and revenue numbers for the UK business, subscriber numbers for Next Gen, and a group cash balance. According to a senior One.Tel corporate lawyer, 'James was obsessed with cash, and if the email was ever late, he would be on the phone straight away'. There was a great sense of urgency about giving the Packers what they wanted.

Jodee Rich claims that from this point on, Mark Silbermann talked to Geoff Kleemann regularly, and James Packer rang Jodee two or three times a day, often calling him at home in the evening as he sat down to dinner with Maxine. He also claims that James knew an enormous amount about what went on in the business. Certainly, he and Kleemann were getting daily cash figures, and there is no suggestion that these lied about how much money One.Tel had in the bank. Nor is there any dispute that they showed One.Tel continuing to consume cash during February, March and April. But there *is* doubt about whether the figures gave a true picture of how bad things were. As any householder knows, you can have money in your account at the end of the month if you stop paying your bills. And that is what One.Tel appears to have started doing sometime in March 2001.

In early February a new staff member had joined the finance team to manage the company's cash resources. A no-nonsense girl, she could see straight away that money was flowing out of One.Tel a great deal faster than it was coming in. Before long, she could also see it might run out altogether. She claims the company hid this problem by deferring payments to creditors.

At the end of every month, this new cash manager prepared a forecast for the next 30 days. To estimate payments, she made a schedule of all the creditors, with the dates they needed to be paid. To estimate receipts, she added up all the bills that One.Tel was sending out, and assessed what percentage of the money was likely to be collected. The combination produced daily cash totals for the month ahead.

At the beginning of March, the forecast showed that cash would run dangerously low before the month was out. She claims that when she showed the figures to Mark Silbermann he told her to change them, saying he had already given cash numbers to the board, which her figures needed to match.

There were two basic ways to manipulate the forecast, the first being to assume that One.Tel would collect more money from its customers. She claims that Silbermann insisted she do this, even though receipts were likely to be lower than usual because the company had stopped doing credit checks on Next Gen customers and there was a growing bad debt problem with local calls.

The second was to defer payment to creditors, and she claims Silbermann told her to do this, too. The combined effect of these changes was to add between $10 million and $20 million to the forecast cash totals.

Silbermann denies giving any such instructions and disputes the nature of the woman's job. 'She was just a record keeper', he says, 'She was not involved in cash forecasting. All she did was the treasury function, managing payments'. He adds that One.Tel paid all its major creditors on time—which is certainly not true.

The woman's other main task was to manage the cash flow on a daily basis, and to update the monthly forecast to reflect the amount of money that had been received. It soon transpired that One.Tel was not collecting nearly as much as Silbermann had told her to assume. She claims that she was now instructed to put more bills on the spike, and to sit with Silbermann each day while he told her who to pay and who to put off.

By the end of March she had prepared a new cash forecast for April—on an Excel spreadsheet—which showed things going from bad to worse. Soon afterwards, she came into work to find a new version on her computer. She claims that when she enquired what it was, Mark Silbermann told her he had sat down with Steve Hodgson the previous evening and made some changes to her forecast, which she had spent the previous two weeks preparing.

There was one change in particular that took her eye: a new 'balancing item' that added $20 million to the forecast total. She asked Silbermann what this $20 million was. He told her to talk to Steve Hodgson. She claims she asked Hodgson what it was, and he said, 'Don't worry about it'. She did worry. She was appalled.

On Wednesday, 4 April, Jodee Rich was a keynote speaker at the Merrill Lynch telecommunications conference in Sydney. Reading from a now familiar script, he told his audience that One.Tel's finances were 'on track as promised'. Once again, he repeated the pledge that the company would have $75 million in the bank at the end of June. The very next day, the company's bank balance was $34 million below that target. Two weeks later, it was $50 million short.

15

Missing Revenue

At no time did I think we were
going to miss our forecasts.

Jodee Rich

Jodee told me in December 2001 that he never believed
One.Tel was going to miss its forecasts—despite all
evidence to the contrary. Even when he repeated the
famous $75 million cash promise on 4 April 2001, he
was still convinced it could be kept. He claims there was
a large amount of revenue stuck in the system—as a
result of billing problems—which was about to flow into
the company's coffers. This 'missing revenue' is Jodee's
justification for failing to tell the board and investors
that One.Tel was at least $20 million behind budget. It
is also Mark Silbermann's reason for not showing the
crucial management accounts to Geoff Kleemann, and
it would presumably be Rich and Silbermann's defence
if they were found to have inflated forecasts of how

much cash the company would have. Keeling and Greaves, of course, have not been prepared to comment, but the claim that a huge amount of revenue was 'missing' is central to the question of whether One.Tel's top management misled the board about the financial health of the company.

The tale of One.Tel's 'missing revenue' is complex and often hard to grasp, but the essence of Rich and Silbermann's story is this. When the One.Tel board was assured on 30 March 2001 that the company was still on budget—and set to keep its promises—it was explained in great detail to James Packer, Lachlan Murdoch and the other directors that at least $28.8 million of revenue was 'yet to be billed' for the first three months of the year. Thus, it was neither necessary nor appropriate to show them the management accounts, which had not counted any of this 'missing' money.

Nor was it therefore necessary to warn the directors that One.Tel was $20 million behind budget—for the simple reason that it wasn't. According to Rich and Silbermann, all this $28.8 million of missing revenue had been identified by late March, so it was perfectly reasonable to assume it would be collected. In fact, it would be billed by One.Tel the following month and, by implication, would be collected soon afterwards.

There are various difficulties with this story. First, the company ran out of cash in early May, despite Rich and

Silbermann's contention that the arrival of this big windfall was going to solve all of One.Tel's problems. Second, if One.Tel did bill an *extra* $28.8 million in April, the revenue for that month should have been far higher than normal, but it was not. Third, if this missing revenue was meant to bring One.Tel back on budget— which is what One.Tel's board was told—the April management accounts should show the company doing exactly that, but they do not. One.Tel's profit actually fell another $11 million behind during the month, and the gap widened further in May. In other words, the figures don't support Rich and Silbermann's argument. Silbermann's response to this, remarkably, is that the management accounts must be 'incomplete', or wrong.

One.Tel's finance team is also not convinced by the 'missing revenue' story. They maintain that One.Tel ran short of cash in early 2001 because the company, and in particular the local call business, was losing millions of dollars more than anyone had bargained for.

The finance team's version of events is that a hunt for 'missing revenue' began in November 2000, when David Barnes and Tim Holmes warned that the Australian operations were behind budget. They say this search gathered pace in February 2001, when the management accounts made it clear that One.Tel had real problems, but the bulk of the 'missing' money was never found.

The missing revenue was believed to be in One.Tel's fixed-wire division, which handled local and long-distance calls from home telephones. This had always been a potential disaster for the company, because it could only make a profit if it recouped its losses on cheap local calls by making money on long-distance. Back in May 2000, the company's analysts had assumed that revenue would be split 40 per cent local and 60 per cent long-distance. But no one had any idea whether this mix of calls was right, and in late 2000 the finance team's figures showed the business was making half as much profit as it should.

When the problem was drawn to Rich and Silbermann's attention, they were adamant that it was not a profitability problem. Their conclusion was that One.Tel's billing system must be failing to charge people for calls, so *revenue* was being lost—even though the figures showed that revenue from the Australian operations was actually ahead of budget.

In January 2001, Silbermann asked one of the company's senior business analysts, who does not want to be named, to look for $10 million in revenue 'missing' from November. She duly dug into the depths of the billing system and came up with some computer tapes containing Telstra call records that had not been properly processed, which accounted for around $6 million.

In late February or early March she was asked to find another $30 million. She was sceptical that so much money could have gone missing, and Silbermann could not explain why he was so sure $30 million was the figure. Her gut feeling was that it was wrong, but she delved into the system again and started to analyse the 'error buckets', where all the calls rejected by the bill runs ended up. If the missing revenue was anywhere, she says, it was likely to be there.

The analyst claims the amounts she found were insignificant. In her opinion, the billing system was charging One.Tel's fixed-wire customers for 99 per cent of the calls they were making. One.Tel's head of billing, Emily Joukhadar, who helped her search for the 'missing' money, confirms this: 'There was not a revenue problem. There were not holes in the billing system, like everyone thought there were'.

Sometime in March, the analyst started looking for an alternative explanation for the budget shortfall, and by early April, she had her answer. It was exactly what One.Tel's finance team had been suggesting since November: the fixed-wire business was only half as profitable as One.Tel's budget had predicted. The mix of calls was all wrong. Instead of the 40:60 split between local and long-distance calls, it was more like 50:50. After the costs of running the business were deducted, there was nothing left.

The analyst reported these findings to Kevin Beck, Steve Hodgson, Mark Silbermann and Jodee Rich in that order. Even at this point Jodee was reluctant to accept she was right, and sent her back to analyse the figures for earlier months. These revealed the even more disturbing news that the fixed-wire business had been making no money since May 2000, when the original budget had been drawn up. Rich then asked her to reconcile her findings with the budget, to see if the business's low profit margins were responsible for the $30 million hole. She and Natasha Nassif from the finance team did the calculations and concluded that they probably accounted for more than $20 million of it.

On Friday, 20 April 2001, some five months after the first warning signs that One.Tel was off track, the two presented their conclusions about the fixed-wire business to Rich, Silbermann, Hodgson and Beck. Only now, the analyst claims, did Jodee accept their argument that 'missing revenue' could not be blamed for One.Tel's cash and profit shortfall.

It seems quite extraordinary that a company the size of One.Tel did not actually know that one of its key businesses was losing money. It also seems quite extraordinary that no one could be sure whether or not $30 million had gone missing. Most of all, it seems extraordinary that the company's top managers could take so long to accept that their company was millions of dollars behind budget, and work out why.

One of those involved believes Rich and Silbermann were 'in denial' about the problem for three to four months: they knew cash was pouring out of the company, and should have investigated the fixed-wire business far earlier, 'but they insisted on believing they were right and everybody else was wrong'.

My own conversations with Rich suggest very little has changed in this regard. I put to him in one of our meetings that One.Tel ended the financial year in 2001 roughly $50 million behind budget. He asks me where I got this figure from—it is from accounts prepared by the liquidator—then insists that it is wrong. 'We were on track for what we told the market', he says.

He later adds, in relation to cash, 'At no time did I think we were going to miss our forecasts'.

Whatever Rich and Silbermann did or did not believe in early 2001 about One.Tel's financial problems, there is little doubt they had a duty to inform the board that the company would miss its financial forecasts unless the missing revenue could be found. Their story, of course, is that they did. One.Tel's non-executive directors and several of the company's senior staff say they didn't. The courts will have to decide whom to believe.

According to One.Tel's finance team, the collapse of the 'missing revenue' story in mid-April left Jodee and his lieutenants needing to pull another rabbit out of the hat, because they now needed to find another $30 million somewhere else if they were to have any chance of keeping the promises Jodee and Brad had made so many times to the market and to One.Tel's directors. Several senior staff, including the analyst, the head of the fixed-wire business and One.Tel's corporate counsel, were told by Jodee to drop everything and work on building a multi-million-dollar damages claim against Telstra.

None of them was convinced that such a claim could be justified. Nor did they really know what they were looking for. And the more they searched, the more they became convinced that One.Tel had no case. 'There was no substance to it. It was thousands, not millions of dollars at stake', says a senior manager who worked on the job. 'It was pretty weak stuff', says another. A third concluded that if anyone or anything was at fault, it was One.Tel's poor management systems.

This was not what Jodee told One.Tel's directors, nor is it what he and his acolytes have since told me. Their story is that the Telstra claim, valued at some $46 million, was not only genuine but was going to bring a large amount of cash into the company. In the meantime, Telstra's alleged crimes against One.Tel—such as failing to deliver electronic billing, or transferring customers with bad debts—could be used as a reason for One.Tel not to pay its next bill from the national carrier.

16

Deep Throat

You don't know me, but I know you. I work at One.Tel. There is a lot of crap people at One.Tel have been telling you.

Email to Geoff Kleemann

During February and March 2001, one of the company's senior accountants watched with mounting frustration as Packer's top finance man, Geoff Kleemann, clearly failed to see what a shocking state the company was in. The accountant was appalled at the cavalier way the business was being run, outraged at the way in which the figures were being manipulated, and astonished that Packer's people were apparently blind to what was going on. It was clear to him and several financial team members that the company was careering towards disaster. He thought long and hard about what was involved, then finally, he sent Kleemann an anonymous email to tell him he was being snowed by Jodee and his team.

'You don't know me', he wrote, 'but I know you. I work at One.Tel. There is a lot of crap people at One.Tel have been telling you'.

The first time this Deep Throat tried to deliver the warning he got the email address wrong—putting only one 'n' in Kleemann—so his missile didn't reach its target. For a couple of weeks he waited for something to happen. Then he went back to the special hotmail account he had set up under the codename Ghostdogperil and sent it off again on 13 April.

His email pointed to a host of specific problems, but the essence of its message was simple: Kleemann was not being told the full story.

> Billing is a mess, months behind. Bad debts are grossly understated . . . the IT team is in chaos. Half of finance have left as well . . . The half-year numbers and subsequent numbers [at One.Tel Australia] are rubbish . . . the assumptions [in the Next Gen business plan] are mostly crap . . . there is a massive hole, approx $170 million [in finance for the new mobile network].

Worst of all was his warning about the subject of most concern to James and Kerry Packer: 'Cash flow: there is a massive hole in this—$21 million—which SH [Steve Hodgson] requests finance staff to "fill"'.

'If you are really interested in finding out what is happening, you need to speak to the second-string players—alone and by surprise—so that they can't be coerced, intimidated into toeing the line.' He then proceeded to name three members of senior management—Mark Silbermann, Steve Hodgson and Kevin Beck—whom Kleemann needed to avoid.

The email was sent on Good Friday. By Tuesday, Kleemann and his team were in the One.Tel office and on the trail, huddling in the corners in an attempt to talk to a couple of the nine 'second-string players' who Deep Throat had identified. At least one senior manager at One.Tel was obviously concerned at this development, asking a woman from the finance team: 'Why were they talking to you? What were they asking? What did they want to know?'.

The email was dynamite, but it seems that the Packers had already decided to act. The day before Ghostdogperil clicked the send button on his computer for the second time, Kerry had called Jodee and Brad into his office for a meeting to tell them that One.Tel was going to run out of cash and to demand a thorough investigation.

It is not entirely clear what prompted this, but Kerry had been worrying about the cash position ever since Jodee 'fucked up' by paying too much for spectrum in March 2000. According to Jodee, there had been increasing tension between James and his father about the family's $400 million investment since that time, which might have come to a head much earlier had Kerry not been so sick he was battling to stay alive.

The big man's health problems had begun in the mid-1980s, when he was whisked into hospital to have a cancerous kidney removed. In 1990 he had all but died from a cardiac arrest during which his heart stopped beating for seven to eight minutes, and the oxygen supply to his brain was cut off. He then underwent triple bypass surgery at St Vincent's Hospital in Sydney, after which he was relatively fit for a few years.

In 1998, his troubles started again: he was flown to New York for emergency surgery on his one remaining kidney and soon afterwards was given a second heart bypass because the first was wearing out. The next year, 1999, he was cut open again so that his arteries could be unclogged. And in November 2000, he was back under the knife once more, at the Royal Prince Alfred Hospital in Sydney, where he was given a new kidney, courtesy of his helicopter pilot and friend Nick Ross.

As if this wasn't enough for any man, he had faced continual problems since that time. Within weeks of the transplant, he was back at the RPA because his body had rejected the new organ, and on two or three other occasions prior to May 2001, he was checked in again for treatment. Several times, it looked like he was going to die. Several times, Australia's papers brushed off their farewell notices, in anticipation of his parting.

On each occasion, Kerry managed to pull through. And every time he did, he turned his mind to One.Tel. In mid-January, as the company's share price sank to its lowest level for more than two years—and well below the average that the Packers had paid—he summoned Jodee Rich to his bunker for an ear bashing. According to Jodee, he told him bluntly: 'You ran out of cash with Imagineering, and it's going to happen again'. He also complained, 'I was right, and now the markets are saying I was right. You blokes never listen to me'.

Meetings with Kerry could be gruelling at the best of times, but this was probably one of the worst. According to Jodee and others, Packer's habit was to invite people for 10.00am and still be going strong at lunchtime. At this point, he liked to ring the buzzer underneath his desk and order his secretary, Carol, to bring in some rare roast beef sandwiches. These were so rare that there were only ever enough for him. For the next ten minutes he would sit there chomping away, while his hungry audience watched in awe. Sometimes, he would ring the buzzer a second time and bark out to Carol that he wanted some more.

Even Jodee, it seems, wasn't game to challenge this display of raw power, but he was not alone in that. There was an unwritten rule that no one left one of Kerry's meetings until he said it was over, and even James dared not argue with this. One executive tells how he absolutely had to get away by 2.30pm from an audience with Kerry that started at midday. He told James this when they went in, and James said it would be fine. It got close to 2.30pm and the man gestured to James that he had to leave. James looked nervous and shook his head. Finally, the man stood up to leave, saying, 'Kerry I really have to go now'. Kerry roared, 'What do you mean, you have to fucking go?'. By this time, James had apparently turned white.

Jodee managed to survive the dressing-down in January, and apparently satisfied Kerry that the company was not yet on the rocks. He maintains that Geoff Kleemann backed him up in the discussion. But it is probably no coincidence that One.Tel was asked a few days later to send daily cash updates to the Packers by email.

Jodee's next grilling from Kerry appears to have been in March, and may well have been triggered by a sudden dip in One.Tel's cash reserves to $35 million. On this occasion, Jodee, Brad, James, Ashok Jacob, Geoff Kleemann and Mark Silbermann all trooped into the RPA and sat by Kerry's hospital bed. According to Jodee, he was sick, cranky and beset with tubes. He was also possibly not at his sharpest. It is not clear whether this session led to any new initiative.

On 12 April, Kerry stumped into action again, demanding a full review of One.Tel's cash position. Even though it was only a week since Jodee had assured the Merrill Lynch conference that everything was fine, the daily emails showed the cash balance had fallen to $37 million. By this time, Kerry also seems to have had several people in his ear about the company. Whatever the immediate trigger, the cash review began in the week after Easter, with two of the Packers' top executives, Martin Green and Darren Miller, helping Kleemann to take a closer look at the books than he had managed since his arrival on the scene at the end of 2000.

But even now, the Packer team did not really get to the 'second-string' players named by Ghostdogperil, such as Tim Holmes and the woman who was managing One.Tel's cash, possibly because they were prevented from doing so. One very senior accountant, who was identified by Ghostdogperil as worth talking to, was caught in conversation with Martin Green and warned off by Jodee. 'I think he was worried what I might tell him', the man says, 'and I must say, it concerned me'.

Nevertheless, it was now blindingly obvious that One.Tel was in trouble. By 19 April, only two weeks after Jodee's promises to the Merrill Lynch conference and three weeks after his assurances to the board that everything was on track, One.Tel's cash reserves had fallen to $25 million, or $50 million short of where the market had been told it would be by the end of June. There was also a big Optus bill about to fall due.

On Monday, 23 April, Jodee was summoned to James Packer's office to be told that more money would need to be pumped into the company. Unless they could sell one of their businesses, it was clear this would have to come from existing shareholders because the chances of raising money from anyone else would be slim.

Lachlan Murdoch claims that it was not until one week later, on 1 May, that he first learned One.Tel was in financial strife. According to an affidavit sworn in June 2001, he received a phone call from James Packer to tell him the company needed an extra $10 million to $15 million 'to reach cash flow breakeven'. Lachlan says he asked James during this conversation: 'Are you starting to lose confidence in the business or is this a timing issue?', to which he claims James replied: 'No, Brad and Jodee don't think there is a problem. It's just a timing issue'.

Another week later, with the Packers' cash review complete, it was clear that much larger sums of money would be needed to keep the company afloat. The PBL team's reckoning was that One.Tel had underestimated its cash requirements by up to $100 million, so that amount of money would have to be found. On Tuesday, 8 May, this conclusion was passed on to Jodee and his team in James Packer's office at Park Street. On one side were Rich, Keeling, Silbermann and Beck, the executive directors of One.Tel. On the other were Packer, Jacob, Miller, Green and the new head of PBL, Peter Yates, who had joined the company just three weeks before.

Fortunately for the boys from One.Tel, Kerry was once again too ill to be there. He had been admitted to hospital, with fears that he might not come out. But even without him it was a sobering couple of hours for Jodee and his team. One version has James telling them that he was 'very disappointed' in their performance. A more colourful account has him accusing them of 'fucking up' yet again. They had promised the board and the market repeatedly that One.Tel would not run out of cash, he said, but it was going to do exactly that. There would have to be a rights issue to bail the company out—priced at 5 cents a share, to raise $132 million—but the company's founders would have to go. In Kerry's absence, Peter Yates was kind enough to pass on a message from the big man: 'This is going to cost you your right testicle', Rich was told.

Mark Silbermann was also singled out for treatment. As he tried to explain the One.Tel Story that there was money in the pipeline which would make it all come right, Ashok Jacob asked him angrily, 'When has any forecast of yours *ever* come right?'. Silbermann apparently arrived back at One.Tel's offices in Castlereagh Street late that afternoon, 'looking shell-shocked'. Jodee was rather less concerned. He and Keeling still owned the majority of One.Tel's shares and had 51 per cent of the votes. They might be in for a rough ride, but surely the storm would blow over? And who could seriously want to get rid of the two men who had made One.Tel such a huge success?

It was now James's job to get on a plane to Europe and persuade the Murdochs to put up another $66 million to underwrite their share of this rights issue. At this moment, Rupert and Lachlan were a world away from all this fuss. The following night, they would be snapped by photographers on the famous red carpet at the opening of the Cannes Film Festival in the south of France, clad in evening dress and flanked by their respective wives. Looking at the pictures today, one sees a splendid scene of family harmony, with the four standing arm in arm, smiling broadly. A newly pregnant Wendi Deng looks plump in a long red dress, while Sarah O'Hare is absolutely gorgeous in cream and gold. Lachlan seems pleased with life, while Rupert—looking every inch the media mogul—is positively grinning.

They all had good reason to be cheerful, of course. The world premiere of their blockbuster *Moulin Rouge* was kicking off the festival; the star, Nicole Kidman, had been staying in their compound, and the director, Baz Luhrmann, was one of Lachlan's best friends. If the two Murdochs had already heard the bad news about One.Tel—and they probably had—they obviously hadn't let it spoil their evening. At this instant, Cannes was the centre of their world, and Australia must have seemed miles away.

In fact, by the time these pictures were taken, James Packer had almost certainly flown in from Sydney and found a moment to take Lachlan aside. According to Lachlan's affidavit, which says (incorrectly) that the meeting took place three days earlier, James told him: 'The position is worse than we thought. One.Tel may need about $50 to $60 million of funding to break even, with a further $70 million as a sensible buffer'.

Lachlan claims he repeated the question he had posed a week before: 'Is there an underlying problem in the business?'. According to Lachlan's affidavit, James again replied: 'No, it's only a timing issue for the business plan to break even. Jodee doesn't think they need it'. Naturally, the rights issue was then discussed, along with News Ltd's willingness to fork out more money. According to his affidavit, Lachlan then said to James: 'They've told the market so many times they don't need any more funds. Even if you raise $1 they will not have any credibility. They will have to go'.

While this exchange between the two mini-moguls was sealing his fate, Jodee was busy spruiking the One.Tel Story to Geoff Elliott of *The Australian*, telling him he loved what he was doing and was proud of the business's success. Naturally, Elliott asked him whether his promise of having $75 million in the bank at 30 June still stood. It is a matter of dispute how Rich replied, and the tape has now been wiped, but Elliott reported him in the next day's paper as confirming that One.Tel was still 'on track'. Lachlan was no doubt surprised to read this in his family's newspaper.

Elliott's article also brought rare good news for One.Tel in the shape of a 50-page report by investment bankers Goldman Sachs, which was headlined: 'Great Start. One.Tel is here to stay'. The bank's analyst Jason Billings had spent many months on this tome and worked hard on the numbers, and in many ways it was a fine piece of work. But its title and conclusion could hardly have been less appropriate: 'The company does not need to raise cash', wrote Billings. 'The company will not need further funding.'

We all make mistakes, of course. In the mid-1970s a British weekly called the *Investors Chronicle*—where I started my journalistic career—made a far worse one than this. The magazine went to press on Wednesday but did not hit the streets till Friday. One famous Thursday, a budget airline called Court Line went spectacularly bust, leaving thousands of holiday-makers stranded and thousands of investors out of pocket. With even worse timing than poor Mr Billings, the *Investors Chronicle* came out on Friday morning, amid news of the disastrous crash, to tell people that the company was sound and the shares were a good buy. I should point out that I was not the culprit.

In retrospect, Geoff Elliott was amazed at how cheerful One.Tel's founder was on that day, given that he knew he was likely to have his company snatched away from him and be branded a business failure yet again. Afterwards, Elliott wrote a short piece in *The Australian*, marvelling at Jodee's demeanour:

The first thing he did when I met him at One.Tel's office . . . was to offer me a Vitamin C tablet. We both had head colds. It was part of the charm of the man. Friendly and smiling, the gesture was straight from the heart. Or was it more a sharp promoter's instinct?

Rich knew he was in the eye of a perfect storm that was about to engulf his company, destroy his reputation for the second time in his life and make enemies of the two most powerful families in the land. You would never have guessed.

In addition to talking up the company, Jodee had been busy trying to sell parts of the business to raise cash. He and Brad had already offered to sell One.Tel's old mobile customers back to Optus, who still provided the service, for around $60 million, without success. They now talked to Vodafone about a possible merger with the Next Gen network, but this also went nowhere.

By Monday, 14 May, James Packer was back from his trip to the south of France. Jodee went round to his Bondi apartment at 7.00am to see him. They had been close friends for a long time, so neither could have looked forward to what James was going to say. In Jodee's words: 'He told me that the rights issue was going to go ahead, and I would have to go. He told me that's what Rupert and Lachlan wanted. And I told him I would do whatever was best for the company. And we put our arms around each other and cried'.

There may well have been other reasons for James to be emotional. In mid-April, as the crisis over One.Tel was coming to a head, Kerry's elder brother, Clyde, had died in California at the age of 65. The day after this meeting with Jodee, James would be escorting his father and mother to the Sydney memorial service. Kerry had been extremely sick, and arrived at the Woollahra church looking thin, pale and fragile. Only a week earlier it had seemed he too might be dying.

The day after the memorial service, James was back on the case, calling in Silbermann and Beck to tell them that Jodee and Brad were resigning as One.Tel's joint managing directors. Somewhat to Silbermann and Beck's surprise, he asked them to stay on. James then rang Lachlan in New York to relay the news that the founders had agreed to go. An emergency board meeting was called for 7.00am Sydney time, Thursday, 17 May. Lachlan would join them on the phone from his office in midtown Manhattan, where it would be late afternoon.

Very few people inside One.Tel had a clue that a show-down was so close. For months, a group of team leaders had regaled each other with horror stories about the state of the business, while waiting for the company to implode, but not even the corporate counsel, Shanti Bergeren, or the head of investor relations, Tracy Cutting, knew until the very last minute that Jodee and Brad were about to be removed. Late on 16 May they found themselves sitting with Jodee and Brad on the 28th floor waiting for draft press statements about their resignations to spew out of the fax machine. The spin doctors and lawyers at News Ltd and PBL had taken over the reins.

Sometime that evening Jodee managed to reach Lachlan in New York. He had been trying for days. Lachlan was 'positive and friendly', but Jodee failed to persuade him he should be allowed to stay on. He went to bed believing he was '90 per cent gone', but optimistic that there was still 'a glimmer of hope'. Brad seems to have already accepted that the battle was lost and appeared to some not to be too concerned that it was ending this way.

When Bergeren and the company secretary, Alicia Parker, arrived at One.Tel's offices at 6.00am the next day, Jodee and Brad were already packing their Rolodexes, papers and personal belongings into big lime-green One.Tel bags. It was normally Parker's job to prepare the board papers, but she still had no idea what was on the agenda. Only now was she told that the meeting would discuss refinancing the company and ask Brad and Jodee to resign.

By the time proceedings began, ten people were gathered in the glass-walled room on the 28th floor that One.Tel used whenever a semblance of privacy was needed. Staff who arrived in the next two hours would be able to see the drama unfold, but only guess at what was being said. Another six people, including Lachlan, Peter Macourt, the chief executive officer of News Ltd, and Ian Philip, News Ltd's chief legal counsel, were linked in via speaker phone. Jodee was disturbed to note that News Ltd, PBL and One.Tel had armed themselves with five lawyers in total.

The first major item on the agenda was the company's cash levels, which Jodee agreed were 'lower than expected'. He had two new explanations for this—Telstra was to blame for some of the shortfall, and the European carriers had caused problems by tightening credit terms—but he also offered his usual assurance that a catch-up in billing would bring cash flooding in. Even now he failed to tell his fellow directors that One.Tel was at least $20 million behind budget.

It's doubtful whether anyone was taking much notice anyway. All the directors had a copy of PBL's cash review in front of them, showing the kitty was empty. And James was quick to remind them that even Jodee and Brad had now accepted there was no chance of One.Tel keeping its promise of having $75 million in the bank on 30 June. Jodee was soon forced to admit that the company had only $20 million left, and had $21 million worth of bills to Telstra and Optus that were already overdue.

The board was then told that if the company was to stay in business, the $132 million rights issue was the only option. As the minutes recorded it:

> Lachlan Murdoch expressed the view that such a fund-raising exercise could only be undertaken once. This view was accepted by the other directors.

> James Packer said that PBL and News were surprised, disappointed and upset, to be put in a

position where they were asked to underwrite an issue, but they were prepared to do so.

With the new funding agreed, they came to the other business of the day: the price that One.Tel's founders would have to pay for the rescue, which the minutes recorded as follows:

RESIGNATIONS OF JODEE RICH AND BRADLEY KEELING

James Packer thanked Jodee Rich and Bradley Keeling for their enormous entrepreneurial vision and hard work, which had taken the company from its small beginnings six years ago to the global organisation it was today. He noted that today marks a new beginning for One.Tel.

Lachlan Murdoch expressed News Ltd's gratitude for the passion and energy of Jodee Rich and Bradley Keeling. They had created remarkable value over the past six years. News Ltd accepts news of their resignation with mixed emotion.

Thus far, it was all going well. Then they hit a problem:

Jodee Rich said that they have not offered to resign, that they believed they had a strong management team. And they believed they should stay. However, they were appreciative of News and PBL's support, so would do what the board believed was right.

Lachlan Murdoch said that he took back every-thing that he had said. Jodee Rich said that he hoped Lachlan was joking. James Packer expressed surprise at Jodee Rich's comments, given his discus-sions with Jodee Rich the previous evening. Lachlan Murdoch said that perhaps he had been misin-formed, as he had understood that an agreement had been reached.

God knows what tension these anodyne sentences conceal. No one had thought for one minute that Jodee would refuse to go—it had all been settled, or so they thought. But they had reckoned without Rich's huge ego, and his conviction that One.Tel would be lost without him. He claims he was also shocked by the brutal way in which they wanted to dispatch him. 'They stuck a resignation letter under my nose and told me to sign it', he says.

But if the corporate hard men from News Ltd and PBL were stirred by this display of stubbornness, they certainly were not shaken. Peter Yates picked up the press release that had been drafted the night before and waved it in front of Jodee's face. Would he prefer it to say that PBL and News had fired him, Yates asked? In the silence that followed, James patted his friend on the leg and asked him quietly, 'How will this achieve your objectives?'.

Even this was not enough to make Jodee throw in his hand, so he and Brad were asked to leave the room, together with Silbermann and Beck. Shortly afterwards, the meeting broke for James to have a private word with Lachlan on another line. According to one eyewitness, he emerged from the boardroom looking distraught and came straight up to Jodee to tell him: 'You shouldn't have done that. You've just made it worse'. He then sat down at an adjacent desk so he could make the call to Lachlan.

When the meeting reconvened ten minutes later Jodee agreed to go quietly. James had apparently told him during the break he would be fired if he tried to put up a fight. Nevertheless, he insisted it be put on record that he did not believe his departure was in the best interests of the company. 'I felt incredibly strongly that I shouldn't go', he says. 'I still feel strongly that the outcome would have been different if I had stayed.'

Brad Keeling also resigned, but agreed, at the board's request, to remain for six weeks to ensure an easier transition. The press release was rewritten to reflect this change. As the amendments were being made, Jodee came out into the big open-plan office, went to his desk, picked up the bulldog clip that he used to hold his money and credit cards, and walked through the kitchen to the goods lift so he did not have to run the gauntlet of his staff. His desk had already been cleared. All the bottles of vitamin pills and herbal tonics had been thrown into sacks or boxes; the dirty tissues had been binned.

There would be no farewells, no tears goodbye, no riotous parties to mark his passing. He would not be back, except with his lawyers. He had built One.Tel from nothing, created jobs for 3,000 people and taken them all for the ride of their lives. Yet few were sorry to see him go. He drove himself back to Vaucluse, then went out on one of his many boats with Maxine. 'We went through Sydney Heads and out to sea', he told me, 'and wondered about life going forward'.

It was still only 9.30am. The Australian Stock Exchange needed to be asked to halt trading in the shares. The staff also had to be reassured; the news could not be allowed to dribble down to the other floors from the top of the building. George Savva, one of Jodee's greatest admirers, had already heard. 'I got very emotional', he says. 'I just got in the car and went home to my family.' He had been so upset that he had broken down and cried in the middle of the office.

The rest of One.Tel's managers and team leaders were summoned to the 28th floor and ushered into the meeting room. It was Brad Keeling's great talent to handle moments like this, and he did it well. His summing-up of the situation was remarkably astute. His message was that an era had ended: he and Jodee were great at starting businesses, but perhaps not so good at running them. The good news, he said, was that more money was being put into the company and the future was secure, so no one needed to worry about their jobs.

The bad news was that some people, including him, would be moving on.

'I will be staying for a short time to help', he told them. 'As for Jodee ... Elvis has left the building.'

17

None.Tel

Like all shareholders we are angry. We've been
profoundly misled as to the true financial
position of the company.

James Packer and Lachlan Murdoch, 30 May 2001

You can say what you like about Rodney Adler—
and many people do—but he knows which way the
wind is blowing. Right up till mid-April he told everyone
that One.Tel was a great company and assured them it
did not need to raise money. Meanwhile, he was busily
selling his shares.

Adler sold in dribs and drabs throughout 2000, then
decided in November to dump another 5 million before
the price fell further. He felt 'there was a lot of repairing
to do' after the battering the company had taken over
the bonus issue, so he wrote to Jodee and James Packer,
offering to resign from the board. They were angry he
was selling and worried that his action might weaken
confidence in the company. He sold, nevertheless, picking

up $2.5 million for the parcel of 5 million shares, and soon found himself under pressure to go. It was clear that the Packers in particular wanted him out. In his own words: 'I wouldn't go so far as to say relationships soured, but there's always the last straw that breaks the camel's back. They needed a reason for me to go, and this was it'.

Adler resigned as a director on 12 April 2001, just before the shit hit the fan. He sold the rest of his shares when the rights issue was announced, because he sensed that the worst was yet to come. 'I just put all 10 million on the market and said, "I'm out of here". I threw them at Foster Stockbrokers and said, "Get what you can for them", and they got rid of 9.4 million at an average price of about 20 cents a share.' Adler's quick thinking brought him another $2 million. But he had made more than 40 times that amount for himself and his family company, FAI, since it had staked $950,000 on One.Tel in 1995. It was probably the best investment he had ever made. He and Rich still talk, but do not appear to be particularly close friends.

Sadly, the poor people who had entrusted their hard-earned savings to Bankers Trust did not do as well as Rodney. By 17 May 2001 their $200 million investment had lost more than 80 per cent of its value. Luckily, the bank's new stock pickers—who had replaced the ones who gave Rich his second chance to lose their clients' money—were smart enough to salvage something from the wreckage. Within two trading days of the rights issue being announced, they too had ditched all their remaining 27 million One.Tel shares.

Someone had to be on the other end of these deals, of course, and no doubt they believed they were getting a bargain because the shares had fallen to a new record low of around 20 cents. The Murdochs and Packers were still standing behind the company, and if the big boys were prepared to risk $132 million then surely it was safe to invest a few thousand.

It was not only a few optimistic punters who felt that One.Tel's prospects were improved by Jodee and Brad's departure. Many of the company's senior staff also breathed a huge sigh of relief. One team leader's reaction was: 'Thank God they've got rid of those guys who were running the company into the ground. Now our hard work will be rewarded. Packer and Murdoch will sort the company out, get the systems working, fix the problems, and put in enough money. They won't let it go down'. Others had similar feelings.

With One.Tel's cash almost exhausted, it was obviously vital that the $132 million was pumped into the company as quickly as possible, but money could not be raised from the shareholders until there was a proper prospectus for the rights issue, with an independent expert's report on the financial health of the company. Consequently, a team of lawyers and accountants from

News Ltd and PBL now started to look at the books in even greater detail than before.

As this 'due diligence' process got under way, life at One.Tel went into limbo. The regular massage team stopped coming, the stationery started running out, and agencies such as the Telecommunications Industry Ombudsman and the Australian Competition and Consumer Commission stopped bothering the complaints team. In this unreal atmosphere, gallows humour thrived. People in the call centre outdid each other with impersonations of Kerry Packer telling James he had been a naughty boy and would get no more pocket money. One wag even sent out a bogus horse-race commentary on the company's voicemail system, which went something like this:

> And Jodee's-Rich-so-he's-not-worried still out in the lead, with Brad's-made-a-Keeling tucked in behind, James-will-you-save-us still waiting to make a move, and Lachlan-ask-your-dad-for-money still trying hard to get on terms.

Initially, Darren Miller and Martin Green, who were once again doing the investigations, told One.Tel's senior staff that all was going to plan. They were finding old unpaid debts in people's bottom drawers, but it was no worse than expected. Green assured the finance team that Packer and Murdoch were committed to putting in money and it was simply a question of how much. This encouraged the 'second-string players' to give them both barrels about how bad the situation really was.

The Packer team's first shock was a document prepared by group financial controller Tim Holmes in April, which suggested that One.Tel would be $50 million behind budget for the year. The second was the revelation that payments to some of One.Tel's biggest creditors were long overdue, so that tens of millions of dollars would be needed, on top of the $132 million, to make the company safe. The third was that a horrifyingly large proportion of the $160 million that One.Tel was owed by its customers appeared to be uncollectable.

The man who gave them this news, Mark Basman, One.Tel's head of collections, told colleagues he had laughed as he showed them the figures. When they asked him what he found so funny, he supposedly replied that he had tried to tell management for 18 months, but no one had listened.

One.Tel's appalling problems with bad debts were much older than this—in fact, they dated from its first year in business. The company had always been vulnerable to the fraudulent, freeloading end of the market because its controls were so feeble, but it had also targeted people to whom cost was paramount: people who struggled to make ends meet. The problem of these people not paying their bills had been made far worse by the introduction of cut-price local calls in November 1999, which had brought another wave of dodgy customers flooding in. For some extraordinary reason, Jodee and George Savva had decreed that One.Tel should not run credit checks on any of these new recruits, so the company had welcomed an army of rejects from Telstra, Optus and AAPT, who either couldn't or wouldn't pay their bills.

Before long, these recalcitrants were being chased by One.Tel's collections department, vividly described by an ex-One.Tel employee in his own unpublished version of the One.Tel Story:

> The collections area was the symbolic garbage dump of One.Tel . . . all the awful decisions in sales, marketing and credit control ended up in the filthy cesspit of collections. It was the collection team's role to chase the fringe dwellers, lowlifes, panhandlers, geriatric gypsies, crooks, beggars, hobos, scam artists, habitual pot smokers, drug addicts, ex cons, failed businessmen, bankrupts, caravan park visitors and any other person whom One.Tel had successfully cornered into this very low-end niche market. These were the same sparkling customers that management had been trumpeting only two, three or four months ago. Anyone who has worked in collections will recognise this variety of customer. One.Tel had far more than its fair share. Lots of these customers disappeared into the atmosphere with bogus names and a constantly

changing address . . . It was described as, 'like trying to catch a puff of cigarette smoke'.

One.Tel did its best to collect money from these people, and had a great system to deal with them. The first line of attack was to leave a message on their mobile phone, telling them their bill was unpaid. The next was to route them through to the collections department whenever they made a call. Shortly afterwards, they would be sent a letter from One.Tel's in-house debt collector, Stoner, Lee & Browning, which was named after the makers of several famous guns: Eugene Stoner was the father of the M16, James Paris Lee was responsible for the .303 rifle and John Moses Browning designed automatic pistols. It was a joke that caused no end of mirth to those at One.Tel who understood it.

Despite all these efforts, some of One.Tel's customers were never going to pay. Yogi Bear, Barney Rubble, Fred Flintstone, Homer Simpson and Astro Boy, who had all been allowed to open accounts with One.Tel and run up bills, were certainly going to prove hard to track down, particularly Mr Bear, whose address was recorded as 'Yellowstone National Park'.

The proper course of action with obvious non-payers was to write them off as bad debts, as any normal company would have done. But Yogi Bear and several of his fictitious friends remained on the debtors' ledger right to the end, suggesting that One.Tel had refused to give up hope of collecting their cash.

As one senior collections team member puts it: 'The bad debts were the ones that Jodee accepted could not be collected. The real figure was always higher. We might tell him that 95 per cent of a category was uncollectable, but he would say he wanted us to collect half of it. So only half would be counted as bad'.

One.Tel sorted its debtors into categories such as 'slow payer', 'final demand', 'summons served', 'bankrupt' and so on. One of these was 'returned mail', where the customer was thought to have done a runner. According to this team member, Jodee decreed that only half of these debts should be declared bad, because he was sure that One.Tel's staff had just got the addresses wrong. Jodee denied doing any such thing.

One.Tel's problem with bad debts became far more serious when the company's results were prepared in June and December, because all provisions and write-offs had to be subtracted from the company's profits or added to the company's losses. A $10 million provision would reduce the company's profits by that amount. Consequently, there was a huge incentive to bolster the figures, especially if promises had been made to the market about how much money One.Tel was going to make. According to One.Tel's unofficial historian:

Senior management would give out clear instructions to one or both of the collections team leaders

to change the profiles for a range of debtors in the worst categories to a profile that would be more collectable. In this way, the amount attached to each profile total would change. It could then be safely displayed to the auditors. Problem solved.

The effect of this exercise was to claim that debts were collectable when they almost certainly were not, so that One.Tel could report bigger profits (or smaller losses) to investors. Three senior people in One.Tel's collections department have subtly different stories of how this was achieved, but all agree that a huge pile of bad debt was swept under the carpet every year from June 1997 to December 2000. Each year, as the business grew, the amount had to be larger and the pile grew bigger. All three claim to have told Steve Hodgson, Mark Silbermann or Jodee Rich that they believed One.Tel's bad debt provisions and write-offs to be inadequate. Their concerns clearly fell on deaf ears. In fact, Jodee denies any warnings were given.

In January 2001, One.Tel's new auditors, Ernst & Young, also complained to One.Tel's senior management that the provisions for bad debts were too low (their working papers show they believed a further $17 million was required). They fought a brief battle to get these provisions increased but were assured by management that the money could be collected.

Such was the background as the Packer team now discovered, to their horror, that the real level of bad debt was far higher than One.Tel's accounts had suggested. One-third of the debts were over 330 days old, more than half were over 90 days old and almost half were already with debt collectors. As a result, Miller and Green believed, the company might be able to collect only $50 million of the $160 million it was owed. This would require a new provision of $50 million, which could be added to One.Tel's losses. Clearly, any forecasts of how much cash the company was likely to collect in coming months would also have to be revised downwards.

Miller and Green's bad news started flowing back to Packer HQ in the middle of the week following the 'rescue' announcement. On the morning of Thursday, 24 May, Peter Yates had breakfast at Sydney's Hilton Hotel with Chris Weston, the head of One.Tel's UK operations. Yates had been told by Jodee that the UK business was having trouble paying its creditors because European carriers had drastically tightened their credit terms. Weston explained that his real problem was that he had been forced to send £10 million ($25 million) to Australia at the beginning of March to ease One.Tel's cash crisis back home. He said he had agreed to do it on the basis that the money would be repaid by 1 May, but it had not been.

Till then Yates had thought One.Tel was just performing poorly and missing a few targets. Now he began to wonder whether the board and major shareholders had been lied to. He talked to Ashok Jacob, the head of the Packers' private company CPH, about Miller and Green's findings and then called a crisis meeting. On the afternoon of Friday, 25 May, he and Jacob met James Packer and his father in Kerry's Park Street bunker. They now knew that One.Tel would need much more than $132 million to stay afloat—perhaps even twice that amount.

They were faced with an unpalatable choice. On the one hand, they could go back to the Australian Stock Exchange on Monday morning saying they had been misled, and announce they were pulling out—which would mean taking some flak, looking stupid and risking legal action. On the other, they could throw an extra $100 million into One.Tel, persuade the Murdochs to do the same, and keep James's reputation intact. However, there was no guarantee that the new mobile network would not need more money further down the track.

It seems the decision was left to James, who had got them into this position and would be in the firing line if One.Tel collapsed. But it is hard to believe that Kerry put absolutely no pressure on him. At the end of a two-hour meeting, James apparently said they should cut their losses.

The first thing to do was tell Ian Philip, News Ltd's legal counsel. The next was to get hold of Lachlan, who was in Los Angeles. Sometime on Saturday, Australian time, Philip managed to get a two-page fax through to him. This did not raise the option of pulling out, but it warned that far more than $132 million could be needed to save the company and listed several reasons why. According to Philip:

The Australian fixed-wire business could be losing between $5 million and $10 million a month.

The UK business, while running well, needs $20 million to pay creditors by June.

The European business has creditors payable in the order of $20 million in the next month or so.

The French business is questionable and other European businesses are unlikely to be profitable.

The billing system does not work.

The remedy, Philip suggested, would be to close some of these businesses, which would involve more money for redundancies. They would also need a new billing system. In the meantime, there was an urgent need to inform the Australian Stock Exchange of the problems. They would also need to get legal advice 'in relation to claims against prior executive directors'. And here was the punch line. As Philip's fax put it:

It appears that the board papers may have intentionally misrepresented cash flows and profitability.

On Sunday morning, Lachlan flew into Sydney from Los Angeles, as he had planned to do for the premiere of

Head Over Heels, in which Sarah O'Hare was launching her movie career. It soon became clear he would be too busy to go to the cinema. He rushed back to his house in Point Piper for a meeting with James Packer and a squad of managers and lawyers from News Ltd and PBL. He was told that News Ltd and PBL might need to pump $300 million into One.Tel to keep it solvent, and that some of this money would have to be used to pay creditors, whose debts were already overdue. According to Lachlan's affidavit of 7 June 2001, this was the first warning he received that One.Tel was unable to pay its debts. It was important from a legal point of view that he should say this, because the Corporations Law carries stiff penalties for directors who allow their companies to continue trading while insolvent.

At 8.00am the next day, Lachlan, James and the rest gathered at Packer HQ for another emergency board meeting. The assembled company included eight directors, seven lawyers, five managers, three outside accountants and Brad Keeling by phone from New York. They were all now told that One.Tel would go bust unless a lot more money was put into the company immediately. The investigation by Miller and Green had revealed that One.Tel would have *minus* $11 million in the bank by the end of the month, and would continue to need between $15 million and $35 million a month after that. In addition, it would need to pay some debts, because more than $80 million were owed to creditors 'beyond normal credit terms'. It would also have to write off another $50 million owed to One.Tel by its customers, which was unlikely to be collectable. Miller and Green said they did not know exactly how much money would be needed to save the company, but it would be 'significantly in excess of $132 million'.

For the second time in a fortnight the ASX was asked to halt trading in One.Tel's shares, pending an announcement. There now seemed very little chance that the company would survive. The company's auditors, Ernst & Young, were given 24 hours to double-check the findings and see if anything had been missed. Another team was dispatched to look for ways to restructure the business, to see if anything could be sold to raise money and cut costs.

Meanwhile, Peter Yates and Peter Macourt were sent to offer Lucent a deal that would keep One.Tel's Next Gen business alive. They had been trying since 18 May to get the US company to help fund the rescue—without success—but were still hopeful that Lucent could be persuaded to kick the tin. It had already spent $650 million on building the new mobile network and had been unable to draw down a cent from the banks because One.Tel had refused to warrant that any part of the network was ready. Yates and Macourt told Lucent that PBL and News Ltd would accept that the network was complete—which would force the banks to hand over the $1.15 billion they had agreed to lend—and guarantee to stand behind it, as long as the Americans agreed to put in another US$75 million to help.

If Lucent said yes, it could have its money, plus a mobile network that was still on air. If it said no, it would miss out on $1.15 billion and be left with a bunch of near-worthless mobile towers and switches. Crucially, it would not have the licence it needed to operate Next Gen itself, because the $523 million worth of spectrum was held in a separate One.Tel company.

It seemed like an offer Lucent could not refuse, but unfortunately there was no goodwill left. The US network builder had been bashed over the head by One.Tel too many times already, and it was hard to get anyone to focus on the proposal in the 24 hours available. On the other side of the Pacific, on the east coast of the USA, a far bigger deal between Lucent and Alcatel was collapsing, and the company's entire energy was focused on preventing it. No one in New Jersey could be bothered about a US$75 million deal in a far-flung outpost like Australia.

The board meeting was due to reconvene at 4.00pm the next day, Tuesday, 29 May, but with the Lucent negotiations dragging on, there was a two and a half hour delay. This gave the lawyers an opportunity to work on the minutes of the 17 May board meeting to ensure they were full and accurate. If legal action were to follow these events it would be important to get the record straight.

When the meeting finally got going at 6.30pm the news was bleak. Yates reported that Lucent had declined to help. Brian Long of Ernst & Young then told them he believed One.Tel would need between $240 million and $370 million to stay alive for six months, by which time it might or might not be self-supporting. The company already had a $3 million unauthorised overdraft at the ANZ, which would blow out to $20 million by the end of the week. It would need $5 million immediately to pay Toronto Dominion Bank, or a $50 million loan would be called in. And since One.Tel was already in breach of its covenants, there was a risk the bank would demand the money anyway.

In these circumstances, the directors were advised that they risked prosecution if they incurred more debts on the company's behalf, because One.Tel was clearly insolvent. This left them two options: put in a couple of hundred million dollars to make it solvent again, or appoint an administrator to take over the company—and let the administrator sell whatever bits of it they could.

There was apparently no discussion about raising more than the $132 million already promised—and the corporate undertaker from Ferrier Hodgson, Steve Sherman, was already on hand to take over.

It felt to some as if it had all been choreographed, and it would be extremely surprising if it had not, as there was a whole raft of people who might be tempted to sue the Packers and Murdochs for failing to bail out the company. Hundreds of investors had bought One.Tel shares on the basis of the two mini-moguls' declaration that the company had a glorious future, and all would now lose their money. Creditors such as Telstra and Optus had also continued to supply the company on the assumption that Packer and Murdoch's support would ensure they were paid. Consequently, James Packer, Lachlan Murdoch, Peter Yates and Peter Macourt were careful to let the other board members make the decision to kill the company when the withdrawal of the $132 million rights issue was put to the vote.

The next morning a new round of press releases went out to announce that the rescue had been cancelled and administrators had taken over. It would be 'business as usual for staff and customers', said Sherman optimistically. 'One.Tel will continue to trade as a going concern.'

The statement from PBL and News Ltd made it quite clear that the $132 million offer had been withdrawn because the company was in a far worse financial position than they had been led to believe. It was 'not as reported to the board on May 17, nor at earlier board meetings, as they understood it'. Nor was there much doubt whom James Packer and Lachlan Murdoch blamed for this. Even though a joint statement named no names, it was pretty clear that they were accusing Jodee Rich and his fellow executives:

> Like all shareholders we are angry. We've been profoundly misled as to the true financial position of the company. We intend to explore all remedies available to us.

It was just like a replay of Imagineering 11 years before. There had been exactly the same assurances from Jodee that the company was fine, precisely the same promises of a glorious future and, finally, the same discovery, when the lid was lifted, that the company was a stinking mess. The only difference was that in One.Tel's case the White Knight was riding off.

Once again, it was left to Brad Keeling to break the news to the staff at One.Tel, who were shocked that their company was again in danger. He left a voicemail on everyone's phone summoning them to the 28th floor, where a couple of hundred people gathered to hear him. It was such a crush in the big L-shaped office that several people were turned away. Standing on a table so everyone could see and hear him, Keeling told them what a great contribution they had made to the company. He also promised to give back half his $7.5 million bonus (the tax man had the other half) to help pay their entitlements if One.Tel's administrator was unable to do so.

There was cheering and applause, but also a fair bit of muttering from the back row. Several of One.Tel's finance team and senior managers, who weren't keen on Brad anyway, knew there was very little risk he would have to pay up. Nevertheless, the next day the papers were full of the story, praising Keeling for his unstinting generosity, and calling on Jodee to do the same. It was a great PR victory for Brad and another setback for his supposed best buddy, with whom he was now barely on speaking terms.

Several times after 17 May, Jodee tried to ring Brad in the office to talk about rescuing the company. According to one close colleague, Brad shook visibly when he took these calls, and resented having to talk to him: 'He was angry and agitated. Jodee still believed he could get the company back. Brad had given up'. Before long, he was telling Jodee he couldn't talk about things anyway because his lawyers wouldn't let him.

Late on Friday, 1 June, two days after the news of One.Tel's collapse, teams of officers from the Australian Securities and Investments Commission (ASIC) and the Australian Federal Police raided the company's Sydney offices. They also descended on the homes of Rich, Keeling and Silbermann, delivering a warning to all three men that they were under the gun.

Even though the raids took place close to newspaper deadlines, the next day's *Australian Financial Review* carried extensive quotes from ASIC's chief, David Knott, who was obviously keen to get maximum publicity for the action. Knott told the paper that his investigators had already spoken to Lachlan Murdoch and James Packer, who had cooperated fully and given useful information. 'They obviously feel quite aggrieved by this', he said, suggesting he saw the two young tycoons as innocent victims. 'We are taking steps immediately to ensure we have access to all relevant records of the company. This is clearly a high priority for us.'

There would soon be more information leaking out. Within a couple of days the *Australian Financial Review* had managed to get hold of the search warrants, which showed exactly whom ASIC was chasing and what it was chasing them for:

> The investigations, which relate to possible criminal breaches of the Corporations Law, centre on former joint One.Tel managing director and founder, Mr Jodee Rich, and the company's finance director, Mr Mark Silbermann.
>
> It is understood that search warrants served by the Australian Federal Police on One.Tel sought evidence on whether Mr Rich had breached S999 of the Corporations Law by making statements or disseminating information that was false or misleading, and which induced people to buy One.Tel shares or to influence the One.Tel share price.
>
> The warrants also sought evidence on whether Mr Silbermann had breached S1307 of the

Corporations Law, which relates to falsification of books 'affecting or relating to the affairs of One.Tel'.

ASIC had heard rumours that One.Tel kept two sets of books and had been contacted by a couple of people who were keen to tell their One.Tel Story. It had also been given the layout of the finance area and told where key files could be found. That Friday, as the raids were taking place, a handful of senior people from One.Tel's finance team gathered for drinks in the Dendy Bar in Sydney's Martin Place. They soon started talking about how they had been asked to change figures. Then they got on to the subject of David Barnes and the blue file, which was locked in the top drawer of a desk on the 28th floor. One of the assembled company slipped away to the toilet for a minute and rang an ASIC investigator—who was at that moment raiding Silbermann's house—to make sure he knew where the file could be found.

These raids, with their suggestions of potential criminal activity by the One.Tel founder, gave the media an excuse to besiege Jodee's house in Vaucluse, and even to stick cameras on cranes so they could see through his windows. They were not the only ones getting in on the act. The Prime Minister, John Howard, told radio station 3AW in Melbourne that he hoped the book would be thrown at One.Tel's bosses—meaning Rich and Keeling. He then laid into them again on Channel 9's 'A Current Affair':

PRIME MINISTER: I think the thing that has really angered people in this situation are those bonuses. They were remarked upon as being extraordinary at the time . . . I mean most people who run companies are honest, straightforward, hard-working entrepreneurial people . . . But . . . these bonuses were $7 million apiece.

MUNRO: And you are calling on Jodee Rich and Brad Keeling to pay it back?

PRIME MINISTER: Yes I am.

The Treasurer, Peter Costello, and his Finance Minister, Joe Hockey, also threw a few well-aimed bricks despite the fact that the tax man clearly had no plans to return his share of the $6.9 million payments made to Rich and Keeling. Strangely enough, no one enquired whether the government might consider returning some of the $523 million it had received from One.Tel for spectrum in March 2000, now that it was no longer being used. A portion of this would have been quite effective in soothing the pain of a few small creditors.

Typically, Jodee Rich was baffled by all the kerfuffle and all this criticism. 'I am amazed that the Prime Minister thinks it's his business to attack me', he told me in late 2001. 'He's even criticised me for having two houses.' He then launched into a speech about how Australia was no good at business and did not value people like him.

But commentators everywhere were struggling to find something nice to say about Rich and his latest corporate catastrophe. Newspapers in the UK, the USA, France, Germany, Holland, Hong Kong, New Zealand, India and Thailand all focused their One.Tel coverage on the huge amounts of money that he and Brad had received from the company before the collapse. Had their journalists known about the two entrepreneurs' other nice little earners, such as the consultancy fees, the royalties, the sale of One.Net and One.Card, and the $62 million return of capital, they would have been even more outraged.

In their stead, the Communist Party of Australia had enough anger for everybody. According to its official *Guardian* newspaper:

> One.Tel is a story of corporate greed, corruption, insider deals, self-aggrandisement by company directors, betrayal of friends and most of all, complete disregard of the workers who made the wealth upon which company directors fed like pigs at a trough.

Within days of being appointed One.Tel's administrators, it was clear that Ferrier Hodgson had no chance of keeping the company trading normally. Steve Sherman had promised that it would be business as usual, but there was absolutely no cash in the bank to keep the company running, and $40 million would have been needed just to keep it going for a month. Worse still, Optus immediately terminated all its agreements with One.Tel and warned people they would be cut off within days. This prompted a wild scramble amongst the other carriers for One.Tel's mobile and fixed-wire customers, with all sorts of threats and special offers being used to induce them to switch. In the marketing war that followed, hordes of One.Tel's customers deserted to rival carriers; others took the opportunity to stop paying their bills. By 4 June, when the administrator produced his preliminary report to creditors, Sherman and his partner, Peter Walker, had already accepted that One.Tel would have to be broken into bits and sold off. By midnight on 5 June, Telstra had pulled the plug on One.Tel's Next Gen and fixed-wire customers, and by 8 June the internet service had also been cut off. By this time, deals had been done to sell off the entire Australian customer base.

On 8 June 2001, the bulk of the company's Australian employees were laid off. Brad Keeling went to each floor of the Castlereagh Street offices to thank people and bid them goodbye. Whether this was the selfless act of a decent man or a good PR strategy, who can say, but he was feted as he made his way through the building. 'It's been great', he told them all, 'I'm sorry it's over'. People were in tears, applauding him wherever he went; girls even asked him to sign their shirts. Till this point he had always played second fiddle to Jodee in One.Tel and remained distant from all but his immediate staff. Now he was emerging as the real dude of the duo. That evening the call centre staff had a party at the Hunter Hotel. When the DJ flashed up a picture of Brad everyone clapped and cheered. When he followed this with a picture of Jodee everyone booed.

Brad's tour of the building was over by late morning, and there was no point hanging around. Some went off to yum cha in Chinatown, others plundered the promotional gear in the basement, such as the lime-green T-shirts, golf umbrellas and seven types of One.Tel hat. One man had his eye on something special. For months he had been feeding a miniature shark in one of the big fish tanks. Fearing for its future—or fancying it for himself—he popped it into a wide-topped water bottle and took it home.

Ferrier Hodgson's switchboard was now besieged. For the next few weeks, One.Tel customers screamed or cried down the phone because they had been sent bills which they had already paid or because a dispute over payment had earned them a bad credit rating and stopped them getting a mortgage. Angry creditors called in too. One of the biggest was Roadhound, a Newcastle-based importer and wholesaler of mobile phones, which was owed $5.8 million. Roadhound had supplied 40 per cent of One.Tel's handsets until early 2001, when One.Tel had suddenly doubled the size of its order. Only after the crash did the company's owner, Ben Sharma, realise that his rivals had stopped dealing with Jodee and Brad's company because they were having trouble getting paid. He was told that his rivals' insurers had refused to keep insuring the debts.

Sharma was angry that others appeared to have known it was crook, and angry that the Packers' people had spent so much time in the company without warning anybody what was happening. Most of all, he was angry with Jodee and Brad, who had kept promising that everything would be fine. Much of what he would like to say can't be printed because of Australia's defamation laws, but the usable bits go like this: 'Jodee Rich and Brad Keeling should be hung, drawn and quartered. This is the second time they've done this . . . There's no way in the world I'll ever deal with them again, never, ever'.

Tech Pacific, which had risen from the wreckage of Imagineering in 1991, may well have wished it had also adopted this rule much earlier. As a supplier of mobiles to One.Tel, it stopped dealing with the company in March 2001 because its debt of $420,000 was overdue. It ended up losing this money.

The Packers and Murdochs, of course, were the biggest losers, dropping $375 million and $575 million respectively, although their shareholders would bear some of this pain. Several in the industry felt they had panicked and should have put in more money so it could be kept going long enough to sell, but the figures showed they had good reason to call a halt. The administrator's second report, published in mid-July, confirmed that One.Tel had survived by consuming bucket loads of other people's money. Since the beginning of 1999, when Australia's two biggest investment families had adopted the company amid so much excitement, One.Tel had gobbled up considerably more than $1 billion in cash. On day-to-day operations alone—that is, excluding investments in such things as spectrum—it had seen off $410 million. It had also, of course, caused Lucent to lose at least $650 million that it had spent on the Next Gen network, and had taken its creditors for a further $130 million.

Despite all this, Jodee had the gall to blame his backers for the demise of the company. It was their failure to put in another $132 million, he maintained, that caused One.Tel to collapse.

When I asked him in December 2001 what brought the company down, he told me: 'One.Tel lost the support of its major shareholders'. When I asked him why this was so, he said that a number of things went wrong in April and May 2001. He repeated his claims that there was $50 million to $60 million caught in the system and that European carriers had tightened their credit terms, and added that the computer running the UK billing system had been stolen. He again denied there were fundamental problems with the business.

'If we had a hiccup', he continued, and he clearly regards One.Tel's cash crisis as only a hiccup, 'I never thought we would lose the support of our major share-holders. It never occurred to me that if it took longer than expected to fix these things it would cause a fatality. Was it a mistake? Absolutely. Did I work hard to keep James Packer included? Yes. I had a false confidence that the shareholders were fully supportive'.

Thanks to this 'hiccup', the great business that One.Tel might have been vanished almost without trace. The UK operations fetched a reasonable price and are still going strong, but the other European businesses were either sold for a song or closed. Meanwhile, the entire Australian customer base, including 200,000-odd customers on the Next Gen network, went or was sold back to Telstra and Optus for a paltry $12 million. It had cost several hundred million dollars to acquire them, and they had never made a profit.

Those with long memories would recall that in early 2000 the UK company Vodafone had paid around $20,000 a head for customers of the UK mobile network Orange. It was a sign of how things had changed in just 16 months that One.Tel's mobile customers were now being passed on to its rivals for a princely $20 a pop, or one-1000th of what some people had been prepared to pay at the height of the boom.

The brand new Next Gen network was repossessed by Lucent, which finally managed to unload it in February 2002 to One.Tel's old rival, Hutchison Tele-communications. Exactly what Lucent got from this deal is not clear, but it certainly wasn't much. The new owners, meanwhile, landed one of the bargains of the new century: 'Lucent is not getting a dollar from us', Hutchison's new chief executive, Kevin Russell, boasted to journalists. A spokesman for Lucent added limply that his company had not lost on the deal.

18

The Blame Game

These matters are likely to
place the marriage under stress.

Jodee and Maxine Rich's financial agreement, May 2001

For someone who continually claimed that money did not matter, Jodee Rich had acquired an impressive array of valuable assets. He and his wife Maxine owned houses, apartments, land, boats, cars, paintings, furniture, a helicopter and a plane, which the Australian Securities and Investments Commission (ASIC) estimated to be worth some $40 million in total. And despite his professed lack of concern about such things, he was obviously prepared to go to great lengths to keep hold of them.

On 31 May, the day before ASIC's raids on his house in Vaucluse and One.Tel's Sydney offices, Jodee struck an agreement with Maxine under the *Family Law Act* to transfer virtually everything into her name. Thus, the

$6 million family home was passed over to her, complete with a promise that he would pay off the $3.7 million mortgage. She was also given the lion's share of Craigend, their unrenovated Darling Point mansion, which Jodee had bought in May 1999 for $14 million.

All the Riches' furniture, worth $338,000, and all their paintings, worth $562,000, including a Lloyd Rees, a Brett Whiteley and a John Olsen, were already Maxine's, as was their $150,000 Porsche 911 convertible, $309,000 in cash, a $650,000 apartment in Darling Point, shares worth $103,000 and Jodee's (or should one say, Maxine's?) offshore powerboat, *Plus One*.

The agreement, and other court documents filed by ASIC, made it clear that Jodee was also handing over to Maxine control of family companies or trusts that owned their hideaway in the Whitsundays, valued at $4 million, the Cessna Citation seven-seater jet, worth an estimated $10 million, the Eurocopter Jet six-seater chopper, worth $2 million and a souped up Holden Commodore. Another $2 million in the Jodee Rich Family Trust would take care of the 'education, main-tenance and advancement in life' of Maxine and Jodee's children. This appeared to be what remained of his $6.9 million bonus.

This left Jodee with half his two other powerboats, half the $1,387 he and Maxine had in a joint account, and a superannuation fund worth $380,000. His promise to pay Maxine an inflation-proofed $1,000 a week in perpetuity would be funded by money left from the sale of Craigend, after paying off the Vaucluse mortgage.

Now you might have thought that you could not make an agreement under the *Family Law Act* unless you intended to separate from or divorce your partner. But the Riches' lawyer, John Landerer CBE, AM, had clearly advised them it was worth a go. A carefully worded explanation of why it was necessary for Maxine to have her hands on the money went like this:

> Jodee's financial affairs have taken a significant turn for the worse, and his financial future is under a cloud. Maxine is concerned that her professional career as a lawyer and public company director may be significantly compromised as a result of the adverse change in Jodee's circumstances.
>
> Additionally, these matters are likely to place the marriage under stress.

Close friends who read reports of this phrasing were amazed that the Riches were even contemplating splitting up: they had been childhood sweethearts, were incredibly close and Maxine seemed devoted to Jodee. Strangely enough, the couple's personal PR man took this opportunity to inform the media that his clients had 'never been closer' and were 'inseparable'.

This no doubt reassured their families that all was well, but it left only one plausible explanation for the asset shuffle: that Jodee was trying to put everything out of the reach of One.Tel's creditors or anyone else who might come gunning for him. Remarkably, the experts reckoned this manoeuvre gave him a good chance of doing exactly that. While Australia's insolvency laws are designed to stop people dodging their debts, it is extremely rare for agreements under the *Family Law Act* to be overturned. At the very least it would be difficult and expensive for Rich's pursuers to get the money back, especially if it were transferred elsewhere.

However, Rich's chances of getting his assets out of harm's way were rapidly reduced by the intervention of ASIC, which was preparing to pounce on him even before news of his property transfers was splashed across the *Sydney Morning Herald*'s front page. Within hours of the headlines appearing, ASIC's counsel asked a New South Wales Supreme Court judge for an immediate order to prevent Jodee or Maxine moving their money offshore or, indeed, anywhere else in Australia.

In the words of Justice Austin, who agreed to freeze their assets for five days until proper arguments could be heard and to slap a $2,500-a-week limit on the Riches' spending:

> The evidence provides reasonable cause for apprehension that the first defendant [Jodee Rich] may have and may be in the course of transferring assets away in circumstances where creditors of the

One.Tel group and of the first defendant person-
ally may be prejudiced.

Justice Austin also ordered Rich to surrender his passport, lest he should decide, as the judge put it, 'to head
off to Majorca or something'. However remote the possibility, no one wanted Jodee to become another
Christopher Skase.

While Austin was delivering this judgment, one of
Sydney's best-known real estate agents, Bill Malouf, was
clinching the sale of Craigend for $16 million to Mel
Gibson's manager, Bruce Davey, who had flown in from
Los Angeles that morning to look it over. By 11.30 that
night, Rich and his lawyers were back in court for an
urgent special session, hoping to persuade the judge to
let the sale go ahead. The media-shy Mr Davey, who had
sent Mel into battle in *Braveheart*, had no desire to get
tangled up in a legal skirmish over Rich's riches. He had
insisted that he would pull out of the deal unless contracts
were exchanged by midnight. Some time in the early
hours of Saturday morning, after various assurances were
given, permission was given for the sale to go ahead.

Within a week, Rich, along with Keeling and
Silbermann, who were also in ASIC's sights, had given
an undertaking to the Supreme Court that made further
freezing orders unnecessary: they would give two weeks'
notice of any sales or transfers of assets, and of any plans
to leave the country. Consequently, ASIC did not need

to convince the judge that there was a prima facie case to be made against the three men over One.Tel's collapse, which was an essential prerequisite for getting the court to take such drastic action. Even so, Justice Austin agreed to make public several key affidavits from ASIC investigators and others, on which the commission was planning to rely.

For the next six months, these would be a valuable guide to the legal actions that One.Tel's various directors might face. The first affidavit, from One.Tel's joint administrator, Peter Walker, suggested the company might have been insolvent since the end of 2000. The second, from ASIC, alleged that Jodee had misled the market with his repeated promises that One.Tel would have $75 million in the bank at 30 June 2001. The third, from Lachlan Murdoch, echoed his earlier claim that he and James Packer had been 'profoundly misled' by One.Tel's management.

The allegations that One.Tel had continued to trade for several months while insolvent were capable of getting all the directors, including Lachlan Murdoch and James Packer, into trouble—and still are. This is because they can be made personally liable for any new debts One.Tel took on, if there were reasonable grounds at the time for thinking that the company would be unable to repay them. Ignorance of the company's financial position would not necessarily be a defence to such an action. Peter Walker, who is the joint liquidator of One.Tel now that it is being wound up, said in July that he believed the company probably became insolvent in March 2001, which would put potential damages in the range of $20 million to $80 million.

James Packer and Lachlan Murdoch are also at risk of being sued by the liquidator for not going ahead with the $132 million rights issue, and for failing to provide a $23 million bridging loan promised to the company on 17 May. There is a case for saying that both were assets of One.Tel on 29 May 2001, when it was placed in administration, because both had been pledged to the company without any conditions regarding its financial health. However, this is likely to be an alternative to any insolvency action, rather than an additional threat.

Whether either of these actions by the liquidator will go ahead depends on the outcome of a civil action brought against Rich, Keeling, Silbermann and One.Tel's chairman, John Greaves. In December 2001, ASIC sought orders from the New South Wales Supreme Court to ban all four men from managing or being directors of any Australian company. It also launched a $30 million to $50 million damages claim against them on behalf of One.Tel's creditors. ASIC's case is essentially that Rich, Keeling and Silbermann concealed the true state of One.Tel's finances from the board during the last few months of the company's life, while Greaves failed to show sufficient care and diligence in his role as director. If ASIC is able to convince the New South Wales

Supreme Court that Packer and Murdoch were denied crucial information, or misled about One.Tel's financial health, the two men would almost certainly have a reasonable defence to anything the liquidator is likely to throw at them.

As this book went to press, ASIC was busy redrafting and apparently expanding its statement of claim in preparation for another court hearing in March. The case is expected to come to trial sometime in the second half of 2002. Clearly, it involves high stakes for all concerned.

19

Rich Kids

Does it matter that I've lost a billion dollars?
Is that what's uppermost in my mind?
What pains me most about the whole One.Tel
saga is that my friendship with James Packer
has been destroyed.

Jodee Rich

Whatever the outcome of the various court cases, James Packer and Lachlan Murdoch do not emerge from the One.Tel saga as the brightest crayons in the box. In the space of just two years they managed to lose nearly $1 billion of their own or their shareholders' money. Yet they also managed to pull the plug on their new mobile network before it was fully operational, and long before it had any chance of making a profit. Having taken a dangerous gamble, they then lost their nerve.

Their argument that they were misled is hardly an adequate excuse. It certainly wasn't a secret that One.Tel was losing hundreds of millions of dollars and gobbling vast amounts of cash. It was also pretty obvious from the start that its backers would need deep pockets to take on the likes of Telstra and break into such a lucrative market. Most of all, it was evident to several people back in October 2000 that the company was likely to run out of money by mid-2001.

One option would have been to pull out then. Another would have been to put in new management. A third would have been to pump in more funds. By the time that James and Lachlan got round to considering these choices, the pressure had increased, they had lost another $200 million, and it was all too hard.

Investors knew One.Tel was in strife months before Packer and Murdoch forced a showdown. So did One.Tel's rivals, customers, head-hunters and the Telephone Industry Ombudsman, to name but a few. So, dare I say, did the financial press. The dogs barked loud and long about this company, and one had to be a supreme optimist to believe Jodee's promises that it was all going to turn out fine. But optimists they certainly were.

An experienced Australian finance director who rejected an offer to run One.Tel's finances in late 2000 says he knew the company was doomed as soon as he walked in the door. 'You could tell just by asking the right questions', he says. 'For example, "What's happening with the cash? Is the company generating enough cash to keep the business going?".' He adds: 'You have to wonder about the Packer people who went in there and had a look around. How the hell didn't Kleemann know what was going on?'.

An outside contractor who worked with One.Tel on a regular basis from 1998 also reckoned it was easy to see the place was a mess: 'It was dreadfully mismanaged, and it was obvious to anyone with an IQ of more than 80 that it wasn't right. You could have seen it in half an hour. I simply don't understand why Packer and Murdoch couldn't spot it'.

One possible explanation is that these two famous rich kids are not as brilliant as their wealth would suggest. Another may be that they refused to listen to warnings. Just two months before One.Tel went down, James Packer sacked his top man at PBL, an experienced, hard-nosed manager called Nick Falloon who was known to dislike Rich and had often expressed doubts about One.Tel. Falloon's crime appears to have been that he didn't share James's new-economy, hi-tech vision. He favoured companies that made profits, produced cash and did not need to be fed hundreds of millions of dollars while one waited for the promoters' promises to come true. Falloon was conservative and sceptical, and was cut out of the loop on One.Tel long before he was cut off.

James Packer, on the other hand, was the truest of true believers. As One.Tel's market value drew close to matching that of the entire Packer empire, one of Kerry's friends claims to have received regular calls from James boasting about the money he was making, and chiding those who had doubted him. One.Tel, it seems, was James's evidence he could match his father and make millions of his own. Then, when the share price fell, James apparently refused to consider that he might be wrong. He continued to hail Jodee as a 'visionary' and a brilliant manager, long after it was clear to others that the company was a basket case.

When One.Tel did collapse James took it incredibly hard. For several weeks he disappeared from the Sydney scene and went to Europe. Many reported that he was seriously depressed; some said he had been banished by Kerry; some even suggested he was talking of suicide. Whatever the truth of these various rumours, it is clear he was doing it tough. James is well liked by those who deal with him and is widely regarded as a decent, honest man, but one former adviser has this to say about him: 'James admires people who have made millions: players, movers and shakers. His motto is, "Whoever dies with the most money wins". He's very immature and he's terrified of his father, desperate to impress him. Kerry can still make him crumble. It is fascinating that he has buckled emotionally over One.Tel. Here's someone who can be quite brutal with other people and he's just buckled'.

Several people describe One.Tel as a power play between father and son—which Kerry eventually won. But even without this dynamic, James's close friendship with Jodee would have made it extremely hard for him to move from being a believer in the One.Tel Story to being a non-believer. It would have been almost as difficult as leaving a cult.

Jodee Rich is a world champion optimist, a powerful and dominating person, and an absolute master of the Blizzard of Hope. He has the capacity to obscure all but the sharpest doubts, and I suspect that James Packer, for all his money and power, was never his match. My own contact with Jodee has been confined to the period since One.Tel collapsed, by which time he had lost around $2 billion of other people's money. When I talked to him, he was being chased by ASIC and pilloried in the press, yet he was still utterly convinced that One.Tel was a brilliant business. Had the company been alive and kicking, with some chance of his forecasts still coming true—as it was from October 2000 to April 2001—I can see it would have been extraordinarily difficult to persuade him that radical changes were needed.

Lachlan Murdoch, who was far more distant than James, might well have been able to tackle Jodee, precisely because he was not so emotionally committed. But he was hardly ever there. Lachlan has been a background figure in this book, because that's all he ever was at One.Tel. His affidavit of June 2001 claims, somewhat surprisingly, that he relied on James Packer to tell him whether News Ltd's $575 million investment was going OK. This is also the impression that Jodee gives of

Lachlan's role: he claims it was hard to get him to take an interest, hard to get him to return phone calls, and hard to get him involved.

One would-be finance director at One.Tel recalls asking Jodee about the two heirs' participation in the business. According to this well-known, well-respected executive, Jodee told him: 'I talk to James quite a bit, but Lachlan doesn't know what's going on, and he doesn't attend board meetings'.

Lachlan's affidavit hums a similar tune. He claims, for example, that his first warning of One.Tel's potential financial troubles came on 1 May 2001, when James Packer called to tell him the business needed more money. If this was the first time he really considered the dangers it shows an extraordinary lack of awareness of One.Tel's problems. This was a business that had the capacity to consume horrific amounts of cash—it was growing fast, paying up to $600 to acquire each new mobile customer, and tweaking the tail of two powerful rivals who were bound to defend their territory.

But even if Lachlan did not understand this (and he surely did) the figures were already showing that money was fast running out. The cash reports to Geoff Kleemann, which Lachlan could have seen, or demanded from One.Tel himself, showed the company's cash reserves were down to $35 million by mid-March and down to $25 million by mid-April. Given that the company had consumed $310 million in nine months, this was surely enough warning that all was not well.

At News Ltd's annual general meeting in October 2001, Lachlan's father Rupert was at pains to emphasise to shareholders—who footed most of the bill for this escapade—that he shared the blame on One.Tel. Thinking in US dollar terms, perhaps, or just a bit vague about anything less than $1 billion, he said: 'You know, it's never nice to lose $300 million. It's a *mea culpa*. We shouldn't have done it, I guess. Or we should have taken more efforts to protect it once we were in. But, you know, it's part of our learning experience, I guess, and compared to some of the wins we've had this year it's not of great significance'.

Maybe $575 million is not of great significance to the Murdochs and their shareholders, but it is staggering that a company could risk so much money and take so little care. One seasoned investor's reaction to the One.Tel collapse in June 2001 was to say that the Packers' and Murdochs' mistake was not to have their own finance director looking after their investment. This was a conclusion Rupert also reached, but only when it was too late and the money was lost. Without one's own finance director it is hard to be sure that proper systems are in place, let alone have confidence that the figures are right.

Those who know Lachlan say he is more like his mother than his father—which is what they also say

about James Packer. He is less aggressive, more intel-
lectual, somewhat Presbyterian. According to his close
friend George Betsis, who is one of Sydney's top advertising men, 'He is not overawed by his destiny. He was
born to rule and has been groomed for it all his life'. He
is also tough and determined, says Betsis, with 'a quiet
intensity to succeed. He doesn't have much tolerance for
failure. He can be very black and white about it'. Hence
his insistence that Jodee and Brad had to go.

Not everyone is impressed by Lachlan's business
acumen. One top corporate adviser who has worked
with him several times describes him disparagingly as
being 'soft left, with a touchy-feely view of the world
that doesn't really fit with his role'. Another management expert, who knew him well in the late 1990s, felt
he would have been happier as a forester. Neither
thought him a natural. And neither rated him as highly
as James Packer.

Nor is Lachlan's track record in business all that
inspiring. The push into Super League in Australia, which
is said to have been his idea, was a disaster that cost the
Murdochs close to $300 million. The internet auction
site GoFish has also come to grief.

As to whether the One.Tel loss will do his prospects
harm, who knows? The Murdochs are a close family
and Rupert is extremely supportive: they are said to talk
daily and often at length. But some believe Lachlan only
has power in News Ltd because of his relationship with

his father, rather than his own talent and authority. And with Rupert showing no signs of abdicating, Lachlan may find himself in the same position as Prince Charles: first in line for succession but in grave danger of missing out. One investment banker who knows the Murdochs well says tartly: 'If I were a betting man I would be having a wager on Wendi Deng. She's ambitious and clever. I wouldn't underestimate her'.

There can't be much doubt that James Packer will take over from Kerry as the head of the Packer empire, even though several who know him insist there have been times when he has worried about being disinherited. But we won't see Kerry crying *mea culpa* over One.Tel like Rupert did, and he is rumoured not to be quite so supportive. One probably apocryphal story has James asking his father what his punishment will be for squandering so much of the family's money, to which Kerry's supposed reply was: 'I'm not going to die yet'.

Shareholders of PBL must wish Kerry would stay alive forever. His instincts on One.Tel were absolutely right: it ran out of cash, just as he feared. Weeks after the collapse, he was said to be skipping in to work, in a better mood than anyone could remember. 'He's as happy as a sandboy', one investment banker observed. 'It has put five years on his life, because it has shown him he's needed.' Insiders at Packer HQ insist he has been generous and gentle with James, and is at his best in a crisis. 'He's happy when things go wrong, because he can do something about it. When things are going well, he's worried that they're about to turn bad', says one.

While James was off the scene—banished or on holiday—Kerry was quick to reassure investors that he was in charge again. In mid-June 2001 he invited a small group of analysts and fund managers to lunch in Sydney's Channel 9 boardroom. Wearing a hearing aid, but looking better than he had at his brother Clyde's memorial service a month earlier, he told his audience he had been in semi-retirement for a few years and had been happy to leave the running of the company to others. But now he was back.

As they tucked in to smoked salmon and lamb roast, Kerry sipped at his mineral water and smoked the odd cigarette. One of his guests thought him 'mentally very sharp, in great form, very across the issues', and felt he was enjoying himself. Only once was the awkward subject of One.Tel mentioned. 'It was a fuck up', Kerry told them bluntly. 'There won't be any more One.Tel's.' They would concentrate on businesses that produced cash and made real profits, and not stray into areas they knew nothing about. When asked where he thought he would be in one year's time, he quipped, 'Well I hope I am still alive'.

But when PBL's annual results were published in August 2001, the great man was suddenly nowhere to be seen. It was left to a pale-looking James to explain to analysts how the family's public company had managed to plunge into the red for the first time in living memory.

It was also his task to assure the world that he and Dad had never been closer. When the meeting was over, he stumbled out of the Hilton Hotel, looking dazed and miserable. He waited in vain for his colleagues to join him, then struck off up the street on his own, pursued by a photographer and a couple of camera crews. After two blocks he stopped abruptly, turned on his heel and retraced his steps, having woken up to the fact that he was heading in the opposite direction to his office.

The collapse of One.Tel was not only tough on Australia's two most famous rich kids. It was also hard on employees, shareholders and creditors of the company, who lost jobs, money and businesses. It was difficult, too, for that other rich kid, Jodee Rich, who was brought down to earth with a spectacular crash for the second time in his business career. Some may feel he deserved it, because there is compelling evidence of a culture of hype, exaggeration, poor management and downright lying at One.Tel for which he was ultimately responsible. But it was his vision that started One.Tel and his passion that almost made it a permanent part of the Australian landscape. Had the sale to Sonera gone through in September 2000, or had Jodee been smart enough to admit earlier that his company was running out of cash, this might have been a very different story. Unfortunately for Jodee, losers don't get to write history.

Many who worked for One.Tel will remember it as the best fun they have had in their working life, as many from Imagineering still do. At his best, Jodee was a great motivator and team builder. At his worst, he insisted everyone do as he said and brooked no argument. Sadly, his greatest strength was also his weakness: entrepreneurs need to ignore warnings from people who tell them things can't be done or they will never take risks; but managers of big, complex companies like One.Tel can't afford to ignore all the advice they are given.

According to Jodee, he has not spoken to his former good mate James Packer since 29 May 2001, the day the corporate undertakers were called in. A few months later the two men ran into each other in Martin Place and mumbled a few awkward pleasantries, but that is all. Jodee claims to be more hurt by this than he is by the demise of the company they dreamed of. 'Does it matter that I've lost a billion dollars?' he asked me during one of our conversations. 'Is that what's uppermost in my mind? What matters to me are relationships. What pains me most about the whole One.Tel saga is that my friendship with James Packer has been destroyed. I was closer to James than I have ever been to any man', he tells me. 'That's what matters. That and the angst this has caused my family.'

Jodee's claim that money matters little to him may soon be tested. The proceedings brought by ASIC will cost millions of dollars to defend and will cost him millions more if he loses. One should also note that while he may be considerably poorer than he was in November 1999, he and his wife Maxine are still sitting on at least $40 million made from One.Tel while the going was good. Keeling, Silbermann, Greaves, Adler and Beck managed to make fortunes too, along the way, from bonuses, royalties or selling shares.

Of course, Rich also escaped with millions from the wreckage of Imagineering in 1990 after causing those who backed him to lose so much. In this sense he is the classic entrepreneur: he placed huge bets with other people's money, and ensured he was first in line to pick up the rewards. In the case of One.Tel, the total net loss suffered by investors, creditors and suppliers amounts to some $2 billion—excluding the very considerable losses suffered by people who bought shares on the stock market and saw their value disappear. The accounts suggest that Rich and Keeling collected almost $115 million between them from One.Tel in the company's short life, the bulk of which would have gone to Rich.

One person who worked alongside the two men at the top of One.Tel and was one of their most loyal colleagues, is disgusted at how Jodee 'feathered his own nest'. Another, who worked for a big institution that backed Rich in Imagineering and One.Tel, is just as disillusioned: 'He took no risk and got all the rewards. Everyone else lost, but Jodee's rich. He's just too smart'.

Typically, Jodee's answer is that he could have made even more money if he had wanted to. He likes to remind people that he did not sell a single share in One.Tel. Naturally, he does not advertise the numerous other ways in which he took millions of dollars out of the company.

Hanging on to his fortune—if he does—will undoubt-edly compensate for the damage to Rich's reputation from the One.Tel collapse. Meanwhile, he continues to protest that he has done nothing wrong and is in no way to blame. Despite two corporate catastrophes he appears to have learnt little or nothing, and least of all humility.

Of course, it is a thin line between self belief and self delusion, and many of those who supported Jodee at One.Tel believe that he has crossed it. Typically, the man himself remains as optimistic about the future as he always was in business. Only once did he admit to me that he was deeply depressed about it all. He was talking about suing Murdoch and Packer—for what I'm not quite sure—and musing about how quickly it had all fallen apart. 'If you had been writing this three months ago, it would have been such a wonderful story, such a success story', he said, wanly. 'That's life, I suppose.' He looked like a man who was at last waking up to the fact that his world had been shattered.

Many months and many meetings later, he was itching to have his day in court, and confident he could clear his name. It will be fascinating to see how he goes, to see if he can sell the One.Tel Story to a judge as bril-liantly as he sold it to James Packer, Lachlan Murdoch, Bankers Trust, stock market analysts and, for a time, just about everyone else.

I have to say, and you may have guessed this already, he did not quite sell it to me.

Epilogue

TeleOne

I wouldn't touch them with a bargepole.

One.Tel creditor asked if he would deal with TeleOne

In February 2002, Jodee's two most trusted lieutenants, Mark Silbermann and Kevin Beck, announced they would be back in business by April with a company called TeleOne, selling long-distance and international telephone services at rock-bottom prices. The new outfit will have a remarkably similar logo to One.Tel, and its name is almost identical. It will use One.Tel assets, snapped up at bargain prices, and will employ several of the old company's former staff. It will even have the dude's dad and sister as its mascots, thanks to Adam Long, Jodee Rich's erstwhile brother-in-law, who has agreed to create them for the new company. It will not, of course, have to pay any of One.Tel's debts.

Whether the new venture can succeed where One.Tel failed, only time will tell, but Australia's two major carriers immediately said they would not be doing business with Jodee's acolytes in any incarnation. 'We would not be leaping into bed with them again', an Optus spokesman told *The Australian*.

'Have they no shame?' a Telstra official inquired, adding, 'They have got Buckley's, because of the obvious link with the company that owed us money'.

Plenty of One.Tel's creditors have vowed to boycott the business. Ben Sharma, the owner of Roadhound, who is owed more than $5 million for mobile phones his company supplied and was not paid for, could barely contain his fury when he heard the news. 'I think it should be illegal', he told me angrily. 'We certainly won't be dealing with them in any shape or form, and I will be advising everyone else in the mobile industry to steer clear of them too.' This probably won't bother Beck and Silbermann, as TeleOne will not be trying to get back into the mobile business. Nor will it be offering local calls, which lost so much money for One.Tel, the company that crashed with them at the wheel.

But TeleOne's dynamic duo may still find friends are scarce. Allied Express, a privately owned courier company in Bankstown, which is owed $224,000 from the collapse of One.Tel, has sworn it will have nothing to do with them. 'I think it's disgraceful', said credit manager Graham Farrell. 'They just pick themselves up, dust themselves off like nothing has happened and start all over again.' Asked whether Allied would do business with TeleOne, he said, 'Absolutely not. I wouldn't touch them with a bargepole'.

Customers may be happier about giving Beck and Silbermann a second go, mainly because they won't have to risk their money as creditors do, but there are plenty of angry punters who feel that One.Chance is enough for Jodee and his boys. The vast majority of people who emailed the *Sydney Morning Herald*'s website after the news was announced expressed scorn or amazement, or a mixture of the two. 'What a joke', one wrote. 'I was a One.Tel customer, and it was the most pathetically run company I have ever used. Let's reward the dodgy bastards by letting them do it all over again to another database of customers.'

'I cannot believe that they are allowed to be back in business', wrote a former One.Tel employee. 'Some staff are going back, I cannot believe that some people are so stupid.'

'What consumer in their right mind would join TeleOne after seeing One.Tel's spectacular flop last year?' another asked.

'Absolutely opposed to any of these people being allowed to operate in managerial capacity in any business ever again', a fourth contributed. 'They burnt a lot of people with their cavalier actions. Don't let them do it again!'

As this book rolled off the presses, TeleOne was busy fitting out new offices in Sydney's Macquarie Street with some of the gear that once made One.Tel staff feel at home. In December 2001, Kevin Beck spent $123,000 at auction on flat-screen monitors, timber desktops, chairs, filing cabinets and computers that had previously graced One.Tel's Castlereagh Street HQ. He even purchased some of the famous fish tanks, which suggests that he, Silbermann, or their unidentified backers, are feng shui believers. More importantly, the new company bought some of One.Tel's Summa4 switching equipment, which was vital in running a telephone business. Needless to say, it picked up this stuff at a fraction of its original cost.

Beck and Silbermann say that the new business is owned by their families—or family trusts—but they are coy about whether anyone is backing them. They have told prospective recruits, in confidence, that TeleOne has $3 million in the bank, and that Jodee Rich is ready to support the company if necessary. Silbermann also told me that the business was funded by 'private equity', whose source was confidential. When I asked whether that meant someone apart from the Beck and Silbermann families, he said: 'No comment'. Interestingly, the registered office of TeleOne Pty Ltd is an accounting firm called Stirling, Warton, Williams, whose principal, John Warton, was auditor of Imagineering in the 1980s. Nowadays, Warton acts as an accountant to Jodee Rich's private companies. Since 2000, he has also acted for Mark Silbermann.

When I asked Jodee Rich in February 2002 whether he was financing TeleOne, he told me that he was not, but had 'steered them towards people who could'. He admitted that he had given Beck and Silbermann advice and would like to be involved in TeleOne 'sometime in the future, if there is an opportunity . . . if my name is cleared'.

It would have been hard for Rich to deny any link. In my meetings with him in late 2001 it became pretty obvious that he was well informed about the new venture. He, Beck and Silbermann were working out of adjacent offices at Ebsworth and Ebsworth, the law firm Jodee uses, in the Glasshouse building in Sydney's King Street, and were frequently on the phone to each other. It appeared that when Jodee called, Beck and Silbermann would come.

Of course, there is no legal reason why Jodee Rich should not be involved in a reprise of One.Tel, even if it does use the company's former assets and trade on its name. He is entitled to be a director of an Australian company unless or until a court rules he cannot, as are Silbermann and Beck. But in light of Jodee's reluctance to be in the thick of it, it is a trifle surprising that his close colleague and co-defendant in the ASIC action, Mark Silbermann, has no qualms.

Silbermann says he will not be a director of the new business but admits he will be involved in managing it. When I asked Kevin Beck what would happen if his partner were to be banned from any involvement in TeleOne, he said: 'We will just have to take it from there'.

On the day of TeleOne's launch, it was Silbermann who fielded most of the questions from the press. On ABC Radio's *AM* program, he was asked by Narelle Hooper: 'How can you justify setting up a new business when your previous activities in One.Tel are still under investigation and indeed ASIC is seeking to have you disqualified as a director?'. Silbermann replied: 'I don't feel responsible in any way for the demise of One.Tel. I think people should look to the major shareholders for that'.

It had a familiar ring to it. Clearly, One.Tel's former finance director thinks that the collapse of the company was not his fault either.

The One.Tel Story in Brief

1 February 1960: John David ('Jodee') Rich is born in New York.

1963: Rich family moves to Sydney. Jodee goes to school at Cranbrook, where he meets Rodney Adler. At 12, Jodee starts his own business, JDR Fisheries, selling tropical fish and leasing aquariums.

8 September 1967: James Douglas Packer is born. He is also educated at Cranbrook.

1978: Jodee studies medicine at Sydney University then switches to economics and law. He and Rodney Adler trade gold together, and write trading software for banks and brokers. Jodee eventually buys Adler out.

1981: Jodee sets up Imagineering. It is part of Studio Australia, a company started by Jodee's father Steven in 1968. Imagineering begins as an Apple retailer, but changes to being a wholesaler of software for IBM, Apple and Commodore, mainly for business customers.

1983: IBM Personal Computer launched in Australia. Imagineering's sales take off.

1984: Imagineering now services 1,500 computer dealers in Australia and has operations in New Zealand. It wins exclusive rights to distribute Lotus software. It has lost money in its first three years but now has annual sales of $10 million and a profit of $500,000.

1985: Imagineering opens offices in Hong Kong, Singapore and Los Angeles. It employs 100 people and claims to be supplying software to 50 per cent of the Australian market. Its sales are now $26 million, and its profit has doubled to $1 million. It is floated on the Australian Stock Exchange (ASX) at $12 million. The float raises only $4.8 million in cash—paid to the Rich Family Trust—because the Riches hang on to 60 per cent of the shares. The offer price is 50 cents a share; net tangible assets are only 3 cents; the rest is 'goodwill'.

1986: Sales almost double to $48 million. The company opens offices in Wellington, Brisbane and Taipei, and expands in Sydney, Melbourne, Hong Kong and Los Angeles.

1987: Sales almost double again to $89 million. Imagineering is now selling its own Ultra PC to Grace Bros, Myer, Kmart, Dick Smith and dealers, and there is a huge backlog of orders. A rights issue raises $8.6 million to fund further expansion. Jodee marries Maxine Brenner, his childhood sweetheart.

1988: Sales more than double to $196 million. A rights issue raises $17 million to fund yet more growth. Bankers Trust puts in $6 million on top of this at $1.50 a share. Offices open in Bangkok, Manila, Seoul, Jakarta, Adelaide, Canberra and Perth. Warehouse space in Sydney is tripled to handle booming PC sales. Debt rockets. Interest rates begin to rise.

March 1989: The market is worried because Imagineering has so much debt. Its shares dive. By August, they are down from nearly $2.00 to 65 cents.

May 1989: Half-year results claim a $2 million profit—up 46 per cent. Small print shows that Imagineering has made a loss. Press release headed 'Continued growth in first half' suggests all is fine.

July 1989: Imagineering puts its year-end back four months, from August to December.

September 1989: Imagineering tells ASX it is negotiating with a potential investor. Shares now 45 cents. Debt mounting. Interest rates still climbing.

October 1989: Hong Kong-based company First Pacific rides to the rescue with $18 million cash, buying roughly one-quarter of Imagineering. Jodee and Steven Rich pick up $3 million of this in a share buyback. They promise the company will make a small profit—up to $4 million—for the year to August. Soon afterwards, Imagineering announces it has made just over $1 million.

November 1989: The profit suddenly becomes a loss of $4 million. First Pacific's accountants have uncovered millions of dollars of expenditure that has been im-properly deferred. Jodee and Steven Rich agree that Imagineering will pay $3 million compensation to First Pacific.

March 1990: Imagineering is in far worse condition than Jodee and Steven Rich have admitted. Results for the 16 months to December show the company's loss is a dreadful $52 million. It has been forced to write off $10 million for bad debts and obsolete stock, and $14 million of 'goodwill'. The accounts get a 'going concern' qualification, which means that the company will be insolvent unless it gets more money from First Pacific and the banks. Jodee tells shareholders that Imagineering is returning to profitability, and that he and First Pacific are getting on famously. In fact, Imagineering is still losing money, is forecast to lose more, and First Pacific has come close to pulling out.

July 1990: Shares are now priced at 12 cents. The ANZ Bank has called in its $38 million loan, and covenants are being breached on loans from the Commonwealth Bank and Westpac, who will pull out too unless First Pacific pumps in another $20 million. An extraordinary general meeting is called to approve a refinancing arrangement that would hand control to First Pacific. Accountants Arthur Andersen tell shareholders to accept or get a maximum of 3 cents a share from a break-up of the company. The refinancing is approved; the Riches lose control.

September 1990: Jodee and Steven Rich are tossed off the board. Jodee goes skiing in the USA and Europe.

February 1991: Imagineering reports another thumping loss of $41 million. By now it has cut staff to 150 from the original 390, shut down its Taiwan computer factory, closed offices and warehouses, and written off a huge amount of obsolete stock.

May 1991: First Pacific privatises Imagineering at 10 cents a share, giving shareholders one-80th of what they paid at the top of the market and one-60th of what Bankers Trust paid in October 1988. An expert report values the shares at *minus* 93 cents, and warns that more losses are on the way. The Riches get 12 cents a share, for a total of $417,600, cashable in April 2001. Jodee has managed to hang on to another $8 million he took out when the going was good.

November 1991: A telecommunications licence is issued to Optus—to operate a mobile and fixed-wire network—breaking Telecom's monopoly of the Australian market.

December 1992: Vodafone is awarded a mobile licence, so there are now three networks.

1994: There are 1 million mobile phone users in Australia, double the previous year.

August 1994: Jodee Rich and Imagineering's former head of marketing, Brad Keeling, decide to start a telephone company 'for normal people'.

September 1994: Bob Mansfield at Optus promises support. So does Jodee's friend Rodney Adler. Rich starts working on a business plan.

February 1995: Optus and Adler's FAI agree to back the new venture, putting in $1.5 million and $950,000 respectively for 28.5 per cent and 18 per cent of the shares. The company will resell Optus mobile services under the brand name 'One.Tel', and pick up $120 in cash from Optus for every customer it signs up. James Packer puts in $250,000 for nearly 5 per cent of the shares. One.Tel's controlling shareholder, Kalara Investments, has around 50 per cent. The bulk belong to Jodee Rich, the balance to Keeling.

April 1995: Keeling sues his former employer, Strathfield Car Radios, in the Federal Court. He had been dismissed from the company in February.

1 May 1995: One.Tel is launched by Rodney Adler. Jodee promises low rates, simple tariffs and one bill for all phone services. There will be no hierarchies, flat management structures, and staff will be encouraged to 'lie on the grass'.

25 May 1995: Strathfield files a cross claim in the Keeling case, alleging fraud.

June 1995: One.Tel has 1,000 customers. Australia-wide there are 2 million mobile phone users, double the previous year.

September 1995: One.Tel has 10,000 customers. Optus starts charging a connection fee to One.Tel, which it has to pass on to customers.

November 1995: Keeling charged with cheating and defrauding Strathfield Car Radio by obtaining bank cheques.

January 1996: Optus forms a new wholesale division. Its boss, Andrew Bailey, is shocked by the generous deal given to One.Tel. His boss, Phil Jacobs, seeing it for the first time, says: 'Shit, we have a problem'. Optus starts trying to get some of its money back.

March 1996: One.Tel has 50,000 customers. Optus sends a letter to One.Tel saying the 1995 deal is too good and it wants to renegotiate.

May 1996: Keeling faces committal in Sydney court on fraud charges. The matter is adjourned.

June 1996: One.Tel's sales reach $65 million, with profits of $3 million before tax.

September 1996: Keeling committal resumes. Magistrate finds that no jury could find beyond reasonable doubt that Mr Keeling had an intention to cheat and defraud Strathfield. One.Tel now has 100,000 customers.

October 1996: Optus sells its One.Tel shares back to the company for $4 million and pays One.Tel compensation of $19.75 million for ending the $120 loyalty payments. With a larger share of the company, the remaining shareholders, including Rich, Keeling, Packer and Adler, are $15.75 million richer. With the valuable Optus bonuses withdrawn, One.Tel now begins to gobble cash.

April 1997: One.Tel launches its One.Net internet service.

June 1997: In its second year, One.Tel's sales have more than doubled to $148 million. It makes a profit of $7.5 million before tax, but only because money from the $19.75 million Optus settlement is still being fed into the company.

July 1997: The telecommunications market in Australia is deregulated. Anyone can now be a carrier.

August 1997: One.Tel starts offering long-distance and international calls. It now has almost 300 staff.

November 1997: One.Tel is floated on the ASX at $2 a share, valuing the company at $208 million. Only $1 million is raised because it is hard to find investors. On paper, Rich and Keeling's stake is now worth $136 million, FAI's $51 million, and James Packer's $17 million.

One.Tel's directors have granted themselves 15 million options, exercisable at 12.6 cents a share, giving them a potential windfall of $28.1 million. In two years' time, the share price and potential gain will have risen 12-fold. Rich and Keeling are in line for $7.5 million apiece; One.Tel's new chairman, John Greaves, former finance director of Optus, is in line for $6.25 million; Rodney Adler for $4.4 million; Mark Silbermann and Kevin Beck (senior One.Tel executives) for $1.25 million.

One.Tel has also paid $2.85 million in consultancy fees to Rich, Keeling, FAI and James Packer, plus $4 million in dividends to the original shareholders, including $2.5 million to Rich and Keeling via Kalara, $941,000 to FAI and $198,000 to James Packer.

Rich, Keeling, FAI, James Packer, John Greaves and Kevin Beck have also retained the rights to two businesses, One.Net and One.Card, from which they will derive substantial royalties. The companies are sold back to One.Tel in July 1998 for $16.9 million.

January 1998: One.Tel launches a 'Global Strategy' to expand into Europe and the USA.

June 1998: One.Tel opens an office in Los Angeles.

August 1998: One.Tel records a profit of $8.8 million before tax, but only by feeding in the $19.75 million from Optus's compensation settlement. It has burnt $8 million cash on its day-to-day operations and spent a further $10.7 million on investment. It has raised more money by issuing new shares to American investors, Coldstream Partners.

One.Tel opens offices in London, followed by Paris, Hong Kong, Amsterdam and Zürich.

September 1998: One.Tel buys mobile spectrum in Adelaide, Brisbane, Melbourne, Perth and Sydney for

$9.5 million. It has always promised it won't own a network, but now it announces it will build one at a cost of hundreds of millions of dollars.

November 1998: One.Tel is desperate for money—it does not have $9.5 million to pay for the spectrum, and the banks won't lend. James Packer and David Lowy each put in $5 million.

December 1998: Rodney Adler sells his family-controlled company FAI to HIH. The Packers' family flagship, Consolidated Press Holdings, buys 16 million of FAI's One.Tel shares for $43 million and another 1.3 million shares from One.Tel chairman John Greaves for $3.8 million. The share price will soar from $2.90 to $10 in early February 1999, producing an instant paper profit of $110 million for James and Kerry. Optus's old stake in One.Tel, sold for $4 million in October 1996, is now worth $300 million.

February 1999: Jodee Rich, Brad Keeling, James Packer and Lachlan Murdoch sell the One.Tel vision to Rupert Murdoch in New York. News Ltd and PBL (the publicly listed companies controlled by the Murdochs and Packers) agree to put $430 million into the company now and another $280 million in the future, in exchange for 40 per cent of the shares. The aim is to build a national mobile network and become No 2 or even No 1 in the Australian market.

$106 million of the Packer–Murdoch money goes to existing One.Tel shareholders in a 'return of capital'. Rich and Keeling pick up $62 million between them— most of which goes to Rich. James Packer collects $6.5 million for his private company, Dorigad, and another $14 million for the family company, Consolidated Press Holdings. Shareholders in News Ltd and PBL help foot the bill.

March 1999: The share price has risen fourfold since the Packers invested in December and from $9.30 to $13.55 in the two days before the February deal was made public. Thirty ASIC and Australian Federal Police raid One.Tel's offices looking for evidence of insider trading. Inquiries focus on Brad Keeling and his father.

April 1999: One.Tel signs a $438 million deal with Lucent to build a mobile network in Sydney and Brisbane.

May 1999: One.Tel signs its 100,000th overseas customer, but the Los Angeles office has closed—el dudo was not a success in the Hispanic community One.Tel was selling to.

Jodee buys the Darling Point waterfront property Craigend for $14 million.

June 1999: One.Tel has not bought enough spectrum for the mobile network it wants to build—which it promises will have 2.5 million customers. No further auction is planned yet. James Packer, Lachlan Murdoch and their lobbyists go into action. Communications Minister, Senator Richard Alston, promises a new spectrum auction will be held in March 2000.

July 1999: The ACCC tells Telstra that it must let companies such as One.Tel offer local calls.

August 1999: One.Tel's annual results claim the company has made a profit of $9.8 million. A closer look suggests it has lost $25 million or more. Just like Imagineering, it's all in the small print: One.Tel has changed its accounting policy to defer $32.4 million of costs incurred in Europe and Hong Kong from setting up businesses and acquiring customers. It has consumed $61 million in cash during the year, of which almost $29 million was on day-to-day operations.

September 1999: One.Tel now has an agreement with Lucent to build a national mobile network at a cost of $1.15 billion (including interest), but it still does not have the spectrum it needs.

November 1999: One.Tel enters the local call market in Australia. It undercuts Telstra by selling calls at a loss, in the hope of attracting customers to its profitable long-distance and international call service.

13 November 1999: One.Tel announces it will bid for Third Generation mobile licences in Europe. This '3G' technology allows TV pictures and the internet to be beamed to mobiles. One.Tel will be competing with companies 100 times its size.

23 November 1999: Lucent announces it will build and finance a European mobile network for One.Tel at a cost of up to US$20 billion. The Murdochs' News Ltd puts another $200 million into One.Tel to fund the Australian and European licence bids. The shares soar again, putting One.Tel into Australia's top 30 companies, with a market capitalisation of $3.8 billion. On 26 November One.Tel shares hit a high of $2.84, making the company worth $5.3 billion—not far short of the value of the entire Packer empire, and roughly 750 times its after-tax earnings. At this moment, on this day, Jodee Rich is worth close to $2 billion.

January 2000: One.Tel announces a pre-tax loss of $22 million for the six months to December 1999.

February 2000: Jodee Rich moves to Paris to develop One.Tel's business in Europe.

March 2000: One.Tel is forced to spend $523 million on the spectrum it needs to build its Australian mobile network. This is ten times what Optus, Telstra and Vodafone paid at the previous auction. Packer and

Murdoch have to cough up another $140 million each to pay for it. One.Tel also raises $340 million from Australian investors, including $200 million from Bankers Trust, who lost all their clients' investment in Imagineering.

3 April 2000: The US Nasdaq market records its biggest ever one-day fall. In Australia, by the end of Tuesday's trading, the local internet index is down 17 per cent from the previous week's high.

6 April 2000: One.Tel pulls out of UK spectrum auction after bidding £2.12 billion. (The winning bids will be more than double that.)

17 April 2000: Dot-com and telco stocks crash again on the Australian market following Black Friday on Wall Street. Merrill Lynch's internet index plunges 31 per cent. Bankers Trust has already lost nearly one-third of its clients' investment in One.Tel.

May 2000: One.Tel launches its Next Generation mobile network in Australia.

August 2000: Results for 1999–2000 show that One.Tel has doubled revenues to $670 million but has plunged to a $291 million loss. It has been forced to count $245 million of advertising and set-up costs in Europe and Australia that it had previously been deferring. It has gobbled up $775 million in cash, of which $169 million has been spent on day-to-day operations. Jodee returns from Europe.

September 2000: A proposal for Finnish telephone company Sonera to invest $1.1 billion in One.Tel for a 30 per cent share falls through. One.Tel forecasts another big loss for the coming year. Keeling and Rich say not to worry: One.Tel will still have $75 million in the bank at the end of the financial year, 30 June 2001.

One.Tel's annual report reveals that Rich and Keeling have received $6.9 million bonuses on top of their $560,000 annual pay packet, despite One.Tel's huge losses. Share price crashes below $1.00.

October 2000: Merrill Lynch in Australia concludes that One.Tel is in danger of running out of cash. Its report says One.Tel may consider selling its mobile network. Interviewed by Michael Pascoe on Channel 9's *Business Sunday*, Keeling says: 'This company's going to be very, very profitable over the next few years'. Rupert Murdoch tells News Ltd shareholders: 'We've got great faith in One.Tel. We wish they had better PR'. James Packer tells *Sydney Morning Herald* journalists at a private lunch that Rich is a visionary, that Brad and Jodee are the best managers in the business and that One.Tel's share price will recover.

November 2000: One.Tel starts Free Time 24x7 which allows customers on its Next Generation mobile network to call each other for free, 24 hours a day, seven days a week. By April 2001, One.Tel's network will be carrying one-third of calls for free.

December 2000: Packer puts his finance man, Geoff Kleemann, into One.Tel to look at the books. According to the accounts, there is $104 million in the bank at December 31, which means $232 million has been used since June 2000.

January 2001: Jodee is summoned to see Kerry Packer and told 'you ran out of cash with Imagineering, and you're going to do it again'. Rich repeats promise that One.Tel will still have $75 million in the bank at the end of June 2001 and will then be generating cash. Shares hit new low of 31 cents.

Macquarie Bank report says One.Tel is worth $3.5 billion. 'There is evidence the business model is going to work', says analyst Andrew Buttrell. The *Sydney Morning Herald* describes it as 'a big call'. *The Australian* calls it 'the most significant endorsement yet from the financial community'. One.Tel's share price doubles within days.

February 2001: One.Tel announces it lost $132 million in the six months to December. Merrill Lynch predicts the company will run out of cash by April. Rodney Adler, still a director, sells 5 million One.Tel shares at 51 cents for $2.5 million.

March 2001: Mid-month, One.Tel's cash reserves fall to $35 million. Nick Falloon is sacked as Chief Executive of the Packers' publicly listed company, PBL, after 18 years.

30 March 2001: One.Tel board meeting is told there will be $91 million cash in the bank at the end of June—$16 million more than earlier promised—and assured that everything is fine. Management accounts show One.Tel is losing millions more than it has budgeted for, but board is not told. Chairman John Greaves resigns.

April 2001: Foster Stockbroking report values One.Tel at $2 billion—78 cents a share—and rates the company a 'Buy'.

4 April 2001: Jodee tells Merrill Lynch telecommunications conference in Sydney that One.Tel is 'on track, as promised'. He claims that European and Australian operations (excluding Next Gen) are already generating cash. Peter Yates, Falloon's replacement at PBL, also gives the company a good rap: 'I am very excited about the One.Tel business'.

12 April 2001: Rich is summoned to see Kerry Packer, who demands a detailed review of how much cash is left. Rodney Adler resigns as director.

13 April 2001: One.Tel whistleblower, 'Ghostdogperil', sends an email to Geoff Kleemann warning him that the company is in trouble and he is not being told the truth.

WorldCom and other carriers in the UK cut credit terms from 120 to 30 days.

19 April 2001: Packer team, led by Darren Miller and Martin Green, begins cash review. One.Tel's cash reserves are down to $25 million.

23 April 2001: According to Jodee Rich, James Packer says One.Tel needs to raise more money with a rights issue.

1 May 2001: James Packer tells Lachlan Murdoch (who is in Europe) that One.Tel needs $10 million to $15 million 'to reach cash flow breakeven'. According to Lachlan Murdoch's affidavit of 7 June 2001, he asks James: 'Are you starting to lose confidence in the business or is this a timing issue?'. James Packer replies: 'No, Brad and Jodee don't think there is a problem. It's just a timing issue'.

8 May 2001: Cash review now complete. PBL team says One.Tel's cash projections are out by $100 million. Jodee Rich, Brad Keeling, Mark Silbermann and Kevin Beck— One.Tel's four executive directors—are summoned to meet James Packer, Ashok Jacob and Peter Yates. They are told they have 'fucked up', there will be a $132 million rights issue, and Rich and Keeling may have to go.

9 May 2001: James Packer meets Lachlan Murdoch at Cannes, where Lachlan is attending the Cannes film festival. According to Lachlan's affidavit, James tells him:

'The position is worse than we thought. One.Tel may need about $50 to $60 million of funding to break even, with a further $70 million as a sensible buffer'. Lachlan asks for a second time: 'Is there an underlying problem in the business?'. James replies: 'No, it's only a timing issue for the business plan to break even. Jodee doesn't think they need it'. Lachlan says: 'They've told the market so many times they don't need any more funds. Even if you raise $1 they will not have any credibility. They will have to go'.

10 May 2001: *The Australian*'s Geoff Elliott brings news of a Goldman Sachs report entitled: 'Great Start. One.Tel is here to stay'. He also quotes Jodee saying that One.Tel is still 'on track' to hit its forecasts. ASIC affidavit of 8 June 2001 cites this as an example of Rich possibly misleading the market. Rich denies saying it.

11 May 2001: Sydney's *Sunday Telegraph* reports that Kevin Beck has sold 1 million shares at 39 cents in the previous two weeks.

16 May 2001: Rich and Keeling meet James Packer at his office and agree to resign. James rings Lachlan in New York to tell him the news. An emergency board meeting is called for 7.00am the next day.

17 May 2001: One.Tel's directors meet at One.Tel's offices in Sydney. Rich, Keeling, Packer, Yates, Beck and Silbermann are there, with a bevy of lawyers. Lachlan

Murdoch and the News Ltd team are on speaker phone. News Ltd and PBL agree to underwrite a $132 million rights issue at 5 cents a share, 28 cents below the previous day's closing price. Rich and Keeling resign. ASX is asked to halt trading in One.Tel shares, pending an announcement. Packer and Murdoch put in a team to examine the financial position of the company, so that a prospectus can be prepared. Press statement from News Ltd and PBL professes great faith in the future of the company.

18 May 2001: Rodney Adler sells 6 million One.Tel shares for $1.21 million. Bankers Trust sells 6.7 million shares for $1.6 million. The following week, both sell more.

25 May 2001: Kerry and James Packer, Ashok Jacob and Peter Yates meet in Kerry's office. They have a new report from their finance team which says One.Tel needs far more than $132 million to stay afloat. It is just like Imagineering 11 years earlier. There are huge bad debts and some creditors have not been paid. They have to decide whether to pump in yet another $100 million and persuade the Murdochs to do the same, or pull out. The decision is left to James: it is to pull out.

26 May 2001: Lachlan is on his way back to Australia. He receives a fax from News Ltd legal counsel Ian Philip telling him that One.Tel may need far more than $132 million, and presenting a long list of problems that have been uncovered. The fax says they need to tell the ASX as soon as possible, and warns: 'It appears that board papers may have intentionally misrepresented cash flows and profitability'.

27 May 2001: Lachlan lands in Sydney and rushes to a meeting with James Packer and top people from News Ltd and PBL. He is told One.Tel may need $300 million, some of which is to pay current creditors. Lachlan says this is his first warning that One.Tel can't pay its debts.

28 May 2001: Another emergency board meeting at 8.00am, in the Packers' Park Street headquarters. Packer's team reports that One.Tel will be bust unless more money is put in immediately. It will have *minus* $11 million in the bank by the end of the month. And $80 million of payments to creditors are overdue. It is using between $15 million and $35 million cash a month, needs an additional buffer of $30 million, and will have to write off $50 million of bad debts. One.Tel's auditors, Ernst & Young, are given 24 hours to double-check the Packer team's findings. The ASX is asked to halt trading in shares for 24 hours. Peter Yates and Peter Macourt (deputy chief executive of News Ltd) are sent to ask Lucent to put up US$75 million to save the company.

29 May 2001: One.Tel board meets at 6.30pm. Lucent has said no. Ernst & Young tell the directors that One.Tel needs $240 million to $370 million to stay alive for the next six months. The company has a $3 million un-authorised overdraft at the ANZ Bank, which will blow out to $20 million by the end of the week. Directors are warned that One.Tel is insolvent and they will be person-ally liable for its debts unless it is given adequate funds. They ask Ferrier Hodgson to take over as administra-tors of the company. There is no discussion about trying to raise more money.

30 May 2001: One.Tel announces that the rights issue will not go ahead as planned and that the company is now in administration. Joint administrator, Steve Sherman, says that it will be business as usual for staff and customers, and that: 'One.Tel will continue to trade as a going concern'. James Packer and Lachlan Murdoch say in a joint statement: 'Like all shareholders we are angry. We've been profoundly misled as to the true finan-cial position of the company. We intend to explore all remedies available to us'.

31 May 2001: As part of a financial settlement under the *Family Law Act* Jodee gives half the $6 million family home in Vaucluse to his wife Maxine and promises to pay off the $3.7 million mortgage. He also gives her control of companies or trusts that own his jet, heli-copter and Whitsundays hideaway.

1 June 2001: ASIC raids One.Tel's offices in Sydney plus the homes of Rich, Keeling and Silbermann. ASIC is investigating whether executives of One.Tel falsified accounts or made false or misleading statements about the company's affairs before its collapse.

7 June 2001: In a sworn affidavit to ASIC Lachlan Murdoch claims to have been 'profoundly misled' about the state of One.Tel's finances.

8 June 2001: ASIC asks the New South Wales Supreme Court to freeze the Riches' assets on the basis that Jodee may be trying to put them out of reach of creditors. Justice Austin agrees, pending a full hearing, and orders Rich to surrender his passport. Mel Gibson's manager agrees to buy Craigend for $16 million, provided contracts are exchanged by midnight. The Supreme Court reconvenes at 11.30pm. Justice Austin allows the sale to go ahead.

11 June 2001: Jodee's father Steven is made a Member of the Order of Australia in the Queen's Birthday honours for services to business and the community.

14 June 2001: Rich, Silbermann and Keeling give undertakings to the New South Wales Supreme Court that they will not dispose of or deal in their assets, or leave the country without giving notice to ASIC. The court releases affidavits from ASIC and the One.Tel joint administrator, Peter Walker, listing the Riches' $40 million assets. Walker says: 'There is a high likelihood that the

Australian companies [in the One.Tel group] were insolvent as at 31st March 2001 and that insolvency could possibly extend back to 31st December 2000 or earlier'.

12 July 2001: Second One.Tel administrators' report to creditors says the company was 'most likely insolvent . . . between March and the end of April 2001'. Any claim against the directors, including Lachlan Murdoch and James Packer, 'may be in the order of $20 million to $80 million'. It suggests possible action against News Ltd and PBL for not proceeding with the $132 million rights issue and a $23 million bridging loan, and for recovery of $90 million of prepaid advertising. The administrators are also examining whether to pursue Rich and Keeling to recover their $6.9 million bonuses and millions of dollars they received for One.Card and One.Net.

24 September 2001: New South Wales Supreme Court relaxes restrictions on Rich, Keeling and Silbermann dealing with their assets, but they still have to give seven days' notice to ASIC if they travel overseas and 14 days' notice if they move assets offshore.

12 December 2001: ASIC begins civil action against Rich, Keeling and Silbermann, alleging that they have withheld financial information about One.Tel from the company's directors and investors. Former chairman, John Greaves, is included in the action, for allegedly breaching his duty of care. ASIC wants all four men disqualified as directors or officers of any Australian company, and is suing them for $30 million to $50 million damages. If it succeeds, the money will go to One.Tel's creditors.

14 December 2001: ASIC lifts travel restrictions on Rich, Keeling and Silbermann. The New South Wales Supreme Court orders ASIC to hand over transcripts of witness interviews and other documents to the trio's lawyers by 4 February 2001.

February 2002: Ex-One.Tel finance director Mark Silbermann teams up with ex-operations director Kevin Beck to start TeleOne. From April 2002 it will be reselling long-distance and international calls, using the dude's dad and sister in its marketing. TeleOne has bought One.Tel office equipment and switch gear from the liquidator at knock-down prices. Telstra and Optus refuse to do business with the new company, along with several One.Tel creditors. Rich says he is not funding it, but would like to be involved if he can clear his name.

March 2002: One.Tel liquidator due to begin public examinations of One.Tel directors, officers and third parties in the Federal Court, Sydney. James Packer, Lachlan Murdoch and Kerry Packer may all be called.

References

Chapter 1

Reines, Rosalind, 23 July 1995, 'The Diary', *Sun Herald*, Sydney, p 142

Cadzow, Jane, 4 August 2001, 'That Rich bloke', *Good Weekend*, p 16

Lawrence, Neil & Bunk, Steve, 1985, *The Stump-Jumpers: A New Breed of Australians*, Hale and Iremonger, Sydney, p 321

Plunkett, Sandy, 5 April 1991, 'The Rich family saga', *Business Review Weekly*, pp 38–42

Chapter 2

Scott, Jeremy, 13 March 1987, 'He's worth $24m and Rich's riches are all his own work', *The Daily Telegraph*

Plunkett, Sandy, 5 April 1991, 'The Rich family saga', *Business Review Weekly*, pp 38–42

Hernon, Fran, 12 September 1987, *Daily Telegraph*

Dalley, Helen, 14 March 1984, 'The Whiz Kid Millionaires', *Australian Business*

Morris, Linda, 28 April 1988, 'The kid who got rich', *Daily Telegraph*

Chapter 3

Plunkett, Sandy, 2 September 1988, 'Imagineering handles too much success', *Business Review Weekly*, p 45

Beagle, Monica, 2 April 1990, 'Sydney millionaire rides bike to work', *Daily Mirror*

Plunkett, Sandy, 5 April 1991, 'The Rich family saga', *Business Review Weekly*, pp 38–42

Chapter 4

Cadzow, Jane, 4 August 2001, 'That Rich bloke', *Good Weekend*, p 16

Lloyd, Peter, 31 May 2001, ABC Radio, 'PM', Sydney

Chapter 8

Lecky, Sue & Mychasuk, Emiliya, 20 February 1999, 'Upwardly Mobile', *Sydney Morning Herald*, p 57

McCrann, Terry, 16 February 1999, 'Lachlan and James dine out on big phone numbers', *Daily Telegraph*, Sydney, p 25

Knight, Elizabeth, 16 February 1999, *Sydney Morning Herald*, Abacus, p 21

Cadzow, Jane, 4 August 2001, 'That Rich bloke', *Good Weekend*, p 16

Lloyd, Graham, 'When Three is Better', *Club Marine Magazine*

'BRW Rich 200', May 1999, *Business Review Weekly*

Chapter 9

Unknown author, March 1721, 'The Second Part of the South Sea Bubble 1721', reprinted by Andrew McFarland Davis in *Colonial Currency Reprints, 1682–1751*, Boston: The Prince Society, 1911, volume II, pp. 304–32

Hale, David, 7 September 2001, 'Can broadband investment revive the US technology sector in 2002?', *The Global Economic Observer*, Zürich Research

Patrick, Aaron, 14 August 1999, 'One.Tel profit leaps 18 per cent', *Australian Financial Review*, p 16

Elliott, Geoff, 14 August 1999, 'One.Tel switch cuts off $25 million loss', *The Weekend Australian*, p 33

Chenoweth, Neil, 21 September 1999, 'Some accounts of the road to Jodee's riches', *Australian Financial Review*, p 1

Elliott, Geoff, 23 August 1999, 'One.Tel faces inquiry by ASX', *The Australian*, p 40

Chapter 10

Durie, John, 25 November 1999, 'One.Tel's price hard to justify', *Australian Financial Review*, p 68

Patrick, Aaron, 20 November 1999, 'Telco Tycoons', *Australian Financial Review*

Elliott, Geoff, 7 March 2000, 'Spectrum stings One.Tel', *The Australian*, p 21

Elliott, Geoff, 2 June 2001, *Weekend Australian*, 'Dear Rod, thanks for the note', p 32

Clifford, Mark L, 15 May 2000, 'The mastermind behind Hutchison's cellular return', *BusinessWeek Online*

Chapter 12

Keeling, Brad, 15 October 2000, *Business Sunday*, Channel 9

Chapter 16

Elliott, Geoff, 10 May 2001, 'Back from the dead', *The Australian*

Chapter 17

Lacy, Christine, 4 June 2001, 'ASIC swoops: $50m loan to One.Tel under scrutiny', *Australian Financial Review*, p 1

Prime Minister, the Hon John Howard MP, 4 June 2001, *A Current Affair*, Channel 9, Sydney

The Guardian, 6 June 2001

Photo and Text Acknowledgments

Acknowledgments are due to the following photographers, authors, publishers and agents for permission to include photographs and extracts of newspaper and magazine articles, books and television transcripts.

Picture Section 1

Page 1	The Fairfax Photo Library (bottom)
Page 2	Russell Stewart
Page 3	Robert Pearce, *Sydney Morning Herald* (top)
	News Ltd (bottom)
Page 6	Peter Morris, *Sydney Morning Herald* (top)
	Cameron Laird, News Ltd (bottom)
Page 7	Adam Hollingworth (top)
	Graham Lloyd (middle)
	Cessna Aircraft Company (bottom)

Picture Section 2

Page 1	Jessica Hromas, *Australian Financial Review* (top)
	Glenn Campbell, News Ltd (bottom)
Page 2	Graham Hely, News Ltd (top)
	Natalie Boog (bottom)
Page 3	Mark Williams, News Ltd (top and bottom)

ACKNOWLEDGMENTS

Page 4   Mark Baker, Reuters
Page 5   Glenn Campbell, News Ltd (top and bottom)
Page 6   Mark Baker, Reuters (top)
             Rohan Kelly, News Ltd (bottom)
Page 7   Austral
Page 8   Dean Lewins, AAP Image (top)
             Mick Tsikas, News Ltd (bottom)
Page 9   AAP Image/Mediakoo (top and bottom)
Page 10   Brad Newman, News Ltd (top)
             Dean Lewins, AAP Image (bottom)
Page 11   Danielle Smith, *Sun Herald* (top)
             Grant Turner/Mediakoo (bottom)
Page 12   Dean Lewins, AAP Image
Page 13   Laura Friezer, AAP Image (top, and bottom right)
             John Grainger, News Ltd (bottom left)
Page 14   Stephen Cooper, News Ltd (top left)
             David Gray, Reuters (top right, and bottom)
Page 15   Barry Chapman, *Sun Herald* (top)
             Stephen Cooper, News Ltd (bottom)
Page 16   Brad Newman, News Ltd (top and bottom)

Cover photo
Jessica Hromas, *Australian Financial Review*

Extracts
BRW Rich 200, 28 May 1999, *BRW*
Cadzow, Jane, 4 August 2001, 'That Rich bloke', *Good Weekend*,
    p 16
Lacy, Christine, 4 June 2001, 'ASIC swoops: $50m loan to One.Tel
    under scrutiny', *Australian Financial Review*, p 1
Patrick, Aaron, 14 August 1999, 'One.Tel profit leaps 18 per cent',
    Australian Financial Review, p 16
Patrick, Aaron, 20 November 1999, 'Telco Tycoons', *Australian
    Financial Review*

Every effort has been made to identify copyright holders of
photographs and extracts in this book. The publishers would be
pleased to hear from any copyright holders who have not been
acknowledged.

Index